The Critique of Management

This book reflects on the nature of business management to contribute to the development of a philosophy and ethics of management. It engages in conceptual engineering of management to delineate the phenomenon of management and, as a result, to open a new perspective on management beyond its self-evident conceptualization.

After questioning the self-evident concept of management, the author develops a philosophy of management with six dimensions of the nature of management: management as participation; management as resistance and responsive action; management as constitution of meaning; management as politico-economic governance; management as non-reductive stakeholder engagement; and management as epistemic insufficient entrepreneurship. These six dimensions of management are taken as points of departure to develop an integrated concept of business ethics, an individual competence for ethical business management, and a concept of ethical codes for corporate social-responsible behavior. This new conception of philosophy of management and business ethics can guide future philosophical and empirical work on the nature of management.

The Critique of Management is an excellent resource for researchers, students, and professionals interested in philosophy of management, business ethics, and corporate social responsibility.

Vincent Blok is associate professor in Philosophy of Technology, Business Ethics, and Responsible Innovation, Wageningen University, The Netherlands. He holds a PhD in Philosophy of Technology from Leiden University. His books include *Ernst Jünger's Philosophy of Technology: Heidegger and the Poetics of the Anthropocene* (Routledge, 2017) and *Heidegger's Concept of Philosophical Method: Innovating Philosophy in the Age of Global Warming* (Routledge, 2019).

"Finally, a book in Management Philosophy providing clear and concise definitions gluing the fields together, making us understand the possibilities and impossibilities of management better".

Anders Bordum, *Copenhagen Business School, Denmark*

"At last, a philosopher looks critically at the idea of management, and some of its associated literature in business ethics. Vincent Blok has done management theory a favor in showing how philosophy can be useful in understanding the basic ideas of management in a sophisticated way".

– R. Edward Freeman, Professor of Business Ethics, Professor Business Administration at the Darden School of the University of Virginia

"Vincent Blok is one of the most important contemporary philosophers of innovation, technology and management. He engages deeply with various expert literatures to tackle important questions in an accessible way. What is management? What is the best it could be? What sort of knowledge can managers use to make decisions? I expect that anyone reading this book, as expert as they might be, will come away with a new insight and a new learning".

– Wim Vandekerckhove, Professor of Business Ethics, University of Greenwich and Editor-in-Chief Philosophy of Management

"This book is one of the most important contributions to the developing field of the philosophy of management in this century. A simple but fundamental question is raised, which many have pondered over - what is management? - and is pursued with a thoroughness that enables the reader to follow the many different facets of the argument, through ancient Greek philosophy to modern critical theory, across political, social and ethical disciplines,, and covering management in the widest range of different contexts. The author builds his position carefully and iteratively over succeeding chapters, to arrive at a broad and comprehensive perspective on the field. This is a book which speaks simultaneously to several audiences: managers in general wishing to understand more deeply the issues involved in their day-to-day decisions, philosophers formulating ways to apply their frameworks to business issues, business ethicists looking for a groundwork for their investigations, management scholars seeking a sound foundation for their ideas, as well as students on MBA and related programmes as they develop their understanding of management. A valuable addition to the literature".

– Paul Griseri, author of *An Introduction to the Philosophy of Management*

The Critique of Management

Towards a Philosophy and Ethics of Business Management

Vincent Blok

NEW YORK AND LONDON

First published 2022
by Routledge
605 Third Avenue, New York, NY 10158

and by Routledge
2 Park Square, Milton Park, Abingdon, Oxon, OX14 4RN

Routledge is an imprint of the Taylor & Francis Group, an informa business

© 2022 Vincent Blok

The right of Vincent Blok to be identified as author of this work has been asserted in accordance with sections 77 and 78 of the Copyright, Designs and Patents Act 1988.

All rights reserved. No part of this book may be reprinted or reproduced or utilised in any form or by any electronic, mechanical, or other means, now known or hereafter invented, including photocopying and recording, or in any information storage or retrieval system, without permission in writing from the publishers.

Trademark notice: Product or corporate names may be trademarks or registered trademarks, and are used only for identification and explanation without intent to infringe.

Library of Congress Cataloguing-in-Publication Data
Names: Blok, Vincent, 1970- author.
Title: The critique of management : toward a philosophy and ethics of business management / Vincent Blok.
Description: New York, NY : Routledge, [2022] | Includes bibliographical references and index.
Identifiers: LCCN 2021032609 (print) | LCCN 2021032610 (ebook) | ISBN 9781032137940 (hbk) | ISBN 9781032140001 (pbk) | ISBN 9781003231875 (ebk)
Subjects: LCSH: Industrial management–Philosophy. | Management–Philosophy. | Business ethics. | Social responsibility of business.
Classification: LCC HD30.19 .B58 2022 (print) | LCC HD30.19 (ebook) | DDC 658–dc23
LC record available at https://lccn.loc.gov/2021032609
LC ebook record available at https://lccn.loc.gov/2021032610

ISBN: 978-1-032-13794-0 (hbk)
ISBN: 978-1-032-14000-1 (pbk)
ISBN: 978-1-003-23187-5 (ebk)

DOI: 10.4324/9781003231875

Typeset in Sabon
by MPS Limited, Dehradun

Dedicated to my students (Teunis Brand, Eghe Osagie, Lisa Ploum, Tjidde Tempels)

Voorburg, The Netherlands January 15 2021

Contents

Acknowledgements

Earlier versions of portions of Sections 4–6 appeared as Blok, V. (2019) "Xenophon's philosophy of management". In: Neesham, C., Segal, S. (Eds.), *Handbook of Philosophy of Management*. Springer: Dordrecht (10.1007/ 978-3-319-48352-8_27-1); Blok, V. (2020) "What is (business) management? Laying the ground for a philosophy of management", *Philosophy of Management* 19: 173–189 (DOI: 10.1007/s40926-019-00126-9). Earlier versions of portions of Section 7 appeared as Blok, V. (2014) "The metaphysics of collaboration: identity, unity and difference in cross-sector partnerships for sustainable development", *Philosophy of Management* 13 (2): 53–74 (DOI: 10.5840/pom201413211); Blok, V., Gremmen, B., Wesselink, R. (2016) "Dealing with the wicked problem of sustainable development. The role of individual virtuous competence". *Business & Professional Ethics Journal* 34(3): 297–327 (DOI: 10.5840/bpej20162173 7); Blok, V. (2018) "Information asymmetries and the paradox of sustainable business models: toward an integrated theory of sustainable entrepreneurship". In: Idowu, S.O. et al., *Sustainable Business Models: Principles, Promise, and Practice*. Dordrecht: Springer, 203–225. Earlier versions of portions of Sections 11–13 appeared as Blok, V. (2020) "Politics versus economics: philosophical reflections on the nature of corporate governance". *Philosophy of Management,* 19(1): 69–87. Earlier versions of portions of Sections 14 and 15 appeared as Blok, V. (2014) "The metaphysics of collaboration: identity, unity and difference in cross-sector partnerships for sustainable development", *Philosophy of Management* 13 (2): 53–74 (DOI: 10.5840/pom201413211). Earlier versions of portions of Sections 14–17 appeared as Blok, V. (2019) "From participation to interruption: toward an ethics of stakeholder engagement, participation and partnership in CSR and responsible innovation". In: Von Schomberg, R. (Ed) *Handbook Responsible Innovation: A Global Resource*. Northampton: Edward Elgar Publishing, 243–257. Earlier versions of portions of Sections 18 and 19 appeared as Blok, V. (2018) "Information asymmetries and the paradox of sustainable business models: toward an integrated theory of sustainable entrepreneurship". In: Idowu, S.O. et al., *Sustainable Business Models: Principles, Promise, and Practice*.

Dordrecht: Springer, 203–225. Earlier versions of portions of Section 21 appeared as Blok, V., Gremmen, B., Wesselink, R. (2016) "Dealing with the wicked problem of sustainable development. the role of individual virtuous competence". *Business & Professional Ethics Journal* 34(3): 297–327 (DOI: 10.5840/bpej201621737). Although I have shifted the focus from competencies for sustainable professionals to competencies for managers in order to fit the material for this book, Section 21 can be seen as co-authored by Bart Gremmen and Renate Wesselink. I am very grateful for their work and inspiration. Earlier versions of portions of Section 22 appeared as Blok, V. (2017) "Bridging the gap between ethical principles and actual responsible behavior: toward a performative concept of corporate codes". *Philosophy of Management* 16(2): 117–136; Blok, V. (2013) "The power of speech acts: reflections on a performative concept of ethical oaths in economics and business". *Review of Social Economy*, 71 (2): 187–208.

After my graduation in philosophy of technology at Leiden University, I worked for several years as team manager at a health-care institution (Centrum Autisme, Leiden) and as CEO of a private research institute in the area of organic and sustainable agriculture (Louis Bolk Institute, Driebergen). It is first of all this type of first-person experience with management practice that helped me to articulate my intuitions in this book. In 2010, I returned to the university and started to work at the management studies group of Wageningen University. In this position, I started to think about management from a scientific perspective. I have learned a lot from colleagues like Onno Omta, Stefano Pascucci, and Domenico Dentoni, who were open enough to collaborate with a philosopher in the area of management science. I am also grateful for the openness and collaborative efforts of other colleagues at Wageningen University, like Bart Gremmen, Renate Wesselink, and Thomas Lans. The collaboration with these eminent colleagues enabled me to contribute to empirical research in sustainable entrepreneurship and business ethics.

At the same time, as a philosopher working in the phenomenological tradition, I was interested to develop philosophical work on management science, next to my empirical work with colleagues in Wageningen. As philosophy of management is a relatively small subdomain, I am very grateful for the openness of this community to support my work. I have such good memories of the various philosophy of management conferences I attended in Oxford, Chicago, and Greenwich over the years, where most of the material presented in this book is also discussed. I would like to thank Nigel Laurie for his dedication and effort to make this conference such a success year after year. I would like to thank Paul Griseri and Wim Vandekerckhove for their work as editors in chief of the philosophy of management journal that published my first article in this field. Later, I joined the community myself and worked as executive editor of the journal. Without this community of great scholars and friends – Cristina Neesham, Frits Schippers, David Carl Wilson, and Marian Eabrasu – much of the ideas developed in this study would not have matured. Another source of inspiration was the working group on business ethics of the Dutch Research School of Philosophy. Guided by eminent scholars like Wim Dubbink, Johan Graafland, Ronald Jeurissen, and Luc Vandeliederkerke, I learned a lot of the great discussions we had over the years.

Finally, I am very grateful for the great discussions with my team of PhD students and post-doc researchers during the years I was working on this book: Daniel Agbeko, Teunis Brand, Jilde Garst, Edurne Inigo, Thomas B. Long, Rob Lubberink, Peter Novitzky, Eghe Osagie, Lisa Ploum, Eugen Popa, Mmapatla Senyolo, August Sjauw-Koen-Fa, Tjidde Tempels, Job Timmermans, Mira Vegter, and Waliou Yessoufou. I am also very grateful that Bart Gremmen, Paulan Korenhof, Thom Long, Julia Rijssenbeek, and Job Timmermans were willing to proofread this book.

Introduction

1 What Is Management?

Today, business management seems to be only a special case of management as a more general human condition. Management is everywhere, ranging from people's self-management to social network management, and from household management to planetary management in the context of global warming. This raises the question what is meant by the concept of business management.

In management theory, the concept has a long tradition. It is normally understood as managerial power and mechanism to control, inspired by the scientific management theory that is still taught in business schools today. Henry Fayol and Frederick Taylor can be seen as the founders of management theory. They introduced scientific management (Taylor, 1911) in general and five functions of management in particular: planning, organizing, instruction, coordination, and control (Fayol, 1949). Further insights in the nature of management were provided by Luther Gulick and Lyndall Urwick; for instance, they extended Fayol's work and coined the POSDC-ORB acronym to indicate the nature of management: planning, organizing, staffing, directing, coordinating, reporting, and budgeting (Urwick, 1952; Gulick and Urwick, 2012). Koontz and O'Donnell developed principles of management as well, such as principles of planning, organizing, staffing, etc. (Koontz and O'Donnell, 1972). These later developments in management theory are also influenced by scholars who indicated the importance of soft skills in management (Mintzberg, 2005), social and informal processes in management (Follett, 1940), or studied management from the perspective of organizational behaviour (Miner, 2002).

In academic philosophy, however, the question what is management received less attention. It is striking that the sub-discipline of philosophy of management never raised the question *what* management *is*. Paul Griseri is, for instance, one of the leading experts in the field. In his *Introduction to the Philosophy of Management*, he introduces in section one "the 'what' of management", but he in fact only answers the question about the "what" of organizations, work, and leadership in this

DOI: 10.4324/9781003231875-101

section (Griseri, 2013). The same tendency can be observed in the *Philosophy of Management* journal. In its first volume, Alan Bray, for instance, raised the provocative question "Why is it that management seems to have no history?" indicating that the practice of management as a corpus of knowledge and skills received only little attention in the literature (Bray, 2001). And, while, in the second volume, Fontrodona and Melé (2002) propose Aristotelian philosophy as a theoretical foundation of management, the history of philosophies of management is virtually absent in subsequent volumes.[1] With this, it is not implied that philosophers are not explored to reflect on issues in management. On the contrary, philosophy of management has a strong tradition in applying ideas of philosophers to management issues, for example: Stoic ideas on ethics of management (Bowden, 2012); Aristotle's ideas on corporate responsibility and management practice (Gimbel, 2005; Hartman, 2015); Dewey's ideas on innovation management (Bordum, 2007); Levinas' ideas on whistleblowing (Loumansky and Lewis, 2013); and Heidegger's ideas on leadership (Krentz and Malloy, 2005). But the ideas of the big names of the philosophical tradition are often not further developed into a full-fletched philosophy of management of Aristotle, Heidegger, or Levinas. This seems to be legitimate, as these philosophers themselves often did not develop an explicit philosophy of management. More importantly, the application and further development of their philosophical insights in philosophy of management did not lead to an answer to the question *what* management *is*.

Why do philosophers with a special interest in *business* management shy away from the question "what is management"? A possible explanation why many non-philosophers define business management self-evidently in terms of managerial power and mechanism of control, while philosophers seem to omit the question "what is management", might be that the concept of management is "highjacked" by political philosophers like Michel Foucault. Foucault framed management as governmental technique that indicates the modern governmentality of the world (Foucault, 2009). On the one hand, it is acknowledged that our understanding of governmentality originates from the Christian pastorate that governs society and is understood as an *oikonomia,* that is, as an administration of society according to the model of the management of a household business (we will come back on this subject in chapter 3). On the other hand, economic management is *a priori* understood from the perspective of political governance as government of populations.[2] With this, the concept of management is already understood from a bio-*political* paradigm and becomes such a general characteristic of all power relations in modern society, that it does not seem to be able anymore to characterize the particular phenomenon of *business* management. This general understanding of the nature of management in our "societies of control" may explain why applied philosophers with a special interest in *business* management shy away from the question "what is management" and, instead, turn to questions like what is work, what is an organization, and what is leadership.

And yet, the question of *what is business management* is legitimate in the field of organization science, business administration, and philosophy of management. On the one hand, we can question whether business management necessarily must be understood from the perspective of managerial power and mechanism of control (Section 6). On the other hand, we can question whether the ideal of management as managerial power and mechanism of control is still feasible if we consider the grand challenges of our time like global warming (Section 7). Either way, if we want to ask the question what management is, we have to put the political paradigm of the conceptualization of management between brackets in order to articulate the particular nature of *business* management. There are also good reasons to follow this strategy. First, if the political paradigm of the conceptualization of management stems from the model of the management of the household business, an *economic* paradigm of management may inform us about the particular phenomenon of *business* management. Second, if we experience discomfort with the self-evident conceptualization of *business* management as managerial power and mechanism of control, we should reflect on this particular context of management and look for alternative conceptualizations of business management that can help us to open up this self-evident notion for philosophical reflection. In this study, we philosophically reflect on the nature of business management to contribute to the development of a philosophy of management. Although we explicitly focus on *business* management in this study, it is assumed that at least some of the dimensions we develop also hold for organizational and public management.

2 Research Questions, Task, and Main Contributions of This Study

In order to answer the question what is business management, we engage in a *critique of management*. In philosophy, *critique* does not only mean that we are critical about the self-evident understanding of management in management science and economics, but *critique* is derived from *krinein*. If Immanuel Kant writes a *Critique of Pure Reason*, what is at stake is the delineation what pure reason means. The question *what* management *is* leads to a *critique of management*, that is the delineation of what management means.

With this, we immediately receive an indication why the efforts in this study are framed as a *philosophy* of management. Traditionally, philosophy is the study of the fundamental nature of reality, existence, and our knowledge thereof. We normally think we know what concepts like human being, freedom, etc., mean. Philosophers question, however, our self-evident understanding of these concepts in order to uncover that we do not know what we mean with these terms, and raise the question *what* human being, freedom, etc., is. For instance, Socrates, arguably the founding father of Western philosophy, discusses with a military general what courage is. He assumes that if you know what a phenomenon like courage means, you should be able to define the term. While the experienced military general thinks that he knows what courage is – standing firm in the battle for instance – Socrates' philosophical method consists in questioning these conceptualizations. He can argue, for instance, that not all instances of "standing firm in the battle" are instances of courageous behaviour. For instance, if you stand firm in the battle with only ten soldiers against 1000 enemies, you might not be courageous but reckless. For instance, if you save a child in a burning house, you are courageous but not standing firm in the battle. The objective of Socrates' philosophical method is to question and, in the end, refute all self-evident assumptions regarding the nature of courage to show that we may *think* that we know what courage is, but in fact do not know it at all. But the purpose of philosophical questioning is not only destructive but also constructive, because the destruction of our self-evident understanding of these concepts enables us to define these concepts anew. A definition states what is a necessary and sufficient condition for something to come under a concept.

A good example of such a definition is the answer to the question what is a human. Traditionally, we define human being as *Animal Rationale* as all humans are animals (necessary condition) that are distinguished from other animals by their rationality (sufficient condition). With the increased insights in the rational, social, and communicative abilities of other animals, we can question this definition and explore new ones, for instance, the idea that human being is the only animal that engages in *trade*. With such a new definition of human being as *trading animal,* we are not only interested in the definition as such but also in the meaning this new conceptualization has for human existence.

Why should we be interested in this type of question regarding the what of business management? Philosophical reflection on basic concepts in the sciences, like the concept of management in business administration, management science, and economics, is important because they are markers for our understanding of the world. Think, for example, of a self-evident notion in our society like "innovation". If we understand innovation as technological innovation which is primarily executed by engineers in private R&D departments and laboratories, then we miss the whole potential of contemporary phenomena that can be associated with system innovation (for instance, agro-ecological innovations), social innovations (for instance, political innovations like online petition websites), or attitudinal innovations (for instance, prevention or lifestyle interventions), as well as the part of the innovation process that can be associated with the diffusion of innovations. Philosophical reflection on the what of innovation can also help to assess whether phenomena fall under the concept or not, for instance, the new paradigm of technological developments and engineering practices that can be associated with *biomimicry,* that is, with the imitation of natural processes in technological design. Finally, philosophical reflection can help to develop a critical attitude towards the self-evident use of the concept of innovation, to highlight contradictions and tensions in its use, and to raise questions regarding the limitations of its use and the conditions of *responsible* innovation. Is innovation good *per se* or should we reflect on its consequences in relation to the problems it intends to solve, the risks involved, as well as the potential negative side effects (Blok, 2020a)?

The philosophical method of questioning management we employ in this study is an *explorative confrontation* with the self-evident concept of management. This method opens up the concept and critically develop our understanding of business management (Blok, 2020b). Our approach is *explorative* because it consists of the articulation of a deeper understanding of philosophical and scientific sources about management. Our approach is *confrontational* because we thereby analyze and disrupt the preconceptions held in the tradition to develop our understanding of business management. We look for historical, epistemological, and ontological accounts of business management that can help to articulate the self-evident conceptualization of management in contemporary business practices. We subsequently explore the limitations and tensions in the definition of management provide by Taylor, Fayol, and others. And we finally engage in critical reflections on the concept to further develop a philosophy of business management. In this, we do not so much look for one univocal meaning of management but for family resemblances amongst various phenomena to provide a critical concept of management.

Although a *critique* of management primarily aims to delineate the phenomenon of business management, it is not limited to such a delineation based on available sources in literature and practice. Contrary to such a *question de jure* that can be found in the work of Kant, our efforts in this study are also *critical.* We critically engage with the philosophy of management beyond its self-evident conceptualization as managerial power and mechanism of control. Both the negative implications of management for profit, managerial power, and managerial control for business life (Section 6) and the limits of managerial control in times of grand societal challenges like global warming (Section 7) make this self-evident conceptualization questionable. Instead of being hemmed in by the structures of its self-evident conceptuality, the task of philosophy of management is to develop new theories of imagination for management science (Tsoukas and Cummings, 1997; Komporozos-Athanasiou and Fotaki, 2015; Deslandes, 2018). In this regard, our study engages in conceptual engineering of management to *delineate* the phenomenon of management and, with this, to open a new perspective on management beyond its self-evident conceptualization.

After questioning the self-evident concept of management in chapter 1, we develop a philosophy of management with six dimensions of the nature of management in chapters 2 to 5: management as participation; management as resistance and responsive action; management as the constitution of meaning; management as politico-economic governance; management as non-reductive stakeholder engagement; and management as epistemic insufficient entrepreneurship. In chapter 6, we take these six dimensions of management as a point of departure to develop an integrated concept of business ethics, an individual competence for ethical business management, and a concept of ethical codes for corporate social responsible behaviour. The six dimensions of the philosophy of management and principle of business ethics can guide future philosophical and empirical work on the nature of business management.

In the next section, we will briefly sketch the research question and main contribution of each chapter.

3 Design of the Study

In chapter 1, we first open up the self-evident concept of management as it appears in philosophical history and contemporary management theory. We first consult the philosophy of management of Xenophon. By confronting his concept of management with contemporary conceptualizations, we provide the first study in which Xenophon's philosophy of management is systematically analyzed from the perspective of business management (Sections 4–5) and challenge the self-evident contemporary conceptualization of management based on his work (Section 6). Xenophon's philosophy of management enables us to criticize the contemporary focus on profit maximization and to articulate an intrinsic relation between business and society. It also enables us to criticize the contemporary disconnectedness of business management and to develop a broader idea of the know-how that is required for business managers. By confronting contemporary conceptions of management as managerial power and mechanism of control with the contemporary context of grand challenges like global warming (Section 7), we subsequently question the contemporary conceptualization of management as establishment and governance of a functioning order; people management and entrepreneurial action. In chapters 2 to 5, we philosophically reflect on each dimension of management to develop a proper concept of management that moves beyond its self-evident conceptualization and solves the identified problems and issues.

In chapter 2, we philosophically reflect on the first three dimensions of the philosophy of management – management as participation (Section 8), management as resistance and responsive action (Section 9), and management as constitution of meaning (Section 10) – and show how these dimensions move beyond managerial power and control, as well as its advantages in comparison with contemporary management theories.

In chapter 3, we broaden our perspective to the notion of management as corporate governance of the functioning order of the business operations. We raise the question whether control is still a feasible ideal of corporate governance and reflect on the implications of the grand challenges of our time for our conceptualization of management as establishment and governance of a functioning order. While corporate governance has been researched from several perspectives, ranging from self-regulation (Gond et al., 2011) to relational governance (Midttun, 2005) to new governance (Moon, 2002), the nature of "governance" within corporate governance is still under-researched. We first introduce the concept of corporate governance from the perspective of economics and politics (Section 11). We then trace the genealogy of the concept of governance based on a selective reading of Giorgio Agamben's work, who has pointed at two interdependent paradigms of governance in the Christian tradition and apply his categories in the context of management as establishment and governance of a functioning order of the business (Section 12). We finally engage in a critical reflection on the concept of corporate governance in times of global warming and develop a new theory of management as politico-economic governance (Section 13). The first contribution of this chapter to contemporary debates on management is that it provides a philosophical account of the nature of corporate governance in general and the economic and political aspects of governance in particular. The second contribution of this chapter is that it provides a philosophical concept of management as politico-economic governance.

In chapter 4, we broaden our perspective on people management as a central aspect of business management. We raise the question whether people management has to be conceptualized differently in light of the grand challenges of our time, as it shows the fundamental differences in value frames, norms, and principles of internal and external stakeholders. In this chapter, we take contemporary debates on *stakeholder engagement, cross-sector partnerships* , and *multi-stakeholder alliances* in management science as a point of departure to reflect on the concept of identity, unity, and difference in these type of collaborations. As many stakeholders have different ideas about the problems and the goals of such collaborations, this could limit collaboration and partnership practices. This raises the issue of how collaboration and partnership practices should be conceived. Contrary to the tendency to harmony, consensus, and alignment amongst stakeholders in most of the literature on partnership and collaboration (Gray and Stites, 2013), we ask which concept of stakeholder engagement, collaboration, and partnership can account for stakeholder inclusion in management practices, while acknowledging and appreciating their fundamentally different judgments, value frames, and viewpoints. To this end, we reconsider the concept of stakeholder inclusion, collaboration, and partnership. We ask how to align different values, norms, and principles of internal and external stakeholders and respect fundamental differences between multiple stakeholders at the same time (Section 14). Our first contribution in this chapter is that we show the *metaphysical* concept of identity, unity, and difference at the bottom of the conceptualization of stakeholder engagement, partnership, and collaboration in the management literature (Section 15). We explore four characteristics of the concept of identity, unity, and difference, which are presupposed in the partnership and collaboration literature. Based on our analysis of these four characteristics, we show the limitations of the metaphysical concepts of identity and difference in the case of collaboration and partnerships with internal and external stakeholders; the metaphysical concept explains why current conceptualizations of stakeholder engagement, collaboration, and partnerships often show a tendency towards consensus and alignment, and cannot deal with fundamental differences amongst stakeholders. Because this tendency towards alignment and harmony turns out to be inappropriate in case of the management of grand challenges like global warming (Hansen, 2006), we subsequently develop a theory of stakeholder engagement, collaboration, and partnership in which fundamental differences are acknowledged and appreciated (Section 17). This concept of partnership and collaboration involves a shift from the cognitive level of primarily understanding other stakeholders, to the behavioural level of actual ethical behaviour in response to their call on us to take responsibility. The second contribution of the chapter consists in the conceptualization of an ethical approach to stakeholder engagement, collaboration, and partnership in management practices. With this, we open a new perspective on the opportunities and limitations of stakeholder engagement and partnership in the context of management practices and provide new directions for managing these partnerships in practice.

In chapter 5, we broaden our perspective on management as entrepreneurial action. We raise the question of whether entrepreneurship has to be conceptualized differently in light of the grand challenges of our time, that is, as sustainable entrepreneurship. We challenge traditional conceptualizations of sustainable entrepreneurship because of a fundamental tension between processes involved in sustainable development and processes involved in entrepreneurship; the concept of sustainable entrepreneurship contains a paradox, because sustainability involves the reduction of information asymmetries, whereas entrepreneurship involves enhanced and secured levels of information asymmetries (Section 18). Our first contribution in this chapter is the introduction of the paradox of sustainable entrepreneurship, which explains the limits of contemporary sustainable entrepreneurial practices. The second contribution of this chapter is the development of a new theory of sustainable entrepreneurship that overcomes this paradox. The basic argument is that environmental problems have to be conceptualized as wicked problems or sustainability-related eco-system failures (Section 7). Because all actors involved in the entrepreneurial process are characterized by their epistemic insufficiency regarding the solution of these problems (Section 7), the role of information in the sustainable entrepreneurial process changes. On the one hand, the reduction of information asymmetries primarily aims to enable actors to become critical of sustainable entrepreneurs' actual business operations. On the other hand, the epistemic insufficiency of sustainable entrepreneurs guarantees that information asymmetries remain as a source of new sustainable business opportunities. This new theory of sustainable entrepreneurship informs the sixth dimension of our philosophy of management as epistemic insufficient entrepreneurship.

Based on the six dimensions of the philosophy of management developed in chapters 2 to 5, we ask for an integrated principle of business ethics in chapter 6. Contrary to most literature in business ethics, which starts with an original disconnect between business and ethics and focusses on the *application* of ethical theory in the particular domain of business management, the philosophy of management that we developed in this study enables us to find our point of departure in the intrinsic relation between business and ethics. Based on the findings of this study, we reflect on the nature of business management to reveal the intrinsic relation between business and ethics and to develop an integrated principle of business ethics. The first contribution of this chapter is that we develop a new theory of business ethics based on the six dimensions of the philosophy of management. By applying our philosophy of management on business ethical considerations, we provide a new argument to reject the free market ideological claim that ethical responsibility has to be excluded from business management. By applying our philosophy of management on ethical considerations, we at the same time move beyond applied ethical approaches in business ethics and, instead, are able to embed ethics in the nature of business management (Section 20).

Subsequently, we ask for the individual moral competencies of the manager that enable him or her to engage in business ethical practices (Section 21). To this end, we explore the meaning of two rather new and unfamiliar *moral* competencies in the field of corporate social responsibility and corporate sustainability, that is, normative and action competence. Because of the complexity of grand challenges like global warming, it is unclear what "normativity" in normative competences and "responsible action" in action competence actually mean. In this chapter, we raise the question of how both these individual moral competencies have to be understood and how they are related to each other. Our second contribution in this chapter is the provision of a virtue ethics perspective on both moral competencies, leading to the virtuous competence of business managers that enables them to engage in grand challenges like global warming and business ethical practices.

Because business ethical practices are not only dependent on the individual manager but also on the institutional context and governance of the business operations, we finally ask for governance structures that secure and enhance business ethical practices. Although codes of conduct and ethical codes are often seen as ways to operationalize ethical principles and norms in the business operations, a major problem is the so-called attitude–behaviour gap; the adoption of corporate codes does, in fact, not necessarily lead to more corporate responsible behaviour. The gap in current research is that we need a theory that explains why corporate codes do not always lead to more corporate responsible behaviour. This theory should provide a concept of corporate codes that in fact enhances and secures actual responsible behaviour in business. The third contribution of this chapter is that it provides a theory of corporate codes that enables managers to enhance and secure corporate responsible behaviour, explains conceptually why codes sometimes fail, and indicates which organizational factors can enhance and secure the effectiveness of corporate codes (Section 22). We provide a performative concept of corporate codes that helps to bridge classical dichotomies like individualist versus collectivist approaches of moral agency (Valasquez, 1983; Werhane, 1985; McMahon, 1995) and restrictive versus empowering ethics (Kjonstad and Willmott, 1995), and opens a new perspective on the interaction between individual moral learning and development and the corporate institutionalization of codes (Constantinescu and Kaptein, 2015).

In the final chapter of this study, we draw our conclusions.

Notes

1 In fact, interest in the history of the concept of management is more often found outside the particular subdomain of philosophy of management, for instance, in Mondzain (2005) and Agamben (2007).

2 According to Foucault, for instance, there are three co-existing types of power relations: (1) legal power in which the sovereign state defines normative codes of what is allowed and what is not; (2) executive power that safeguards the obedience to the legal system, like police and penitentiary detention systems; (3) biopolitical power as government of populations (Foucault, 2009). In biopolitical power, "the massive, compact disciplines are broken down into flexible methods of control" (Foucault, 1979: 211).

1 Setting the Scene: Opening Up the Self-evident Concept of Management

One way to open up the concept of management for philosophical reflection is by tracing the different meanings it has in history. Historical analysis can help us to question the self-evidence of the current association of management as managerial power and mechanism of control, to deconstruct the presupposed concepts that always already structure our understanding of management, and to explore the sedimentary conceptual structures which show themselves in the words and notions we self-evidently use in our understanding of management practices.

Although most philosophers in the history of philosophy did not develop an explicit philosophy of management, there seems to be at least one exception. One of the first philosophical conceptualizations of business management occurred in the work of Xenophon (2013). In *Oeconomicus*, published around 385 B.C., Xenophon introduces a dialogue between Socrates and Critobulus, a wealthy young man, and Ischomachus, a noble and successful manager, about *oikonomia*.[1] *Oikonomia*, as Xenophon understood it, is not comparable with our contemporary understanding of economics and is primarily concerned with household management (Deslandes, 2018). The fact that *oikonomia* originally concerns household management, rather than economics, may also explain why economists are often hesitant to read Xenophon as an economist (Lowry, 1979). The domain of the household is not limited to the private sphere of the house in which we live, but extents to all property that enables the owner of the household to make a living. This legitimizes us to take Xenophon's philosophical reflections on household management as a preliminary philosophy of business management. In this chapter, we first explore Xenophon's philosophy of management (Section 4) and the knowledge, skills, and virtues that good management requires (Section 5). Subsequently, we confront Xenophon's conceptuality with the self-evident understanding of management in contemporary management science to open-up the self-evidence of the concept of management for critical reflection, first by considering it from the perspective of Xenophon's work (Section 6) and then by considering it from the perspective of the grand challenges of our time like global warming (Section 7). Our reflections will raise particular questions

DOI: 10.4324/9781003231875-1

that challenge the self-evident conceptualization of management in terms of managerial power and mechanism of control.

4 Xenophon's Philosophy of Management

One of the first philosophical conceptualizations of management occurred in the work of Xenophon. In the *Oeconomicus*, business management concerns the totality of the assets of the owner. Although these assets are a necessary condition to make a living, it is not a sufficient condition as these assets have to be managed in order to become profitable and generate wealth for the owner (Xenophon, 2013: 1.15, 3.1–3.3). What are the main characteristics of business management that can be found in Xenophon's work? In this section, we identify the main characteristics of management based on our reading of the *Oeconomicus*. In this effort, we abandon the contextual factors that can be found in Xenophon's work, as he lived in an agricultural society and in a period where management mainly concerned the management of slaves.

Establishment and Governance of a Functioning Order of the Business in Order to Make Profit

A first characteristic of business management concerns the functional order and ordered arrangement of the business. The business is led by a superintendent (*episkopos*) who is in control of the business, even in case of accidents and unforeseen situations, so that it's ordered functioning is guaranteed and maintained. This control of the manager is compared with a ship:

> Now I saw this man in his spare time inspecting everything that is needed as a matter of course on the ship. I was surprised to see him looking them over and asked what he was doing. "Sir", he answered, "I am looking to see how the ship's equipment is stored, in case of any accident, or whether anything is missing or mixed up with other equipment". (Xenophon, 2013: 8.15–16)

Business management is understood here as the establishment and governance of a functioning order in which all natural resources have their proper place, all human resources have their proper task and role,[2] and the business manager regulates and governs the proper use of these natural and human resources in order to make profit. This involves the structuring of the business and the assignment of an appropriate place to each part of the business. Xenophon speaks about grain that has to remain dry and wine that has to remain cool, but we can extent this to the appropriate design of the production and distribution process of a business, the structure of business units, etc. Next, it concerns the placement of employees in this functioning order. The first characteristic of business management that we can discern is the establishment and governance of a functioning order of the business in order to make profit.

Establishment and Governance of a Functioning Order of the Business in order to Evoke Public Admiration

A second characteristic of business management occurs if we consider the ordered functioning of the ship we encountered before. In first instance, the establishment and governance of a functioning order of the business enables the manager to act appropriately in times of setback or unforeseen circumstances that threaten the survival of the ship in stormy weather. But another aspect of this functioning order is that it constitutes a "paradise" of beauty that evokes admiration (Xenophon, 2013: 4.13, 4.21). We can think of Xenophon's example of the ship in which all equipment is well stored – for example, rope is not lying around but well-ordered and organized – and that provides peace of mind and energy to work in, but we can easily extend this example to well-established organization structures in which all disparate tasks and roles work together as one (Xenophon, 2013: 8.7). Xenophon provides the example of a chorus:

> A chorus is a combination of people; but when its members do as they please, it becomes mere confusion, and there is no pleasure in watching it; but when they move and sing in an orderly fashion, then those same people at once seem worth watching and worth hearing. (Xenophon, 2013: 8.3)

This order is not only a functional order but evokes admiration because of its beauty – everything is more beautiful when set out in order according to Xenophon (2013: 8.20) – and nothing is so good for human beings as order (Xenophon, 2013: 8.3). It is important to acknowledge that for the Greeks, the beautiful does not only has aesthetic but also moral significance. The second characteristic of business management that we discern is that the manager establishes and governs the functioning order of the business in such a way that its (beautiful) order evokes public admiration.

Establishment and Governance of a Functioning Order of the Business to Serve Both Private and Public Interests

A third characteristic of business management is that the ordered functioning of the business does not only serve the private interests of the owner of the business – for example, a grand harvest – but also the public interest of society. A farm does not only provide food and luxury by which people live and enjoy their live but also the environment in which public services can be practiced. Xenophon provides the example of agriculture that enables man to work on the land *and* prepare them to defend the state:

> She gives increased strength through exercise to those who labour with their own hands and hardens the overseers of the work by rousing them early and forcing them to move about briskly. For on a farm no less than in the city the most important operations have their fixed time. Again, if a man wants to defend his city by serving in the cavalry, farming is his most efficient partner in furnishing upkeep for this horse; if in the infantry, it energizes his body. (Xenophon, 2013: 5.4–5, 11.17)

We can easily abstract from this particular context and argue that management establishes and governs a functioning order that serves simultaneously private – sales of food products – and public purposes – serving a healthy society by promoting a healthy lifestyle. In the end, business management is not a goal in itself but should enable the business manager to serve the interests of his or her friends and the state according to Xenophon (2013: 6.9). Only those who serve the state and are loyal to society are held in the highest esteem by the state (Xenophon, 2013: 6.10). The third characteristic of business management that we can discern is that the business manager establishes and governs the functioning order of the business in such a way that it integrates public and private interests.

Engagement in the Business Operations via Direct Labour

In order to establish and govern the functioning order of the business, the manager has to engage in the business operations himself via direct labour according to Xenophon. This seems to be strange for a business owner in the Greek context, as labour is scorned and held in low regard in ancient Greece (Xenophon, 2013: 4.2). But Xenophon is more positive about direct engagement in the business operations of the business manager via direct labour – planting, for instance (Xenophon, 2013: 4.22–24) – as it contributes to their happiness as purpose of life (*eudaimonia*) (Xenophon, 2013: 4.25). The joy of direct labour provides satisfaction and self-confidence, as their mastery in the production of the products and services that the business provides matures.[3] Another aspect of the positive assessment of direct labour may be the double purpose of business operations that we encountered before, for instance, farming (private interest) and preparing to defend the state (public interest). One other important reason for direct involvement in labour is that an important task of managers is to teach their employees, which requires know-how as we will see. Here, direct labour is not a goal in itself but serves the manager's aim to fulfil his or her role as business manager and his or her role as public servant. The fourth characteristic of business management is the involvement of the manager in the business operations via direct labour.

Engagement in the Business Operations via the Work Done by Other People

The fifth characteristic of business management concerns the manager's engagement in the business operations via the work of other people, that is, the management of his or her subordinates to perform all roles and tasks in a proper way. His or her task is to give subordinates a proper role and task and manage them in such a way that they are not imprisoned and enforced to perform their task in a proper way, but that they are free and willing to work for the business manager (Xenophon, 2013: 3.4).

At a first level, he has to cooperate with his wife in order to become successful according to Xenophon. Although Xenophon argues that the business manager has to instruct his wife in the right way of doing things (Xenophon, 2013: 3.11), and with this, may make the impression that he sees his wife merely as subordinate like Aristotle,[4] it is clear that Xenophon is in fact very positive about the role of the wife in business management and that he stresses cooperation and partnership with her in growing the business:

> I think that the wife who is a good partner in the household contributes just as much as her husband to its good; because the income for the most part is the result of the husband's exertions, but the expenses are controlled mostly by the wife's management. If both do their part well, the estate is increased; if they act incompetently, it is diminished. (Xenophon, 2013: 3.15)

If we abstract from classical role models, we can argue that Xenophon highlights here that the business manager cannot maintain the functioning order of the business all by himself.[5] Because he is focusing on sales, for instance, he needs first of all to cooperate and partner up with other managers who manage expenses. The maintenance of the functioning order of a profitable business requires a team of managers that "mutually service" (Xenophon, 2013: 7.19) each other and form a partnership, balancing income and expenses, external and internal affairs, etc. As it is clear that for Xenophon, the wife contributes equally to the success of the business, we can abandon his literal connection of males as manager of the external affairs and females as managers of the internal affairs (Xenophon, 2013: 7.20–7.26) and highlight the functional difference between the management of income, for instance, marketing and sales, and the management of expenses, for instance, procurement. Next to performing his or her own specific role as manager of income or expenses, for instance, the manager has to manage a management team together with other managers in order to make the business profitable. The management of a management team is the first level of engagement of the business manager with business operations via the work of other people.

At a second level, the business manager has to establish a management system because he or she cannot control everything himself, for instance, in case of other branches of the business that are not under his or her direct control. One way to maintain the functioning order of the business is by establishing internal rules and regulations that all employees have to comply with, for instance, maxims and governance procedures that safeguard right behaviour. Xenophon provides examples like "thieves shall be punished for their thefts" (Xenophon, 2013: 14.5), but we can easily abstract from these examples and extent it to other and also more positive core values of a firm like honesty and integrity. It is interesting to observe that Xenophon focusses on the content of these rules, for instance, that the maxim we just mentioned makes greed unprofitable to the offender and benefits the upright employee (Xenophon, 2013: 14.6).

At a third level, the business manager maintains the functioning order of the business by assigning proper roles to trusted middle managers that send him reports about their business performance, and that can perform the management tasks in the name of the business manager. This middle manager should have the same personal characteristics as the business manager as owner of the assets, for instance, self-control and eagerness to improve the business (Xenophon, 2013: 9.11–12, 14.1; see Section 5 for the further discussion of the competencies of the manager). The business manager is the superintendent who oversees and governs the middle managers so that they adhere to the arrangement of tasks and roles, and inspects the performance of the business (Xenophon, 2013: 9.14–15, 14.1). Like the business manager oversees and governs the middle managers, the middle managers oversee and govern the employees. Also, these middle managers are seen as partners of the business manager:

> We also taught her to be loyal to us by making her a partner in all our joys and, if we had any trouble, inviting her to share that too. We trained her to be eager for the improvement of our estate by making her familiar with it and by allowing her to share in our success. And we developed in her a sense of justice by giving more honour to the just than to the unjust, and by showing her that the just live in greater wealth and freedom than the unjust. (Xenophon, 2013: 9.12)

A key task of the business manager is to select the middle managers who are attentive to the business affairs. He or she selects those who have a passion for making money and have a desire to win the approbation of the business manager (Xenophon, 2013: 14.9) and avoids those who are hard drinkers, sluggards, fall desperately in love (Xenophon, 2013: 12.11–15), and remain dishonest even though they are well treated. He or she has also to review the performance of the middle managers and to reward high performance and to honour them, and to punish low performance. It is important to see that for Xenophon, reward does not only consist in the provision of monetary rewards but also in the promotion of good performing middle managers in the scale of honours (Xenophon, 2013: 4.7). This can be done formally via promotions in rank, but also informally by giving trust, by entrusting an important task, and by providing honour to particular employees.

This does not mean however that the business manager can delegate all roles and tasks to the middle management. According to Xenophon, as the business manager experiences best the profits of good management and the losses of bad management, some management tasks can only be performed properly by the business manager himself or another member of the management team and cannot be delegated to the middle managers or employees. Although Xenophon does not provide examples, we can think of management decisions that can have a major impact on the profit and loss of the business.

One can negatively argue that the principle–agent problem explains why the business manager cannot delegate all management tasks to the middle managers, for example, that the business manager as owner of the assets (principle) can never be sure whether the middle manager (agent) will act in his or her best interest or will be tempted to serve his or her own interests instead. More positively formulated, however, one can also argue that the business manager cannot delegate all management tasks to the middle managers because of the considerable importance of teaching and training, as we have seen. This requires his or her leading by example and therefore, his or her direct engagement in the business operations anyway. This brings a fourth level of engagement with the business operation via the work of other people to light, namely people management of the employees of the branches that are under his or her direct control. At this level, management consists in leading subordinates in such a way that they obey willingly and contribute to the profitability of the business, instead of running away in times of setback (Xenophon, 2013: 3.4, 4.19). This requires not only the ability to manage inflowing and outflowing streams of resources, to superintend the value adding process performed by employees, but also rewarding good behaviour and punishment of employees who are misbehaving (Xenophon, 2013: 7.42). Rewarding employees does not only consist in monetary rewards, but also in showing that being obedient is more advantageous for the employees, and by providing particular rewards that are valuable for the individual employees; the one who loves nice cloth is more rewarded by a nice robe, according to Xenophon (2013: 13.6–9). Furthermore, it also involves a differentiation in rewarding, by providing the better employee with superior gifts. Direct people management also involves the skill to care for the employees (Xenophon, 2013: 7.37), as those who are cared for feel grateful and more loyal. As a consequence, the employees will follow the business manager and serve his or her interests. And according to Xenophon, this ability to lead employees that are willing to follow constitutes a good manager[6]:

> Those you may justly call high-minded who have many followers of like mind; and with reason may he be said to march "with a strong arm" whose will many an arm is ready to serve; and truly great is he who can do great deeds by will rather than by strength. So too in private enterprises, the man in authority – foreman or manager – who can make the workers eager, industrious, and persevering – he is the man who gives a lift to the business and swell the surplus .... But if at the sight of him they stir themselves and a spirit of determination and rivalry and eagerness to excel falls on every workman, then I should say: this man has a touch of the kingly nature in him. (Xenophon, 2013: 21.8–10)

Training and Teaching of Employees and Middle Managers

As said, the direct engagement in people management is not a purpose in itself but establishes the know-how of the business manager that enables him to teach the middle management. The middle manager cannot learn to be a good superintendent if the teacher (the business manager) himself models inattentiveness according to Xenophon (2013: 12.18–19). It is primarily "the master's eye" that makes the middle manager good (Xenophon, 2013: 12.20), and this requires at least some direct engagement in the actual business operations of the business manager. With this, a sixth characteristic of business management emerges, namely training and teaching of employees and middle managers. The business manager has to manage his or her subordinates by teaching them how to perform particular skills well, such as producing a grand harvest, making bread out of grain, cloth out of wool, and to superintend and take care of the business. We can easily abstract from Xenophon's examples of the agricultural sector and extent it to any value adding process in business life. By teaching an employee how to make cloth from wool, for instance, the manager doubles the value of the employee because he or she is able to add more value by making cloth from wool, than only the production of wool, for instance (Xenophon, 2013: 7.41). Teaching also concern teaching of loyalty to the business manager, although loyalty is best learned by rewarding those who contribute to the prosperity of the business.

Acknowledgement of the Fundamental Limitations of Management and the Role of Risk and Misforture

Although the business manager establishes and governs a functioning order of the business, Xenophon acknowledges the fundamental role of risk and misfortune. However well the functioning order of the business is established and managed, foresight of future affairs is fundamentally limited, and it is always possible that unforeseen circumstances occur. On the one hand, the emergence of unforeseen circumstances explains why a business needs a well-managed functioning order, in which all employees blindly know where to find equipment and resources to adequately address challenges, like a ship that is assaulted by a hailstorm. We can easily abstract from Xenophon's examples of hailstorms and frosts that impact agricultural practice and argue that managers have to deal with imperfect foresight and contingency. On the other hand, although the establishment and governance of a functioning order helps to manage the business well in case of an accident, Xenophon acknowledges the fundamental limitation of the role of management. In the context of Greek society, this acknowledgment leads to management practices to propitiate the Gods and to ask the blessing of the Gods before engaging in business operations (Xenophon, 2013: 5.19–20). This acknowledgment of the fundamental limitation of the role of management of the functioning order of a business is the seventh characteristic of business management.

Proper Asset Management in order to Increase Profit and Pleasure

The eighth characteristic of business management concerns the extension of the business by proper asset management. Proper asset management, on the one hand, prevents that all assets are fixed in buildings, etc., and are therefore not available and usable to make a profit or that these assets are out of direct control (for instance, in foreign countries) but instead are arranged carefully in the proper place and managed to make profit (Xenophon, 2013: 3.3). On the other, asset management consists in the acquisition of new low performing sites and to make them profitable in order to sell them later on for a higher price, next to autonomous growth of the business via good management practices. It is important to notice that the purpose of these acquisitions is not only to make profit but also for reasons of pleasure:

> "Well farmed land", he would say, "costs a lot and can't be improved;" and he said that where there is no room for improvement there is not much pleasure to be got from the land: landed estate and livestock must be continually improving to give the fullest measure of satisfaction. (Xenophon, 2013: 20.23)

But the aim of business management is not to increase property as such. The aim of business is to satisfy the wants of the business manager (Xenophon, 2013: 2.4) *and* to serve his or her friends and the state: "Surely those who can maintain their own estate and yet have enough left to adorn the city and relieve their friends may well be thought affluent and powerful man" (Xenophon, 2013: 11.10). And even when Xenophon seems to suggest that the increase of property is a purpose in itself, this increase is limited by the condition of self-control, which prevents greed and impulsive behaviour, by the condition of fairness and honourability (Xenophon, 2013: 7.15, 11.8), and by the condition of providing pleasure.

Proper Asset Management in order to Serve Society

The ninth and last characteristic of business management is therefore that management is conditioned by the human needs of the business manager as owner of the assets on the one hand, which may be different for each individual manager (Xenophon, 2013: 2.4), and by his or her service to society on the other.[7] Xenophon provides examples like the entertainment of foreign guests, playing the benefactor to the citizens and contributing to the defence of the state (Xenophon, 2013: 3.6), but we can easily generalize these examples towards a serving role of business to society. According to Xenophon, those business managers who cannot afford these services will be punished by the public (Xenophon, 2013: 2.7).

In Table 1.1, we summarize the nine characteristics of business management that we encountered in Xenophon's work in this section.

5 Key Requirements of Business Managers According to Xenophon

After having identified the key characteristics of business management according to Xenophon, we can also identify the key personal characteristics of the business manager. Although management is a branch of knowledge (*episteme*) according to Xenophon (2013: 1.1), it in fact concerns the *practice* to employ the assets – arable land, for instance – in a particular spatial-temporal context and in such a way that they become profitable – provide a rich harvest, for instance. Business management then does not only involve knowledge – for example, understanding the "what" of farming – but also skills – for example, understanding the "how" and "when" of farming (Xenophon, 2013: 15.8) – as well as the right virtues to successfully operate as a farmer and produce a grand harvest – for example, being attentive and able to govern employees, for instance (Xenophon, 2013: 15.5). Just like knowledge and skills, also these virtues are a necessary condition of successful business management according to

Table 1.1 Nine characteristics of management that can be found in Xenophon

1 Management concerns the establishment and governance of a functioning order of the business in order to make profit.

2 Management concerns the establishment and governance of a functioning order of the business in order to evoke public admiration.

3 The establishment and governance of a functioning order of the business serves both private and public interests in an integrated way.

4 Management consists in the engagement of the business manager in the business operations via direct labour.

5 Management consists in the engagement of the business manager in the business operations via the work done by other people.

   a. Collaboration and partnership with other business managers in a management team.

   b. Establishment of a management system with internal rules and regulations that employees have to comply with.

   c. Assigning proper roles to trusted middle managers.

   d. Direct people management of employees and/or middle managers.

6 Management consists in training and teaching of employees and/or middle managers.

7 Management acknowledges the fundamental limitations of the establishment and governance of the functioning order of the business, and acknowledges the fundamental role of risk and misfortune.

8 Management consists in proper asset management in order to increase profit and pleasure.

9 Management consists in proper asset management in order to serve society.

Xenophon. He identified various virtues of the business manager, for instance, eagerness (in opposition with unwillingness), diligence (in opposite to idleness), moral courage (in opposite to moral cowardice) care (in opposite to negligence), and self-control (in opposite to gambling and consorting with bad companions; Xenophon, 2013: 1.16–1.20).

In modern language, we can frame these three components of knowledge, skills, and virtues in terms of the individual competencies to use the assets of the business in a particular context and situation (We will come back on this subject in Section 21), so the combination of knowledge (*episteme*), virtue (*arête*), and skills (*technè*) that enables an individual business manager to fulfil his or her tasks successfully.[8] We will now discuss the three components of these individual competencies of business managers as we can find them in Xenophon's work.

Knowledge Involved in Management Practices

Xenophon argues that business management concerns a branch of knowledge by which business managers can increase their business (Xenophon, 2013: 6.4). A first part of this knowledge concerns the knowledge as described by the nine characteristics how to establish and govern the functioning order of the business. Business management builds in this respect a field of knowledge as the manager has to understand the job and how and when to do it. Otherwise, a doctor could do the job of a manager as well (Xenophon, 2013: 13.2).

This knowledge of business management is required for three reasons: first, this knowledge enables the business manager to engage in various dimensions of business operations himself (associated with characteristics 1, 2, 3, 7, 8, and 9). Second, this knowledge enables the business manager to manage the middle managers and employees (characteristic 5). Only a manager who has knowledge about the what, how, and when can govern his or her middle managers and employees in a proper way according to Xenophon: "The greatest lesson to learn is how each job ought to be done; and you added that if a man doesn't know what to do and how to do it, no good can come of his management" (Xenophon, 2013: 15.2). Third, this knowledge is required to enable the business manager to teach and train the middle managers:

> Of course I try to train them myself, Socrates. For the man has to be capable of taking charge in my absence; so why need he know anything but what I know myself? For if I am fit to manage the farm, I presume I can teach another man what I know myself. (Xenophon, 2013: 12.4)

A second layer of knowledge concerns the sector-specific expert knowledge of the domain in which the business manager is operating, for example, the what, how, and when of farming (Xenophon, 2013: 15.6). This is required for two reasons. First, this knowledge enables him to engage in the business operations via direct labour himself (characteristic 4). Secondly, a large part of the work of the business manager consists in teaching, for instance, teaching how to generate a grand harvest in farming. This requires the business manager to have particular expert knowledge about farming, for instance (Xenophon, 2013: 7.41). Only if the manager knows what, how, and when to do farming, that is, when his or her mastery of farming is established and matured, he or she is able to teach and manage employees that are involved in farming practices (characteristic 6). In this respect, his or her mastery of the products and services that are produced by the business comes first and is primary, while his or her mastery of his or her employees is secondary. At the same time, the manager should be open to learn from others as well, even his or her employees: "Stand before the loom and be ready to instruct those who know less than you, and to learn from those who know more" (Xenophon, 2013: 10.10).

Xenophon explores the knowledge that is required for farming, for instance, knowledge about the nature of the soil as fertile soil for the produce, the particular plants that can grow properly in a particular region, the right time for sowing and reaping, given the nature of the soil and the local climate. This indicates that the knowledge that is required is not only the knowledge of the what (theoretical knowledge) but also knowledge of the when and how (practical knowledge) that is developed through practice. This sector-specific expert knowledge holds for the what, how, and when of farming but is different in each specific sector.

Another aspect of this practical knowledge is that it is combined with action. Xenophon indicates that many people may know, for instance, the best way of marching in formation through an enemy's country, but that only a few carry it out accordingly. The good manager does not only have knowledge about what ought to be done in a specific situation but also takes care that it is actually done this way (Xenophon, 2013: 20.14). Xenophon calls this attentiveness (Xenophon, 2013: 20.6), a competency that clearly resonates with the modern competency of action competence, that is, the ability to actually take responsibility (see Section 21). Attentiveness is characterized by the ability to oversee the work that has to be done and by taking care that the business operations are actually effectuated according to the planning, by planning the work and by effectuating it accordingly (Xenophon, 2013: 20.18).

A further cognitive aspect is the ability of the business manager to acknowledge the limitations of his or her individual competencies, and the acknowledgment of roles and tasks of other members of the management team that have to be balanced in order to maintain the functioning order of the business. There are different roles that have to be played in the business and the perfect balance and partnership can be threatened if one of the managers is only focusing on his or her own role or task, neglecting the importance of the others. "But because both must give and take", good managers are characterized by "memory and attention" (Xenophon, 2013: 7.26). Why?

> Just because they are not equally well endowed with all the same aptitudes, they have the more need of each other, and each member of the pair is the more useful to the other, the one being competent where the other is deficient. (Xenophon, 2013: 7.28)

Memory (mneme) is the retention of the managers' own role and task, for instance, production, and attention (*epimeleian*) is the ability to acknowledge the importance of the role and task of other managers to maintain a profitable business, for instance, sales. This idea is confirmed by Xenophon's argument that the good manager requires the power to practice self-control to acknowledge the necessary balance and partnership between the different roles and tasks to maintain a profitable business (Xenophon, 2013: 7.26).

Skills Involved in Management Practices

Xenophon repeatedly indicate particular skills of the business manager, like the ability to train middle man and employees (Xenophon, 2013: 5.14); the ability to govern man by rewarding those subordinates who act properly and punish those who are disobedient; the ability to motivate and encourage his or her subordinates (Xenophon, 2013: 5.16); a large part of management concerns the skill to maintain the functioning order of the business. Xenophon speaks about the manager as superintendent that guards the rules and regulations of the firm, inspects the business and the task performance of the employees. This skill overlaps with practical knowledge and constitutes manager's attentiveness.

Virtues Involved in Business Management

Throughout Xenophon's work, several virtues of the business manager are discussed. Business management requires self-control in general (Xenophon, 2013: 7.15) and particular control like eagerness (in opposition with unwillingness), diligence (in opposite to idleness), moral courage (in opposite to moral cowardice), and care (in opposite of negligence) (Xenophon, 2013: 1.18–19). The (middle) manager should be loyal (Xenophon, 2013: 12.5), avoid gambling and consorting with bad companion (Xenophon, 2013: 1.20).

According to Xenophon, the good manager is characterized by the practice of specific virtues, as a virtuous manager will be honoured by his or her employees, and better manages the business (Xenophon, 2013: 7.43). Xenophon identifies particular virtues, like high-mindedness. Further, the manager should act in an integer way by showing himself as he or is and without finery because otherwise he or she could deceive people (Xenophon, 2013: 9–10). It is not a problem and even desirable if the manager looks healthy because he or she is doing physical exercises – Xenophon refers to management by walking around, which also strengthen the health of the manager (Xenophon, 2013: 10.11–12) – but it should be real health and no finery like makeup, high heels, etc., to make a better impression or to pretend to be something more than he or she actually is.

A final aspect of the manager's virtues is his or her acknowledgment that his or her success is not only dependent on his or her own performance but dependent on the Gods that grant prosperity to the one who knows his or her duties and is thoughtful and careful accordingly (Xenophon, 2013: 11.8). The business manager prays for health, esteem in the city and wealth, for instance, and acts and behaves according to these prayers (Xenophon, 2013: 11.8), for example, he or she acts as the best possible version of him- or herself. He or she honours the Gods by helping his or her friends if they need anything and supply what the state lacks (Xenophon, 2013: 11.9–10). In short, the business manager acts according to the way he she wants to be seen by the Gods. We can frame these virtues in terms of integrity, sincerity, and modesty.

In describing the individual competencies of business managers, we do not distinguish between knowledge, skills, and virtues of business managers and middle managers but provide a complete list of possible knowledge, skills, and virtues that are needed. Although one could expect that knowledge how to establish and govern the functioning order of the business is more important for the business manager than for the middle manager, both require people management skills, attentiveness, and virtues like self-control. Xenophon is rather explicit in this, when he argues that in case a business manager assigns a middle manager to perform part of the tasks in his or her name, the same characteristics of self-control, memory, and attention are applied to the middle managers (Xenophon, 2013: 9.11).

Another issue that has to be taken into account is that according to Xenophon, nonetheless the important role of teaching and training, this does not imply that he believes that all knowledge, skills, and virtues can be learned. People management skills, for instance, are partly a gift that is required next to teaching:

> Mind you, I don't go so far as to say that this can be learned at sight or at a single hearing. On the contrary, to acquire these powers a man needs education: he must be possessed of great natural gifts; above all, he or she must be inspired. For I regard this gift as not altogether human but divine – this power to win willing obedience: it is manifestly a gift of the gods to the true votaries of self-control. (Xenophon, 2013: 21.11–12)

Finally, according to Xenophon, the competencies of the business manager that are identified in the *Oeconomicus* are not only applicable to *business* management but also to military management and political management.[9] On the one hand, this shows already that business or economic management is integral part of the political management of the state (We will come back on this subject in chapter 3). On the other hand, it raises the question which of these competencies are particularly applicable on *business* management only.

In Table 1.2, the various knowledge, skills, and virtues that can be found in Xenophon's work are summarized.

6 Questioning the Self-evident Conceptualization of Management from the Perspective of Xenophon's Philosophy of Management

It is striking that this early conceptualization of management resonates pretty much with the management theory provided by Henry Fayol.

Table 1.2 Knowledge, skills, and virtues (competencies) of business managers that can be found in Xenophon

Knowledge:	• Knowledge how to establish and govern the functioning order of the business, how to manage people, etc.
	• Sector-specific expert knowledge, e.g. the what, how, and when of farming.
	• Practical knowledge to effectuate and to actually engage in the business operations.
	• Self-knowledge of the limitations of the knowledge and skills of the business manager.
Skills:	• Training skills.
	• People management skills (e.g. reward and punishing, motivation and encouragement, taking care).
	• Maintenance skills (e.g. guarding rules and regulations, inspection).
Virtues:	• Self-control, eagerness, diligence, moral courage, care, loyal, and high-mindedness.
	• Integrity, sincerity, and modesty.

According to Fayol's management theory, management has five functions: planning, organizing, instruction, coordination, and control (Fayol, 1949). If we compare Xenophon's philosophy of management with the functions of management according to Fayol's management theory, we see that planning, organizing and control correspond with the first characteristic of business management that we can find in Xenophon's work. Instruction and coordination correspond with the fifth characteristic we can find in Xenophon's work. We can even argue that Xenophon's conception of people management already moves beyond the mechanistic perspective of management that is often associated with scientific management and prefigures the people-oriented perspective that is introduced by the human relations school (Mayo, 2003).

Xenophon's characteristics of management also resonate pretty much with contemporary definitions, for instance the one that can be found in the Oxford Dictionary of Business and Management. Management in the verbal sense concerns the act of managing an organization or a part of it in order to make most effective use of available resources, and management in the substantive sense concerns the people involved in these type of managerial activities, that is, the directing, planning, and running of the business operations (Law, 2009; Statt, 2004). According these definitions, management (1) concerns an organizational skill to establish and govern the functional order of the organization that is taught at business schools, which corresponds with the first characteristic of business management that we found in Xenophon's work; (2) it concerns the ability to motivate subordinates, which corresponds with the fifth characteristic of business management that we found in Xenophon' work; (3) it has an entrepreneurial sense and concerns the recognition and exploitation of new business opportunities, which corresponds with the eighth characteristic of business management that we found in Xenophon's work. Another similarity is that management is generally seen as something that can be learned by training, which corresponds with the sixth characteristic of business management that we found in Xenophon's work, although the extent to which people management can be taught remains disputable (Law, 2009).

In sum, the comparison between Xenophon and contemporary definitions of management show three areas of commonality: (a) management consists in the establishment and governance of a functioning order of the business; (b) management consists in the engagement in the business operations via the work done by other people; (c) management consists in proper asset management and entrepreneurial action in order to serve business and society. At the same time, Xenophon's philosophy of management enables us question contemporary definitions of management as managerial power and mechanism of control.

Management for Profit

While currently, business management is mainly focussed on the establishment and governance of a functioning order of the business to make profit, Xenophon shows the intrinsic relation between business and society. The aim of business management is not only to evoke public admiration (second characteristic of Xenophon's concept of business management), which requires that the business operations both serve private and public interests in an integrated way (third characteristic of Xenophon's concept of business management), and that private profits are partly spend to serve society (ninth characteristic of Xenophon's concept of business management). This concept of management challenges not only contemporary conceptualizations of the differences between private and public management in political philosophical debates. It also challenges current business management practices that primarily aim at private interests and their redistribution via tax payment and philanthropic activities and calls for the active engagement and integration of societal interests in the business operations in order to increase corporate social responsibility (CSR). CSR, seen from Xenophon's perspective, should be integral part of business management in order to evoke public admiration. We could frame public admiration in modern terms as being responsive to societal needs in order to receive a social license to operate by the public (we will come back on this subject in chapter 3).

It also requires that business managers integrate both private and public interests in their business operations and solve tensions between economic and societal values. While private interests often prevail over public interests in contemporary business management – think of the example of the food industry that often contribute to public health problems (e.g. obesity, type 2 diabetes; Tempels et al., 2017a) – Xenophon challenges us to integrate private and public interests in business management – think for example of food firms that engage in food innovations for public health and serve the common good (Garst et al., 2018). In Section 10, we take this contested area of management as the point of departure to move beyond contemporary conceptualizations of management for profit and reflect on management as constituting meaning.

Management as Managerial Power

According to contemporary definitions, management concerns the act of managing an organization in order to make most effective use of available resources. The manager is an efficient and powerful agent according to traditional management science in general and scientific management in particular (Fayol, 1949; Taylor, 1911). Management concerns a skill that can be learned at business schools and this skill enables the individual professional to direct, plan and control the business operations. Although the roles and tasks of business management can be combined with other professional tasks, it often involves a strict division of labour between the manager of the business operations and the workforce, and a strict division of labour between the knowledge and skills of the business manager – leadership and finance for instance – and sector specific or disciplinary knowledge and skills of the workforce. In this respect, the manager remains external to the primary process of the business operations, and this separation of the primary process ensures the differentiation between hierarchical levels on which the manager is dependent. Further, by withdrawing him- or herself from the primary process in which the workforce is highly dependent on each other, the manager becomes independent and manages and controls the primary process via instrumental control systems (management by numbers).

This conception of management can be contrasted with Xenophon, who highlights the necessity of sector specific expert knowledge and skills of the manager, and the necessity of the involvement of business managers in the business operations via direct labour (fourth characteristic of management that we can find in Xenophon's work). On the one hand, the strict division of labour in contemporary conceptualizations of management may explain the instrumentalization of management in contemporary business management, and the disconnection and distance between business management and the business operations at the work floor. On the other hand, Xenophon's concept of business management can help to reconnect and integrate business management and execution. In this the particular knowledge, skills and virtues that Xenophon propose may help to develop a broader set of individual competencies and know-how that is required for business managers. In Section 8, we take this contested area of management as the point of departure to move beyond contemporary conceptualizations of managerial power and reflect management as participation.

Management as Mechanism of Control

While the role of risk and misfortune is normally acknowledged in modern conceptualizations of business management, the radical fallibility and vulnerability of management is often not systematically reflected upon in the literature (Deslandes, 2018). It is often taken as something that can be managed and controlled, for instance by risk management practices. Xenophon's conception of management can help us to acknowledge the fundamental limitations of business management and the vulnerability of the manager, that is, the fundamental role of risk and misfortune and the impossibility to establish full control; there is no such thing as Taylor's "one best way" to operate the business. This possibility of failure fundamentally limits the ambition of business managers to establish and maintain full control of the business operations. On the one hand, this idea challenges contemporary business management practices that primarily aim to increase power and control and substantiate the so-called "control societies" in the industrial age (Deleuze, 1992, 1997). On the other hand, the acknowledgement of failure, risk and misfortune may rehabilitate the role of business management as ability and capacity that involves know-how, actual engagement and virtue.

In other words, Xenophon's concept of business management helps to acknowledge the limitations of management control, that is, the fundamental role of risk and misfortune and the impossibility to establish full control (seventh characteristic of management that we can find in Xenophon's work). In this respect, Xenophon can be seen as prefiguring some aspects of Fiedler's contingency management theory, especially his acknowledgement that there is no absolute best way to manage the business, and the situational character of the management style of the manager (Fiedler and Garcia, 1987). In Section 9, we take this contested area of management as the point of departure to move beyond contemporary conceptualizations of management as mechanism of control and reflect management as resistance and responsive action.

Based on this first round of reflection on the nature of business management, we cannot draw conclusions regarding these three contested areas of management yet. But by comparing characteristics of business management provided by Xenophon with the self-evident understanding of business management in contemporary management theory, we open up this concept for further philosophical reflection in the next chapters.

7 Questioning the Self-evident Conceptualization of Management from the Perspective of the Grand Challenges of Our Time

We continue our reflections on the self-evident conceptualization of management by concentrating on the three common characteristics in Xenophon and contemporary definitions of management that we found in the previous section; management as establishment and governance of a functioning order of the business; management as engagement in the business operations via the work done by other people; management as proper asset management and entrepreneurial action. We concentrate on the societal role of business to question these three characteristics of management.

The societal role of business is not only argued for by Xenophon, who sees an intrinsic relation between business and society (Section 4). Also, in our contemporary society, it is increasingly acknowledged that firms are not only economic institutions but at the same time moral institutions that contribute to society at large; they embody strategies and operations that involve moral decisions regarding the good or right way of production and consumption of their products and services. The core of Corporate Social Responsibility (CSR) lies in their commitment to perform ethically in business life. CSR is however nothing straightforward, as becomes clear if we consider the grand societal challenges of our time like the Covid pandemic, world poverty and global warming. These pose several challenges for our understanding of the responsible management of these challenges.

Global warming is for instance such a grand challenge business managers have to deal with. Firms are increasingly seen as part of the problem while they should become part of the solution. Nowadays, 93% of the CEOs see sustainable development as an important feature of their firm's future success (Accenture, 2010). Initially, Corporate Social Responsibility (CSR) with regard to sustainable development was motivated by public responses to irresponsible business activities and pressures from NGOs (Porter, 2006), and consisted mainly in cosmetic improvements of the corporate image of the firm in order to safeguard their market position. Today, it is increasingly seen as a source of competitive advantage (Málovics et al., 2006). Over the last few years, we have seen a tremendous increase in sustainably produced goods and services, balancing economic, socio-cultural and environmental aspects. Furthermore, CSR or more in particular, corporate sustainability, has become increasingly important in our Western society. By engaging in sustainable development, firms respond to the expectations of their stakeholders in order to enhance and secure their license to operate (Gunningham et al., 2004). Corporate social responsibility can therefore be seen as a business approach to sustainable development, in which firms voluntarily integrate sustainability into their business strategies.

At the same time, managing CSR with regard to sustainable development is difficult because sustainability is a so-called wicked problem. Wicked problems are complex, ill-structured, and public problems, like international terrorism, climate change and poverty, and cannot be solved in traditional ways or by simple solutions. According to Rittel and Webber (1973), who described the concept of wicked problems as opposed to tamed problems for the first time in 1973, these problems are not called wicked because they are themselves ethically deplorable. Rather, the term means that these problems are difficult to pin down. They concern complex systems in which cause and effect relations are uncertain or unknown. Rittel and Webber (1973) specified ten characteristics of wicked problems. Examples include the fact that there is no definitive formulation of a wicked problem, that solutions to wicked problems are not true or false but better or worse, that wicked problems have no stopping rule, that is, that the problem solver does not know when an acceptable solution to the problem has been found, etc. (Batie, 2008).

It is not difficult to recognize that sustainable development is such a wicked problem (Wick et al., 2011; Grunwald, 2007; Swart et al., 2004).[10] On the one hand, the famous definition of sustainable development from the Brundtland report – *Our common future* – (World Commission on Environment and Development, 1987) seems to be quite simple, stating that the use of resources today should not constrain the use of (non-renewable) resources in the future. If, however, we take the biophysical finiteness of the earth into account and, with this, the fact that every resource will eventually be exhausted, it becomes clear that the problem is difficult to pin down and highly complex, just like its solution (Peterson, 2009). Several authors have indicated that global warming is such a highly complex problem because it concerns global and interconnected issues like climate change, increasing populations and changing consumption patterns, which cannot be solved in traditional ways or by simple solutions (Brennan, 2004; Ehrlich and Ehrlich, 2009). Further indications of this wickedness can be found in the dispersion of causes and effects – emissions of greenhouse gasses (GHG) are produced in a particular geographical area but have global effects – in the fragmentation of agency – there is no centralized system of global governance to tackle this global problem, while local agents have the tendency to serve their own (unsustainable) interests (Harding, 1968) – and in institutional inadequacy – local enforceable sanctions to enhance and secure more sustainable behaviour is limited by the current, mainly national institutional context (Gardiner, 2006; Jamieson, 2007). Some authors even call global warming a super wicked problem:

> Time is running out; the central authority needed to address them is weak or non-existent; those who cause the problem also seek to

> create a solution; and hyperbolic discounting occurs that pushes responses into the future when immediate actions are required to set in train longer term policy solutions. (Levin et al., 2010: 2)

In such a context, it is difficult, if not impossible, to conceptualize how managers of corporate social responsibility, who have a broad variety of perspectives and interests, accept responsibility "to maintain a non-declining set of opportunities based on possible uses of the environment for future members of their communities" (Norton, 2000: 1043). In fact, it is not possible to satisfy the needs of the current generation *without* changing the conditions for future generations. On the one hand, we cannot propose definite solutions if we do not have a definite problem description. On the other hand, all proposed solutions remain finite and provisional compared to the complexity and depth of the sustainability problem itself. In this sense, we can never reduce sustainability to a finite set of particular "problems", nor say that these problems can definitely be solved, that is, that sustainability is fully achieved.

These problems also occur at the level of the production processes of firms. Current production and consumption patterns – think of nano-particles in food products, batteries in cell-phones and plutonium to power pacemakers – can be expected to impact future generations in a way that firms can never experience, predict or manage. Manager's foresight of future developments is fundamentally limited while their current knowledge of responsible solutions is insufficient and may always have unintended negative consequences. The lack of foresight and the possibility of unexpected negative side effects reveal the *epistemic insufficiency* of managers who intent a good or right way of production and consumption, while they presuppose that they know what is right and wrong in business life. In other words, managing corporate social responsibility with regard to sustainable development is limited by the wickedness of grand challenges like global warming and our epistemic insufficiency regarding the possible side effects of our interventions to take responsibility (DeMartino, 2011).

While the epistemic insufficiency of managers makes clear why grand challenges pose serious problems for managers engagement in corporate social responsibility regarding sustainable development, the reality of these grand challenges also makes clear why business managers ought to commit to CSR. This raises the question who is in charge to take responsibility for grand challenges like global warming. A first possible response consists in the idea that business managers themselves are able to address these challenges. Sustainability related governance mechanisms like sustainability standards and codes of conduct can be seen as successful instruments developed by business managers in order to enhance and secure more corporate social responsibility with regard to sustainable development (Andersen and Skjoett-Larsen, 2009; Mamic,

2005). A second possible response consists in the call for political action by governmental institutions to enhance and secure more corporate social behaviour by the introduction of new rules and regulations, whether or not on a global level.

In both responses, it is self-evidently presupposed that we are currently "out of control" and that control can be established and secured again by more established forms of public or private governance. The question is however whether "control" is still a feasible ideal of business management if we acknowledge the epistemic insufficiency of managers regarding the good or right way to produce and consume. This raises the question what implications the very nature of the grand challenges of our time – both their wickedness and our epistemic insufficiency to manage them properly – has for our conceptualization of management. We will see below how wicked problems like global warming challenge the three common characteristics in Xenophon and contemporary definitions of management: management as establishment and governance of a functioning order of the business; management as engagement in the business operations via the work done by other people; management as proper asset management and entrepreneurial action.

Management as Establishment and Governance of a Functioning Order

So far, we encountered business management as the establishment and governance of a functioning order in which all natural resources have their proper place, all human resources have their proper task and role, and the business manager regulates and governs the proper use of these natural and human resources in order to make profit (Section 4). This effort to govern the functioning order of the business can be operationalized by planning, organization and control (Section 6). This conceptualization of business management is challenged by the very nature of grand challenges like global warming. Because global warming is a wicked problem, it is questionable whether managers of corporate social responsibility with regard to sustainable development are in *control* of this problem, while their epistemic insufficiency makes it questionable whether they can *plan* and *organize* its solution. Simple planning and control mechanisms are not available because the cause and effect relations are either unknown or uncertain. In the context of contemporary grand challenges, it is no longer self-evident that management consists in the establishment and governance of a functioning order. It raises the question what implications the wickedness of the grand challenges of our time and our epistemic insufficiency to properly manage these challenges have for our conceptualization of management. In chapter 3, we take this contested area of management as the point of departure to move beyond contemporary conceptualizations of management as establishment and governance of a functioning order and reflect on management as politico-economic governance.

People Management

If business management is understood as the engagement in the business operations via the work done by other people (Section 4), which can be operationalized by the people-oriented perspective of management (Section 6), this conceptualization is also challenged by the very nature of grand challenges like global warming. It challenges the idea that management consists in the assignment of tasks and roles to human resources in order to establish and govern the functioning order of the business. Facing grand challenges like global warming, managers first and foremost have to *engage* in *collaboration* and *partnerships* with internal and external *stakeholders*. While people management assumes that in the end, the manager take responsibility for corporate social responsibility with regard to sustainable development and assigns roles and tasks to human resources to that end, the reality is that many different internal and external stakeholders have different ideas about the problem and the scope of the responsibility of the firm to address these problems. For a firm like Neslé, corporate social responsibility may consist in cleaner production and consumption processes (e.g. waste reduction, sustainable sourcing and recycling), while employees and environmental NGOs may question the role of firms in the Western capitalist system. For a firm like Unilever, corporate social responsibility may consist in the increase of welfare conditions of animals that are used for food products, while employees and animal welfare NGOs may question the role of animal production and consumption in general. The different value frames held by different employees and other internal and external stakeholders pose a challenge for people management. In this context, it is no longer self-evident that management consists in the engagement in the business operations via the work done by other people. It raises the question what implications the wickedness of the grand challenges of our time and our epistemic insufficiency to manage these challenges have for our conceptualization of management. In chapter 4, we take this contested area of management as the point of departure to move beyond contemporary conceptualizations of people management and reflect on management as non-reductive stakeholder engagement.

Management as Entrepreneurial Action

If business management consists in proper asset management and entrepreneurial action (Section 6), this conceptualization is also challenged by the very nature of grand challenges like global warming. The contribution of entrepreneurs to sustainable development has been increasingly receiving attention in the literature (Hall et al., 2010; Klewitz and Hansen, 2014; Parrish, 2010; Thompson et al., 2015). Sustainable entrepreneurship is defined as entrepreneurs' quest to contribute to the supply of innovative environmental products and services with the potential of substantial market success, societal change and changed market conditions (Schaltegger and Wagner, 2011). Whereas traditional entrepreneurs are primarily motivated to address commercial needs and add economic value, without specific concerns regarding sustainability, sustainable entrepreneurs are primarily motivated to address sustainable needs (Trivedi and Stokols, 2011). And whereas traditional or commercial entrepreneurs discover and exploit primarily profitable business opportunities to address customer needs (Shane, 2003), environmental problems are the primary source of profitable business opportunities for sustainable entrepreneurs (Dean and McMullen, 2007). The distinction between profit-driven entrepreneurs and sustainable entrepreneurs is not dichotomous however, but rather a continuum ranging from a purely sustainable to a purely profit-driven orientation (Austin et al., 2006). In fact, many entrepreneurs are profit oriented and at the same time generate environmental and social impacts.

In this, the manager involved in entrepreneurial action seems to combine the best of both worlds by initiating those activities and processes that lead to the identification, evaluation, and exploitation of profitable business opportunities (i.e. entrepreneurship) in order to contribute to sustainable development. In their framework for recognizing opportunities for sustainable development for instance, Patzelt and Shepherd (2011) identify additional knowledge of the natural environment, in addition to motivation and entrepreneurial knowledge, as crucial to being able to identify business opportunities for sustainable development. Environmental problems are seen as additional sources of new business opportunities, just as contributing to the solution of environmental problems can be seen as adding to the economic value-adding process in eco/entrepreneurship (Dean and McMullen, 2007). Sustainable entrepreneurs are thereby expected to be better able to balance economic (profit), social-cultural (people), and environmental (planet) interests by entrepreneurial action. In this respect, one can argue that sustainable entrepreneurial action builds a specific category of management as entrepreneurial action in times of global warming.

The question is, however, what consequences the wicked problem of global warming has for our concept of entrepreneurial action. Is the presupposition of a win–win, in which economic and environmental interests can be integrated in sustainable business models, legitimate, or is there a fundamental tension between processes involved in sustainable development and processes involved in entrepreneurial action (Hahn et al., 2015; Van der Byl and Slawinski, 2015)? The very nature of grand challenges like global warming challenge the win–win paradigm of sustainable entrepreneurial action and shows a fundamental tension. This tension can be found in the notion of information asymmetries and their impact on sustainable entrepreneurship.

Information asymmetries can be defined as the situation in which at least one actor in an economic exchange has more or better information than the other actors. The tension in the concept of sustainable entrepreneurial action can be preliminarily formulated in the following way: sustainable development involves the reduction of information asymmetries, because it enables collaborative action with multiple stakeholders for sustainable action. At the same time, entrepreneurial action requires enhanced and secured levels of information asymmetries in order to achieve and secure competitive advantage. This tension between sustainable development and entrepreneurial action raises the question what implications the wickedness of the grand challenges like global warming and our epistemic insufficiency to manage these challenges have for our conceptualization of management. In chapter 5, we take this contested area of management as the point of departure to move beyond contemporary conceptualizations of management as entrepreneurial action and reflect on management as epistemic insufficient entrepreneurship.

Key Knowledge, Skills, and Virtues of the Business Manager

In Section 5, we indicated that the particular knowledge, skills and virtues that Xenophon propose may help to develop a broader set of individual competencies and know-how that is required for business managers. At the same time, this conceptualization of the key requirements of business managers is challenged by the very nature of grand challenges like global warming.

Over the past few years, individual competencies for the management of corporate social responsibility with regard to sustainable development have received increasing attention in the business ethics, education, and sustainability literature. Competence is the combination of the individual knowledge, skills and attitudes which enable managers to perform certain tasks and achieve specific goals, for instance regarding sustainability. Although the focus has been mainly on the educational context, significant progress has been made on conceptualizing key competencies for sustainability in recent years (Barth et al., 2007; de Haan, 2006; Willard et al., 2010; Wiek et al., 2011; Rieckmann, 2012).

In the business management context, Dentoni and colleagues (2012) and Lans and colleagues (2014) have developed and tested a framework of seven competencies required by managers of corporate social responsibility with regard to sustainable development: systems-thinking competence, foresight-thinking competence, strategic management, embracing diversity and inter-disciplinarity, interpersonal competence, normative competence, and action competence. Anticipatory or foresight thinking is for instance important to assess the future impact of business operations (Wiek et al., 2011), while systemic thinking is important to assess the interrelation and interdependency between several factors involved in interventions to manage sustainable development in alignment with the business operations (Rieckmann, 2012).

The first five of these competencies are relatively familiar in management, business, and entrepreneurship literature. However, normative competence and action competence are rather new concepts. Normative competence enables the manager to assess and improve the sustainability of social-ecological systems on the basis of a set of fixed values and principles. Action competence is the "capability ... to involve yourself as a person with other persons in responsible actions and counter-actions for a more humane world" (Schnack, 1996: 15). In contrast to the other competencies for managing corporate social responsibility with regard to sustainable development, both normative and action competence can be considered moral competencies; they concern norms, values and beliefs which define what is right and wrong concerning corporate social responsibility with regard to sustainable development, and enable managers to take the right decisions and behave in a responsible way.

At first sight, the introduction of two moral competencies seems strange, since normativity, as generally understood in the philosophical literature, has to do with a central kind of action-guidance; one cannot recognize normativity without being at the same time motivated to act on it. Nevertheless, one can argue that the acknowledgement of our ethical responsibility is one thing, but that our actual taking action on this responsibility is something else, as numerous examples in business management clearly showed (think for instance of a banker who clearly knows that manipulating interest rates is violating the norm, but who does not necessarily act upon this knowledge). The difference between the two moral consequences can be conceived therefore in the following way: based on normative competence, managers can be *held responsible* for corporate social responsible practices, while based on action competence, managers can *take responsibility* for corporate social responsible practices. Can these two competencies be added to the key skills and competencies identified by Xenophon?

The wickedness of grand challenges like global warming raises the question how the moral competencies for corporate social responsibility with regard to sustainable development have to be understood. On the one hand, sustainability is a normative concept because it doesn't describe the world as it is, but the way it *should* be (Hahn, 2009). But on the other hand, if sustainable development has to be understood as a wicked problem, the norms and values required of the various stakeholders are not readily available or at least conflict with one another. And if this is the case, it is not clear which norms and values should guide the management of corporate social responsibility with regard to sustainable development. In other words, if sustainable development is considered a wicked problem, it is unclear what "normativity" in the normative competence and "responsible action" in the action competence of the manager actually mean.

This tension between the normativity of both moral competencies and the wickedness of global challenges like global warming raises the question how the knowledge, skills, and virtues of the business manager have to be understood. In chapter 6, we take this contested area of management skills and competencies as the point of departure to develop an integrated concept of business ethics to manage corporate social responsibility with regard to sustainable development (Section 20), including a concept of individual virtuous competence (Section 21) and a performative concept of ethical codes and codes of conduct (Section 22).

Conclusion

In this chapter, we opened up the self-evident concept of management as it appears in philosophical history and in contemporary management theory. We first consulted Xenophon's philosophy of management and identified nine characteristics of business management (Table 1.1; Section 4) and identified key requirements of the business manager (Table 1.2; Section 5).

By contrasting Xenophon's philosophy of management and contemporary management theory, we first identified three areas that challenge the self-evident conceptualization of management as managerial power and mechanism of control from the perspective of Xenophon's philosophy of management: management for profit; management as managerial power and management as mechanism of control (Section 6). Subsequently, we challenged three common characteristics of management that were found in both Xenophon and contemporary management theory from the perspective of the grand challenges of our time: (a) management consists in the establishment and governance of a functioning order of the business; (b) management consists in the engagement in the business operations via the work done by other people (people management); and (c) management consists in proper asset management and entrepreneurial action (Section 7). We also challenged the conceptualization of the key requirements of business managers based on the very nature of grand challenges like global warming in this section.

Although management as managerial power and control can be found in textbooks in management and economics, and describe more or less contemporary management practices, the consultation of Xenophon's philosophy and insights in the very nature of the grand challenges of our time provided six contested areas of business management. Based on the six contested areas in management we encountered in this chapter, we now open up the self-evident conceptualization of business management for philosophical reflection in the next chapters. In each chapter, we take one or more contested areas of management that we identified in this chapter as the point of departure in order to build on but also move beyond contemporary conceptualizations of management as managerial power and mechanisms of control and develop a critical dimension of our philosophy of management. In Table 1.3, an overview of the contested area's and the new conceptualization that will be explored in each chapter is provided.

In chapter 6, we take the philosophical conceptualization of management we developed in this study as the point of departure to develop an integrated concept of business ethics to manage corporate social responsibility with regard to sustainable development, including a concept of individual virtuous competence and a performative concept of ethical codes and codes of conduct.

These new dimensions of the philosophy of management are not only the product of philosophical reflection but can be found in practice as well. They only have a different status as they substantiate our

Table 1.3 Opening up the self-evident conceptualization of business management

Contested Area's of Business Management		Dimensions of the Philosophy of Management	Chapter
Management for profit	→→→	Management as constituting meaning	2
Management as managerial power	→→→	Management as participation	2
Management as mechanism of control	→→→	Management as resistance and responsive action	2
Management as establishment and governance of a functioning order	→→→	Management as politico-economic governance	3
People management	→→→	Management as non-reductive stakeholder engagement	4
Management as entrepreneurial action	→→→	Management as epistemic insufficient entrepreneurship	5

opposition to the dominant concept of management as managerial power and mechanisms of control that is still taught in business schools today and opens up a new perspective on business management. The normative, rather than descriptive nature of these new dimensions of management is not at all problematic, as the development of new theories of imagination for management science is necessary to prevent that we remain intellectually imprisoned by the structures of its self-evident conceptualization (Komporozos-Athanasiou and Fotaki, 2015).

Notes

1 At first sight, it seems to be strange to consult Socrates' vision on business management, as he is normally seen as very negative about profit-making and business (Plato, 2013). Because the historical comparison between the Socrates of Plato and Xenophon is beyond the scope of this study, we purely focus on Socrates contribution to the question what is (business) management as it appears in Xenophon's *Oeconomicus* here.

2 Although Xenophon himself explicitly talks about slaves, we conceive the term in more neutral terms as subordinates. On the one hand, Xenophon's description of the role and treatment of slaves resonates with modern ways of treating employees as we will see. On the other, both slaves and employees can be formally seen as subordinates of the business manager who is the owner of the assets.

3 While historically, direct labour is primarily associated with pain and suffering, Xenophon associates it with joy and pleasure. This may be explained by the fact that he, as business manager, is *free* to engage in direct labour while his or her employees are necessitated to engage in direct labour in order to survive. This may also explain why Karl Marx criticized Xenophon's "characteristic, bourgeois instinct" (cited in Strauss, 1989: 203). At the same time, we could argue that Xenophon's appreciation of direct labour helps us to criticize the disconnection between the workforce and the management level that can often be observed in contemporary bureaucratic organizations (see Section 6).

4 According to Aristotle, females are naturally subordinate because of their limited rationality (Aristotle, 1944: 1260a9–15).

5 In this, Xenophon deviates from the classical idea that in economic affairs, "the rule by many is not good; one should be master, one be king", which can be found in Homer's *Illias* and is cited and confirmed by Aristotle *Metaphysics* (Aristotle, 1933: 1076a3ff).

6 Xenophon wrote another book on leadership, based on his experience of a military campaign in which the Greeks fled for the Persians by fighting their way back to Greece (Xenophon, 1989). Although there are several overlaps between Xenophon's *Oeconomicus* and *Anabalis*, a further comparison between the two works is beyond the scope of this chapter, which focusses on business management in general and not on leadership only. See for an analysis of Xenophon's concept of leadership, Humphreys (2002).

7 Xenophon is against profit maximization as such and his notion of the limitation of the economic sphere by the political sphere resembles Aristotle's conceptualization in this respect (Aristotle, 1944). The further comparison between Aristotle and Xenophon is beyond the scope of this chapter.

8 Framing the particular *episteme* involved in business management in terms of individual competency solves an interpretation problem (Bragues, 2007), as

Xenophon calls management an *episteme* and a *technè* in this book, and is actually consulting a good practitioner in management in the second half of the book, and is not only looking for universals or ideas that can be applied in different cases of business management. Although Agamben is right in his observation that management is less epistemic and more a way of being (Agamben, 2007: 17), he misses this threefold notion of competency as a combination of *episteme, arête,* and *technè.*

9 The question whether political and economic management can be reduced to each other in a general concept of management that holds for both domains, or whether the two remain separate aspects of steering is beyond the scope of this chapter. (We will come back on this subject in chapter 3.)

10 Although we conceptualize sustainability as a wicked "problem", this does not imply that we see sustainability as one single problem. The wickedness of wicked problems means that they have to be conceptualized at a systems level and therefore involve a range of interdependent problems, like climate change, global waste and nutrition streams, pollution of land and water, etc.

2 Management as Participation, Responsive Action, and Constitution of Meaning

In chapter 1, we critically reflected on management as managerial power, as mechanism of control and as focussed on profit maximization (Section 6). Our consultation of Xenophon's insights in the nature of management enabled us to open up this self-evident concept for philosophical reflection. In this chapter, we continue our reflections by focussing on the act of management itself. The point of departure of this chapter is the assumption that we do no justice to the nature of management if we only conceive the phenomenon from the perspective of its utility, that is, the idea that the nature of management can be conceived based on its effects, for example, management of effective use of resources, serving private, and public interests. Management is primarily a social relation which involves actual action and behaviour. For this reason, we concentrate on the three contested areas of management that we identified in Section 6 as points of departure in order to build on but also move beyond contemporary conceptualizations of management as managerial power and mechanisms of control.

Regarding the self-evident notion of management as managerial power, it became clear that contemporary conceptualizations of management involve a strict division of labour between the manager and the workforce. This division of labour may explain the instrumentalization of management in contemporary business management and the disconnection and distance between business management and the business operations at the work floor. At the same time, Xenophon's concept of business management enabled us to reconsider this disconnection. The integration of business management and sector and domain-specific knowledge and skills enables the manager's involvement in the execution of the business operations. In Section 8, we take this contested area of management as the point of departure to philosophically reflect on the nature of management as participation as a first critical dimension of our philosophy of management.

Regarding the self-evident notion of management as mechanism of control, it became clear that the radical fallibility and vulnerability of management is often not systematically reflected upon in the literature.

DOI: 10.4324/9781003231875-2

While it is assumed that risk and fortune can be managed and controlled, Xenophon's conception of management helped us to acknowledge the fundamental limitations of business management and the vulnerability of the manager, that is, the fundamental role of risk and misfortune and the impossibility to establish full control. In Section 9, we take this contested area of management as the point of departure to philosophically reflect on the nature of management as resistance and as responsive action as a second-critical dimension of our philosophy of management.

Regarding the contemporary focus on profit maximization and on private interests of business management, Xenophon's insights in the aim of business management to evoke public admiration was identified as third-contested area. Instead of the sole focus on profit maximization, business managers are required to both serve private *and* public interests in an integrated way. In Section 10, we take this contested area of management as the point of departure to philosophically reflect on the nature of management as constitution of meaning as a third critical dimension of our philosophy of management.

8 Management as Participation

As we have seen in the previous chapter, management is often conceptualized as external to the primary process of the business operations (Section 6). The business manager manages and controls the primary process via instrumental control systems. We can frame this externality and instrumentality of management practices in terms of a *loss of participation*, that is, as a loss of participation in the primary process of the business. We can argue however that the participation of the manager in the primary process is actually important. This loss of participation of management is often criticized for its focus on computation and calculation, resulting in high levels of bureaucracy. First, because comparability requires standardization, the loss of participation of management can be criticized because it neglects the singularity of the individual managers and employees in favour of general governance mechanisms and common corporate goals (Robert, 2001; see also Section 12). Second, following from the first objection, the loss of participation of management can be criticized because it neglects the moral impulse of individual managers (Bauman, 1989) that leads to unethical behaviour in management practices (Jackall, 1988). Third, because of the emerging gap between the management level and the workforce level, the loss of participation of management can be criticized because of its lack of understanding of and feeling for the professionals that are involved in the primary process.

For these reasons, we question the loss of participation in many contemporary management practices and open a new perspective on management as participation in the primary process of the business operations.[1]

Business management is a particular domain of knowledge, but the proper use of this knowledge, for instance via teaching and coaching of employees, requires experience as well. Management can be seen as expert knowledge, that is, proven knowledge based on experience, which requires the participation of the manager in the primary process to constitute know-how, that is, his or her actual engagement in the primary process of the business to produce a product or service for instance. The know-how of management does not only concern practice-based knowledge how to plan and control the business operations, but first and foremost, the practice-based knowledge how to make the product the business sells on the market. This know-how not only enables the business manager to teach and manage his or her employees, but also to enjoy the pleasure of engagement in the primary process of the business operations. Furthermore, this know-how enables the manager to appreciate the beauty of the functioning order that is accomplished under his or her supervision, next to his or her ability to plan and control the business operations in a proper way. In other words, while current management practices may be characterized by a loss of participation, we would argue that this loss of participation is not a necessary characteristic of the nature of management and that management is in fact characterized by participation.[2]

As participation is a relational term, management as participation raises the question who is participating in management. We can argue that management as participation is self-referential, that is, embedded in the manager's abilities or capacities, in his or her ego or self. The ego or self of the manager is the singular condition that determines in which business he or she is involved. This singular condition can be found in the manager's particular disciplinary interests (healthcare or engineering for instance), in his or her personal or family history (gender differences, family businesses or regional industries for instance), in his or her physical or cognitive abilities (talents in math or communication for instance), etc. The self or ego of the manager is the singular condition that constitutes a range of possibilities for action and behaviour, while it closes off others. All actual activities the manager engages in remain embedded in the ego or self of the manager as centre of his or her participation in the business operations. Most often we do not pay attention to the self-referentiality of management, but only in case of a discrepancy between the manager's abilities and his or her actual performance, for instance in case of a manager of a healthcare institution without any professional experience as health professional, or in case of a manager of a bio-industry firm who took over the family business but does not have any affinity with animals. This shows that the ego or self of the manager is not a passive receptor of experiences that subsequently engages him or her in management practices, but that this self is always already intentionally involved in the business practices and is determining which business opportunities for action and behaviour he or she can take advantage of, and which not.

With this self-referentiality of management, we do not want to claim that management as participation is primarily subjective. If the self of management is characterized by a relational term – that is, participation in the primary process – we can formally argue that the self of this relation is not given prior to the relation; management is practice-based know-how, which means that the actual participation in the business operations constitute the self or ego of the manager at the same time, namely his or her know-how. In fact, management as participation means that the self of the manager and the primary process which he or she manages are co-constitutive (we will come back on this subject in the next subsection).

This first dimension of our philosophy of management – management as participation – enables us to question the loss of participation of management that can be encountered in many contemporary management practices and opens a new critical perspective on the nature of business management. The transition from the loss of participation of management to management as participation provides a first critical dimension of our philosophy of management.

9 Management as Resistance and Responsive Action

How can we further characterize the act of management? What initiates this act? The notion of failure may provide an appropriate starting point to reflect on the question what initiates the act of management. It is often argued that business management starts with a problem, for instance, suboptimal processes or dissipation of resources in the production process. This problem is addressed by the act of management. We can also think of a problem that is experienced by consumers – for example, the lack of connectivity – that is addressed by the introduction of new products or services – for example, the cell phone. In this respect, managers can be seen as problem solvers. In case of a market failure, these problems provide opportunities for the manager to establish a profitable business. In others, like in green entrepreneurship, the point of departure of new business activities is found in ecosystem failures like climate change.

What these cases of profit- and sustainability-driven businesses have in common is that the act of management is initiated because of the experience of a problem or failure that is found in the world. This problem provides a business opportunity for the manager and may lead to profit if the business is successful, but also to social or sustainability benefits in case of social enterprises for instance. Another commonality is that instead of facing the reality of this problem or failure in the world, and instead of bending to the facts just because they are real, the manager is oriented towards opportunities that are not real yet but can become real due to his or her act of management. This means that management is not so much characterized by the managerial power to control the steady state (Section 6). On the contrary, management is characterized by resistance, namely resistance against the world as it currently is organized and arranged, and by the manager's decision to change the world; the manager experiences a problem or failure in the world and decides not to leave it this way but to initiate new business operations or to change current business operations in order to address this problem. In case of a profit-driven business, this resistance and decision to change the world can be found in a gap in the market that the business manager solves by developing new products or services that meet customer needs. In case of a sustainable business, this resistance can be found in resistance against sustainability-related ecosystem failures and in the decision of the manager to take the responsibility to change the world by engaging in sustainable entrepreneurial action (see Section 18).

The idea that management is characterized by resistance and the decision to change the world opens another perspective on management as mechanism of control. As argued earlier, business management is often understood in terms of the managerial power to control the steady state; it concerns the functional order and ordered arrangement of the business that is led by the manager who is in control of the business, so that its efficient functioning is guaranteed and maintained. Although control is definitely important to sustain the business and serves the survival of the firm, it is also criticized for its focus on computation and calculation and neglectance of the individual professional in favour of bureaucratic control as we have seen. We can prevent this criticism by arguing that management as mechanism of control has to be balanced with another aspect of management that can be associated with resistance and action to change the world; business management involves the decision to change the world and can be associated with pro-active firms like Unilever that take their corporate social responsibility with regard to sustainable development and initiate a *sustainable living plan* as normative anchor point for the business operations. In this way, management as resistance and action enables us to conceptualize the nature of business management beyond mere control, namely as resistance against problems or failures in the world and the desire to change the world in order to address these failures.

The decision to change the world does not accept the status quo and results in an acting out upon this desire to change the world, rather than bearing and managing this impulse. Management is not only focussed on control but involves a new beginning to address the problem or failure in the world. This beginning is conditioned by the problem or failure that the manager experiences. At the same time, the manager is the *arché* of this beginning and the one who initiates the acting out to address the problems or failures in the world that he or she experiences.

Management as resistance and acting out to change the world implies the structural role of contingency and the possibility of misfortune in management. Every acting out is performed in an environment in which also other actors operate, like customers, suppliers and competitors. This means that acting out at the same time suffers from the acts by others, and this explains why the acting out of the manager may lead to an unlimited variety of consequences. On the one hand, what comes out of the acting out of the manager cannot be calculated upfront and always has unexpected elements in it, as its beginning is determined by the singularity of the self-referentiality of the manager (Section 8). On the other hand, the success of his or her acting out is not guaranteed. There is always the risk of failure, for instance the risk of bankruptcy or misfortune. To the extent that the success of the acting out of the manager to exploit new business opportunities is fundamentally incalculable, managerial decision-making processes are not processes that can be fully determined and calculated via the various steps involved in decision-making processes but remain fundamentally contingent. This structural contingency involved in management as acting out can partly be controlled by management but cannot be fully lifted. In this respect, contingency and the possibility of misfortune are structural characteristics of management as acting out to address the problems or failures in the world.

Because the fundamental uncertainty of management as acting out can never be fully controlled by managerial power, we can argue that business management is in need of the public approval that provides the firm a social license to operate. This approval by society can be gained if the acting out of the business manager is at the same time responsive to social needs, next to profitability, for instance. In case business operations might have unforeseen consequences for employees or consumers for instance, this responsiveness may require that the manager becomes responsive to these concerns in the (re)design and execution of the business operations. In other words, because the act of management is always intrinsically exposed to the possibility of misfortune, the acting out of management to solve problems or failures in the world should at the same time be characterized by his or her responsiveness to societal needs and concerns. In fact, acting out and responsiveness belong together and are mutually dependent, as acting out alone can change the world without any guarantee that the way the manager addresses problems and failures in the world is societally desirable. At the same time, responsiveness alone can consists in the acknowledgement of a problem or failure in the world without any actual engagement in its solution. Only in responsive action, the manager engages in such a solution of problems or failures in the world that is societally desirable. With this responsiveness of manager's acting out, we can substantiate the idea that management has not only economic significance but also moral significance.

With this characteristic of management as responsive action, we also encounter another aspect of the self-referentiality of management. The self or ego of the manager is existentially involved in his or her choice for responsive action. The manager existentially chooses and engages in responsive action without certainty about his or her future success or misfortune. In other words, the self or ego of the manager is at stake in his or her decision to take responsibility for the problems or failures he or she experiences in the world. The self of the manager emerges only in this choice that decides about his or her future prosperity or distress. This capability to act in a risky and uncertain environment can be framed in terms of the action competence that we encountered already in Section 7. It is a moral competence of the manager to take responsibility for problems and failures in the world, which involves the manager's belief that he or she is capable to change the world by addressing these failures in a responsible way. (We will come back on this subject in chapter 5 in connection with management as epistemic insufficient entrepreneurship.) To the extent that management starts with resistance against problems or failures in the world, the desire to change the world is the impulse for his or her decision to engage in responsive action to change the world to address this failure in a responsible way. In this respect management as responsive action is existentially embedded in the disposition or *ethos* of the manager to do the right thing and how to live the good life. One can think of managers like Yunus Grameen who started his microcredit bank primarily to solve a societal issue.[3]

The second critical dimension of our philosophy of management – management as resistance and responsive action – enables us to question the disconnection between business management and the *ethos* of the manager, that is, his or her knowledge about the good life. It also enables us to question the lack of attention for the structural role of uncertainty and possibility of misfortune in our conceptualization of business management. With this, we open a new critical perspective on the nature of business management as resistance and responsive action. The transition from management as control to management as responsive action provides a second critical dimension of our philosophy of management.

10　Management as Constitution of Meaning

While currently, business management is often understood in terms of the establishment and governance of a functioning order of the business in order to make profit, we questioned the sole orientation on profit already in the previous section; the existence of social enterprises and sustainable businesses already show that profit may be an important condition for firm survival, but does not necessarily define the nature of business management. We can argue that a pure focus on profit maximization is only a special case of the performance of business management as responsive action. This raises the question in what the primary performance of business management actually consists if it is not profit.

We open a new perspective on the primary performance of business management if we reflect for a moment on Xenophon's conceptualization of management. Business management is understood here as the establishment and governance of a functioning order in which all natural resources have their proper place, all human resources have their proper task and role, and the owner of the assets regulates and governs the proper use of these natural and human resources in order to make profit. In first instance, this functioning order of the business enables the manager to act appropriately in times of setback or unforeseen circumstances that threaten the business operations. It also constitutes a "paradise" of beauty that evokes admiration, for instance the ship in which all equipment is well stored and provides peace of mind and energy to work in (Section 4).

It becomes clear that the particular performance of management consists in the establishment and governance of a functioning order. Only within such an order, resources can have their proper role and function. The establishment and governance of order indicates that the manager has a very specific performance next to his or her participation in the primary process as first dimension of our philosophy of management (Section 8) and his or her engagement in responsive action as second dimension of our philosophy of management (Section 9). The particular production of the manager does not only consist in the production of new or changed products and services to address problems or failures in the world, but in the production of order.

What is order? Negatively said, we can argue that the production of order has nothing to do with the production of products or services, or metaphysically understood beings. The ordered functioning of a firm concerns a meaningful arrangement of these beings, in which these beings have their proper place. This arrangement of beings is not attached to these beings themselves, but the orderly arrangement of the primary process of the business to produce particular products and services assigns all resources their proper place; there is not a particular arrangement attached to wood or iron, but in a primary process to produce hammers for instance, wood and iron have their proper place, while wool or grain would not have such a proper place in this particular primary process. If Xenophon associates this orderly arrangement of the business operations with a paradise of beauty that evokes admiration, it is the orderly arrangement of the physical and natural resources – the rope, the net, and the sailor in case of the ship – that constitutes a meaningful whole that relates all these separate beings to each other and brings them together in a world for fishing for instance, that enables the act of fishing. Not the production of goods – that is, fish – is the primary task of the business manager, but the constitution of a meaningful world order for the business operations. This meaningful arrangement of the business operations is beautiful, not these resources that have their proper place in this meaningful world of fishing. In this case, fishing is the organizing principle in light of which the business operations function as a meaningful order in which natural and human resources have their proper place. But we can also think of businesses that embrace sustainability as normative principle in light of which the business operations are (re)designed.

Positively said, therefore, we can argue that management originates from the experience of dis-order and consists in resistance against this dis-order by the articulation of order. The primary performance of management consists in the constitution of a meaningful arrangement of the business operations in which all natural, arteficial, and human resources have their proper place, role, and task and are arranged in such a way that they enable the manager to act out and produce new or changed products and services. This meaningful arrangement of the business operations is not naturally given, nor produced by the managerial power to control the business but is the primary performance of the business manager. With this performance, the natural resources of the business receive their proper place, all human resources involved receive their proper task and role, and even the manager as regulator and governor of the proper use of these natural and human resources receives his or her proper place for the first time.

We therefore frame this particular performance of business management as constitution of a meaningful world for the proper execution of the business operations, for instance a meaningful world for fishing, producing hammers, etc., that enables the business manager to address the problems or failures that he or she experiences in the world. With this, the intimate relation between the world of business and the world of society it operates in and is responsive to becomes clear; business in society means that the world of the business operations is constituted in such a way that they are responsive to problems or failures in the world of society. At the same time, the world of business and the world of society never coincide, as the world of society is characterized by a plurality of (competing) businesses that constitute a multiplicity of co-existing but different worlds of businesses in society. The world of the different businesses may partly overlap with each other, but the world of society is always beyond the actual world that is constituted by the individual business manager, and always remains open for new beginnings or new configurations of responsive actions by a new generation of managers.[4]

With this, we encounter another aspect of the self-referentiality of management. The self or ego of the manager is not only the subject of the constitution of a meaningful world of the business operations. He or she indeed establishes and governs the orderly arrangement of the business, in which the human resources involved in the business operations have their proper place and are at home, but is also object of this meaningful world; it gives the manager his or her proper task and role in the business operations as well. This means that the meaningful arrangement of the business operations is not constituted once and for all, but only is realized in the actual execution of the maintenance of this meaningful arrangement by the participation and responsive action of the manager.[5] With this dual role of the manager as subject and object of the constitution of a meaningful world for the business operations, the importance of business integrity as congruency between the principles of the business and its operations, as well as management integrity as congruency between the manager's role as subject and object of this meaningful arrangement of the business, becomes clear (see further Section 22).

This third critical dimension of our philosophy of management – management as constitution of a meaningful world for the business operations – enables us to question the main focus on profit that can be encountered in many contemporary business practices, and opens a new perspective on the primary performance of business management. The transition from management for profit to management as constituting meaning provides a third-critical dimension of our philosophy of management.

Conclusion

In this chapter, we critically reflected on three contested area's in business management, based on our comparison of Xenophon's conception of management with contemporary definitions of managerial power and mechanism of control, namely: management as managerial power, management as bureaucratic control, and management as profit maximation. Based on our reflection on these contested area's in management, we opened up the self-evident conceptualization of business management for philosophical reflection in this chapter. We developed three critical dimensions of the philosophy of management that progressively move beyond the self-evident conceptualizations in current business practices: management as participation; management as resistance and responsive action; and management as constituting meaning. These three critical dimensions of the philosophy of management move beyond the self-evident conceptualization of management as managerial power and control and highlight the importance of three new dimensions of management.

Notes

1 If we positively characterize management as participation, we do not take the notion of participation in the sense developed and criticized by Levinas (1969). According to Levinas, participation is radically opposed to ethics, which is responsive to the singularity of another person. Participation is always characterized by the reduction of the otherness of the other person to the same in favour of a common ground in which the singularity of the other is neglected in favour of their commonality. In fact, we agree with Levinas' criticism of participation as we develop a concept of management as non-reductive stakeholder engagement, collaboration, and partnership in chapter 4. Here, we highlight another aspect of participation as relation to the self as engaged actor, instead of a relation to the other (Stiegler, 2005).

2 A legitimate question is what explains the loss of participation in many contemporary management practices. One could point at the ambiguity in the Greek and Latin conceptualization of action: "To the two Greek verbs *archein* ('to begin', 'to lead', finally 'to rule') and *prattein* ('to pass through', 'to achieve', 'to finish') correspond the two Latin verbs *agere* ('to set into motion', 'to lead') and *gerere* (whose original meaning is 'to bear'). ... In both cases the word that originally designated only the second part of action, its achievement – *prattein* and *gerere* – became the accepted word for action in general, whereas the words designating the beginning of action became specialized in meaning, at least in political langue. *Archein* came to mean chiefly 'to rule' and 'to lead' when it was specifically used, and *agere* came to mean 'to lead' rather than 'to set into motion'. Thus the role of the beginner and leader, who was a primus inter pares (in the case of Homer, a king amongst kings), changed into that of a ruler; the original interdependence of action, the dependence of the beginner and leader upon others for help and the dependence of his followers upon him for an occasion to act themselves, split into two altogether different functions: the function of giving commands, which became the prerogative of the ruler, and the function of executing them, which became the duty of his subjects" (Arendt, 1958: 289). This split in the meaning of action may explain why management is primarily associated with a loss of participation. A full answer to this question would require, however,a broader reflection on the political economy in which contemporary management functions, and is therefore beyond the scope of this chapter (I will come back to this topic in chapter 3).

3 As this section focusses on the nature of business management, we identify responsive action as general characteristic of management. This characteristic forms the basis of particular business ethical reflections on the role of business management. But contrary to management as participation of the self of the manager in the business operations, responsiveness does not necessarily imply any participation of the other in the business operation, which involves a reduction of the other person (or society at large) to the interests values of the business manager. Ethical responsiveness can consist in responsive action to address societal problems and failures without any participation, but in response to the call of the other person (or society at large; we will come back on this topic in chapter 4). The further exploration of the business ethical implications of our concept of management as responsive action will be discussed in chapter 6.

4 This plurality of worlds also shows why the responsiveness of the world of business to the world of society does not necessarily imply any participation of the world of business in the world of society, but constitutes a multiplicity of

co-existing worlds that enable social responsibility for the problems or failures of the world without any participation. We will come back on this subject in chapter 4.

5 This double role of the manager as subject and object of acting out might originate from the Christian idea that *oikonomia* is both assignment and fulfilment of the assignment (Agamben, 2011: 22). See Section 12 for a further exploration of the Christian roots of management.

3 Management as Politico-economic Governance

After questioning the self-evident conceptualization of management from the perspective of Xenophon in the first chapter, we questioned it from the perspective of the grand challenges of our time (Section 7). In the context of contemporary grand challenges like global warming, it is no longer self-evident that management consists in the establishment and governance of a functioning order. As management involves an intrinsic relation between business and society, as we have seen in the previous chapter, while society faces grand challenges like global warming today, we questioned whether managers can *control* this problem, while because of their epistemic insufficiency, it is questionable whether they can *plan* and *organize* its solution (Section 7). We raised the question what implications the wickedness of the grand challenges of our time and our epistemic insufficiency to properly manage these challenges have for our conceptualization of the management of the corporate social responsibility regarding sustainable development. In this chapter, we take this contested area of management as the point of departure to critically reflect on management as establishment and governance of a functioning order of the business operations and to move beyond contemporary conceptualization. To this end, we reflect on management as politico-economic governance as fourth dimension of our philosophy of management.

Like in the first chapter, the point of departure of our reflection is found in the historical analysis of the different meanings of the concept of management as governance of the business operations in history. In this, we are indebted to Giorgio Agamben's *The Kingdom and the Glory*, which contains an intellectual history of the genealogy of the Western concept of governance. In this book, Agamben points at two interdependent paradigms of governance in the history of the Western world; kingdom and governance, sovereignty and economy, and law and order (Agamben, 2009, 2011). Agamben's philosophical project as a whole – *Homo Sacer* – can be read already as a philosophy of governance, namely as a philosophy of human life as it is included and at the same time excluded by political power (Agamben, 1998). But because we are mainly interested in a positive concept of management as governance of

DOI: 10.4324/9781003231875-3

the *business* operations as fourth dimension of our philosophy of management, our philosophical reflections in this chapter do not consider Agamben's philosophy as a whole,[1] but examine his genealogy of the concept of governance only in light of our effort to develop such a positive concept of management as governance. This strategy is legitimate, as Agamben's philosophy of human life is notoriously abstract and nowhere explicitly considers governance in more applied fields like business ethics and philosophy of management, while he himself framed his book as genealogy of *economy* and government. This strategy explains why we do not provide a full account of Agamben's philosophy of human life in this study. Instead, we provide a philosophical reflection on the nature of management as governance of the business operations in discussion with a selective reading of Agamben's genealogy of governance in order to articulate a positive philosophical concept of management as governance that can inform our philosophy of management.[2]

In Section 11, we first introduce the concept of corporate governance by exploring the economical and the political responses to the call for governance mechanisms to deal with the grand challenges of our time. These responses are then reviewed from the perspective of Agamben's genealogy of the concept of governance (Section 12). Finally, we engage in a philosophical reflection on the concept of management as politico-economic governance as a fourth critical dimension of our philosophy of management (Section 13). To this end, we develop four characteristics of management as politico-economic governance.

11　Management as Corporate Governance and the Perspectives of Economics and Politics

Corporate Governance is traditionally defined as a system by which the tasks and responsibilities within a firm are divided by both informal as well as formal mechanisms for directing and controlling the business objectives, the strategy and the operations of the firm (Abor and Adjasi, 2007; Uhlaner et al., 2007; Roelofsen et al., 2015). We encountered this idea also in Xenophon, who argued that the manager guards the rules and regulations of the firm (Section 4). Although management as governance of the business operations traditionally concerns the governance of the relation between the firm and its shareholders, and mainly focusses on financial control (revenue streams, market share, return on investment, etc.), nowadays it includes other stakeholders as well. Stakeholders are a broad range of groups or individuals who can affect, or are affected by, an organization, both internal such as suppliers, customers, employees, and external such as governments and NGOs (Freeman, 1984). By including other stakeholders as well, governance can focus on social and environmental objectives as well, next to financial objectives (sustainability, integrity, ethics, etc.; Abor and Adjasi, 2007). In contemporary conceptualizations of management, governance is therefore defined "as the system by which firms are directed and controlled and as a set of relationships between a firm's management, its board, its shareholders and its other stakeholders" (European Commission, 2010).

Management as governance of the business operations can be seen as an instrument to enhance and secure corporate social responsibility (Aguinis and Glavas, 2012; Taneja et al., 2011; Jones, 2009; Kallio, 2007). There are various mechanisms of governance that can be deployed by the business manager, like integrating CSR objectives in strategy development (Melewar and Karaosmanoglu, 2006), the alignment of resource management (human resources, financial resources, etc.) and CSR objectives (Filatotchev et al., 2006), the embedding of CSR objectives in a shared vision and the core values that constitute the organizational culture of the firm (Uhlaner et al., 2007), the monitoring of responsible behaviour by the introduction of codes of conduct and accountability reports (Filatotchev et al., 2006), etc. (Roelofsen et al., 2015).

The development of a broader perspective on the governance of the business operations beyond shareholder value corresponds with wider developments in society. Traditionally, a strict distinction was made between the role and function of political actors – governance by the state as creation and maintenance of the political order – and economic actors – corporate governance by business managers as creation and maintenance of the economic order. This distinction originates from Aristotle, who proposed a strict opposition between the private sphere of the household and the public sphere of the state (Aristotle, 1944).[3] In the so-called network society, however, the monopoly of the state to produce social regulation and judicial norms is no longer self-evident.[4] It is increasingly replaced by a more complex network of non-state actors (firms, NGOs, etc.), which are themselves loci of political activity (Castells, 2000).

This trend towards the network society is strengthened by increasing globalization. Because the primary responsibility for economic, socio-cultural, and environmental aspects is allocated to different actors in society – the profit sector on the one hand and governmental organizations, NGOs and civil society on the other – it is argued that the governance of complex societal problems like global warming presuppose the active involvement of and partnership with society (Hens and Nath, 2003). It involves the transfer of governance responsibilities from national governments to global networks of multiple actors like multinational enterprises (MNEs) and global NGOs. With these trends, a new type of governance emerges. Such political arrangements beyond the nation state and beyond its authoritative power to enforce the law, which instead rely primarily on non-hierarchical forms of steering and non-coercive power, can be understood as *governance without government*. An example of this emerging type of governance can be found in the collaboration between the World Wildlife Fund (WWF) and Unilever, who developed a long-term program for sustainable fisheries. This initiative, which is known as the Marine Stewardship Council, is a certification scheme that enhances sustainable behaviour of suppliers, fisheries, and seafood shops.

One can critically argue that this modern concept of governance without government leads to a sovereignty *of* the market. Sovereign parliamentary and legislative power of the nation state is becoming recessive and is increasingly dominated by the market power of globally operating MNEs; increasingly, states become dependent on market actors, which challenge the idea of the sovereignty of the state; increased levels of privatization, deregulation, and marketization transformed the relation between the political actors – for example, the sovereign state – and economic actors – for example, firms – significantly over the years. Accordingly, we may argue that instead of a sovereignty *over* the market, we nowadays see a sovereignty *of* the market.

In times of crisis – think of the financial crisis in 2008 for instance – this ability of business managers to take responsibility becomes questionable. At the micro-level, self-regulation by business managers becomes questionable if one considers scandals like Volkswagen's manipulation of pollution emissions tests in the United States notwithstanding all kinds of corporate environmental policies. At the meso-level, we see a structural negative impact of industries on the environment. At a macro-level, firms are sometimes seen as "externalization machines", which makes CSR a contradiction in its own terms (Bakan, 2005).

These crises raise all kinds of questions regarding the sovereignty *of* the market and call for a new political sovereignty *over* the market. This means that it is assumed that political action is needed to enhance and secure corporate social responsible behaviour of firms. It is either called for *political* CSR, that is, a political legitimation of firms by incorporating deliberative democratic practices in the governance of their business operations (Scherer and Palazzo, 2011). Or it is called for a bigger role of political governance as authoritative enforcement of corporate social responsible behaviour by the introduction of new rules and regulation (Assländer and Curbach, 2017). This call for the rehabilitation of the role of state regulation seems to be legitimate, as business managers have the tendency to serve their own interests, while national or even global governance is needed to serve the commons.

The question is, however, whether political actors can govern and control the market in the globalized and complex world we currently live in. Or is it the other way around that large corporates control the state, as political actors are influenced by the lobby activities of firms and are influenced by the financial market of credit providers, ratings agencies, etc. This "paradox of regulation" shows the interdependency and interconnectedness of sovereign states and firms (Majone, 1994; Haines,

2011). This paradox leads to the question whether the traditional opposition between the sovereign power of the Nation state and the economic power of managers governing firms is not a mere pre-supposition that never existed in reality. If such a classical opposition is merely a supposition, we can no longer call for political CSR or for the rehabilitation of the role of political governance. On the contrary, it raises questions regarding the nature of this interrelation between sovereign states and managers governing firms (Tempels et al., 2017b). How do we have to conceptualize governance in this context and what are the consequences for business management?

In the next section, we turn to the intellectual history of the concept of governance by Giorgio Agamben to answer these questions. On the one hand, Agamben can help us to trace the presupposed distinction and even antagonism between political and economic governance in the philosophical and theological tradition. Agamben enables us on the other hand to reflect on the interrelation between political and economic governance and can inform our philosophical concept of management as politico-economic governance, because he rejects such a strict dichotomy.

12 Agamben's Genealogy of Governance and its Application in Governance Practices

Instead of taking a position in the debate whether there is a sovereignty *of* the market or a sovereignty *over* the market, we philosophically reflect on the two types of governance and their interrelation in this chapter. To this end, we consult *The Kingdom and the Glory*, a book on the genealogy of the concept of governance by Giorgio Agamben. In this book, Agamben asks for "the ultimate structure of the governmental machine of the West" and argues that the two types of sovereign political governance and economic governance originate from two dominant paradigms in Christian theology, namely political theology and economic theology (Agamben, 2011).

Even for readers who are not familiar with the Christian tradition, the difference between the two paradigms in theology can easily be understood. One of the traditional theological problems was how to reconcile the *unicity* and sovereign power of God with the *trinity* of the Father, the Son and the Holy Spirit, and with this, the reconciliation of the absolute and transcendent being of God with his providential and rescendent organization and administration of the world via his Son and the Holy Spirit (Agamben, 2007). Political theology, on the one hand, concentrates on the nature of God and asks for his unicity, transcendence, and sovereign power. This leads to a theory of the sovereignty of God. This paradigm of Christian theology is called political theology, because the theory of the sovereignty of God is juridico-political – God governs the world through the institution of universal rules, principles, and norms, as opposed to the execution of this sovereign power by the application of these principles in management practices – and leads to contemporary theories of sovereignty.

Economic theology, on the other, concentrates on Gods relation to the created world. *Oikonomia*, as the Greeks understood it, is far removed from our contemporary understanding of economics, but concerns household management (Deslandes, 2018). This administrative paradigm defines *oikonomia* originally. While *oikonomia* originally concerns the administration of the household as it is opposed to politics as governance of public life (Aristotle, 1944), the economic theologians take the word *oikonomia* to designate the immanent order of the administration of divine life, and the governance of its creatures, that is, God's divine plan of salvation. The difference between sovereignty and economy is that the first is ontological – it concerns the *being* of God – while the second concerns God's *praxis* – it concerns his administration and management of human life on Earth. According to Agamben, this administration is not dependent on a set of (sovereign) rules or principles, but is the result of situational and pragmatic considerations that can be different in different situations (Agamben, 2011: 17–18).[5] "*Oikonomia* is presented here as a functional organization, an administrative activity that is bound only to the rules of the ordered functioning of the house (or of the firm in question)" (Agamben, 2011: 18). While Aristotle sees this *oikonomia* functioning in the ordered arrangement of the household, the economic theologians transposed this concept into the theological field in which it acquired the meaning of a divine plan of salvation (Agamben, 2011).

The theological problem how to reconcile the unicity of God with the Trinity can now be solved: as the being of God is concerned, he is absolute one, but as the actions of God are concerned and the way he manages the world, he is three. More important for our discussion in this chapter is that although the economic theological paradigm is in first instance non-political, following Aristotle's strict distinction between economics and politics, the economic notion of divine providence and management of the world is transposed to the political governance of men. The theological distinctions between the being of God (sovereignty) and the actions of God (*oikonomia*) were transposed to the governance of men, that is, kingdom as sovereign non-executive power (*auctoritas*) and administration and management as executive power (*potestas*; Agamben, 2011).

If we apply Agamben's categories in the contemporary context of management practices, we recognize the distinctions he traced in the intellectual history of the West.[6] The idea that "the King reigns but doesn't govern" is for instance transposed from the theological domain to the domain of political governance of men, and can be recognized in contemporary monarchies where the sovereign power of the king reigns without having any executive power. And in corporate governance of publicly listed firms for instance, we recognize this distinction in the separation between the executive board and the non-executive board. In other words, Agamben's conceptualization of the economic theological paradigm of governance next to the political theological paradigm explains common dichotomies in political life - kingdom and government, being and action, *auctoritas* and *potestas*, *ordinatio* and *executio*, law and order, etc. – and explains the genealogy of management as economic governance in contemporary liberal democracies in the West, as well as the present domination of economy and management over all aspects of social life (Salzani, 2012; Whyte, 2013).

We now return to Agamben's reading of the genealogy of governance to further clarify the relation between economic and political governance. By tracing the theological origins of our notion of governance, Agamben not only explains why contemporary governance has taken the form of management as economic governance – theology conceives divine life as *oikonomia* (providence as divine government of the world) – which is transposed to the government of men. It also explains why governance always has these two aspects associated with being and action which cannot be reduced to each other – kingdom concerns the ontological level of the *being* of God while government concerns the practical level of the *actions* of God – while they also cannot be completely separated – as the son of God, Jesus cannot be "lower" than God and is godlike himself. The being of God concerns the sovereign transcendent power to establish normative principles according to which reality appears as established order, and the actions of God concern the economic administrative power to manage this established order in light of these normative principles (Agamben, 2011: 81). In profane governance of life on Earth, we can recognize this inseparability of both types of governance according to Agamben; a governance structure that is only characterized by sovereign power would be ineffective and impotent, while a governance structure which is only characterized by economic power would be groundless and anarchic (Agamben, 2007). Therefore, both aspects constitute governance as "bipolar machine" according to Agamben, that is, of sovereign or legislative power through universal laws, principles, and norms, and of economic or executive and managerial power that applies these laws and principles in practice.[7]

If we apply Agamben's concept of governance as bipolar machine in the context of our discussion of the duality of governance that we introduced in the previous section, it can help us to reflect on the relation between political and economic governance. If we see a dominance of economy over politics as a result of deregulation, privatization, and marketization, that is, an economic sovereignty *of* the market instead of a political sovereignty *over* the market economy, then Agamben's categories can help us to diagnose the current situation. On the one hand, his categories help us to conclude that the current dominance of economics over politics testifies of an economic type of governance that is not limited by sovereign principles but is an-archic, a political "empty" type of governance which can be associated with limitless capitalism (Whyte, 2013). On the other hand, his categories can help us to understand that the dominance of economics over politics doesn't imply an "end of politics" and ultimate victory of capitalism, but that it is embedded in the historical tension between sovereignty and *oikonomia*, which constitutes this bipolar machine of governance. Based on this reading of Agamben's genealogy of governance, we then could argue for the rehabilitation of sovereign or political power in order to limit the economic governance associated with capitalism.

And yet, such a rehabilitation of political power would miss a more fundamental problem that Agamben has with the classical notion of sovereign governance as political legislative power to establish universal rules, norms, and principles. Agamben argues that such an establishment of governance by sovereign power involves a "state of exception" (Agamben, 2005). We turn now briefly to Agamben's notion of the state of exception in order to deepen our understanding of the concept of sovereign governance.

In political life, the sovereign can always decide on the exception or take an extra-legal decision, for instance in case of a crisis. In such a crisis, the sovereign can decide to temporarily suspend the applicability of the law or, in case of a revolution, to suspend the old law and replace it by a new law based on an extra-legal decision (Humphreys, 2006). Based on many examples in legal history, Agamben shows that such a state of exception is exceptional in history, but increasingly becomes the "paradigm of government" in the West (Agamben, 2005: 7). For Agamben, the philosophical significance of the state of exception consists in the acknowledgement that a law, norm or principle functions as an inclusion and exclusion criterion.

A classic example is the foundation of the Greek democratic political system, which consisted in the suspension of the old law and the introduction of a new law that in fact includes free men in the political-legislative system and excludes women and slaves. With this, it becomes clear that any law or principle acknowledges the law's outside – the law that defines what is free man implies at the same time the existence of behaviour that falls outside this definition. Women and slaves as such "outlaws" drive the constitution of the legal system and the execution of extensive power to integrate them within the system – whether by punishment and sanctions or by education and cultural assimilation – and at the same time, the remaining "outlaws" are reduced to "bare life" of an a-political existence.[8]

If we apply Agamben's notion of the state of exception of sovereign governance in the context of management of corporate social responsibility, we easily see what is at stake. If global warming is framed as a grand challenge and threat of humanity, as is indicated in many books and reports, and if a "rhetoric-reality" gap exists between political statements about the climate actions needed and the lack of corporate social responsible action in practice, one can question the ability of business managers to take responsibility to address this global problem and call for political action. At the same time, one can question whether the current democratic institutions are able to actually address these type of grand challenges (Flinders and Wood, 2014). Not only do we not have a systematic politics of climate change (Giddens, 2011), but we can even question whether climate action can be made in liberal democratic societies because of the self-interest of the powerful elites and/or the relatively short time horizon of democratic policy makers (Shearman and Smith, 2007; Flinders and Wood, 2014). This emergency of the grand challenge in combination with political inaction may call for a state of exception, that is, authoritative interventions by the state. A country like the United States could for instance install a system of global climate controlling satellites, while using undemocratic procedures (Oels, 2012). With this sovereign political intervention, a law defines what is sustainable performance (e.g. integration of both economic and environmental sustainability for instance) and what falls outside this law (e.g. environmental unsustainable behaviour performed by firms that are solely focussed on economical sustainability). These firms, that can be seen as "outlaws", drive the constitution of the legal system and the execution of extensive power to integrate them within the system. The call for an "authoritarian regime" to politicize the climate change challenges (Shearman and Smith, 2007) testifies of such a sovereign attempt to capture and control this anomy by bringing this "outside" of the law under the jurisdiction of the law.

Although the current institutional inadequacy to tackle global warming (Gardiner, 2006) may provide arguments for the installation of such an authoritarian climate politics, Agamben's categories show that such a state of exception, which is inherent in sovereign power, would reduce the individual responsibility of business managers – the sustainable entrepreneur or responsible manager – in light of the totalitarian claims by the universal laws, rules, or principles.[9]

If we apply Agamben's concept of the state of exception of governance in the context of management as governance of the business operations, we recognize these inclusion and exclusion mechanisms as well. Firms nowadays form multi-stakeholder alliances and cross-sector partnerships together with research institutes and NGOs in order to address complex societal issues. The governance of these partnerships is difficult because of the different value frames and roles of the actors and the power relations involved. In the literature, various governance interventions are proposed to deal with these issues, such as value frame fusion (Le Ber and Branzei, 2010) or constructive conflict (Cuppen, 2012). As we will discuss in chapter 4, most literature on the management of these collaborations and partnerships have the tendency to harmony, consensus, and alignment amongst multiple stakeholders, while fundamental differences amongst these stakeholder are insufficiently taken into account.

Based on Agamben's work, we could explain this tendency to harmony and consensus as the result of the state of exception, that is, of the introduction of a norm or principle for inclusion and exclusion by the business manager, in which the fundamental differences amongst stakeholders are neglected in favour of their commonality. The state of exception in management as governance of the business operations is further confirmed by inclusion and exclusion tactics in the framing of the problem and in the selection tactics of stakeholders and partners for collaboration; radical stakeholder groups are often excluded from the collaboration while modest stakeholders are included.

Also, at the organizational level, the state of exception can be found in management as governance of the business operations. Corporate governance introduces general procedures and norms, which show what is seen as important for a firm, for instance profit and sales, but also social and environmental aspects. The state of exception is found in the disciplinary power of corporate governance initiatives in which the singularity of the individual employee or manager and his or her value frames and norms are neglected in favour of common corporate goals (see also Section 8, where we encountered this issue in terms of a loss of participation). Standardization for instance makes comparability possible but implies the neglectance of the singularity of individual managers and employees (Robert, 2001).

Because the state of exception is inherently involved in management as governance of the business operations, we can understand why the criticism of the current dominance of economic governance *over* political sovereignty – which can be associated with the inability of market economies to perform ethically in business life – cannot simply be solved by calling for the rehabilitation of sovereign or political power in order to limit economic governance. In such a situation, business managers may seem to engage in corporate social responsibility due to political interventions, but they in fact subscribe consciously or unconsciously to the state of exception as well, in which their individual responsibility is neglected. This raises the question how we can engage in management of corporate social responsibility with regard to sustainable development without neglecting the individual responsibility of the managers involved.

With the help of Agamben's conceptuality and our application of his categories in the context of management as governance of the business operations in this section, we can now re-reconsider the sovereignty of the market that we discussed in the previous section. Based on

Agamben's conceptuality of the bipolar machine of governance, we can first of all argue that the diagnosis of a sovereignty *of* the market is wrongly stated because there is no such thing. Sovereignty concerns the ontological level of universal rules, principles, and norms, and we have seen that economy concerns the practical level of administration and management. So, if we want to frame the diagnosis, we have to frame it as an age of economic governance *without* sovereignty. From the perspective of Aristotle, economic thinking which is not limited by the political ideals of the good life is not economic in the proper sense of the word, but a limitless accumulation of wealth. This is called *chrematistics*. Interestingly enough, *chrematistics* is pretty much comparable with what we nowadays see as the liberal market economy.

Second, however, we could argue against such a diagnosis of an economic governance without sovereignty based on Agamben's conceptuality:

> Today, we could say that the act of government or execution has the primacy, it is clear, the crisis of parliamentary and legislative power is evident everywhere. It is like dead, legislative power doesn't exist anymore in Europe or the United States, an absolute primacy of government. But anyway – even in this case – both poles are there: so one pole can prevail on the other, like now it is the case for government and executive power, but nevertheless they must be there, otherwise no government, there is another form of power. (Agamben, 2007: 5)

Why? If we take the idea of governance as bi-polar machine serious, we have to reject the idea of an economic governance by business managers without sovereignty. Also, in the current hegemony of economic governance, the role of sovereign power is still important. This is confirmed by the current practice of deregulation and marketization that goes hand-in-hand with the enlargement of the whole legal system (sustainable development goals, carbon pricing systems, etc.). Economic and sovereign power in fact go together and build this bi-polar machine.

Third, based on Agamben's conceptuality, we could criticize a strict distinction between sovereignty and economic governance today. A strict differentiation between economic and political institutions is merely apparent because all actors are political/economic from this perspective, are determined by this bi-polar machine.[10] The marketization of global warming in the bio-based economy and the politization of firms, ranging from lobbying activities to political CSR for sustainability, can illustrate these trends. This corresponds with the idea that regulation in the network society cannot be seen any longer as state intervention, but as part of a political-economic constellation of power in which political and economic actors are intertwined and mutually dependent. It is clear that the call for a bio-based or circular economy for instance is not merely political or economic. This calls the whole dichotomy between sovereignty *of* the market versus sovereignty *over* the market into question and calls for the acknowledgement that politics and economics do no longer represent two separate domains where one of the two is sovereign over the other. It rather shows that economic institutions are always already political *and* economic; always involve already political and moral statements about what is good and wrong, what for instance are good relations of business and society, good ways of production, distribution and customer relationships, etc. Examples are the free market as a norm in either economic and political life, or the sole economic role of economic actors in society as a principle.

Our analysis in this section shows that in a fundamental way, the question about the political legitimation of management as governance of the business operations, whether it is found in political CSR within economic institutions or in political limitations of economic institutions, always comes too late. Management as governance of the business operations is always already guided by a bi-polar machine of governance, whether this is found in "internal" corporate sovereignty (mission statements and core values for instance that guide CSR policies) or in "external" political sovereignty (governmental rules and regulations that enhance and secure corporate social responsibility of firms). We could argue that sovereign governance and economic governance have to be understood as di-polarities where no clear line can be drawn between political and economic actors as if they were two different substances. In fact, the continuous oscillation between political and economic tendencies constitutes a field in which both rely on each other and are in continuous tension (Raulff and Agamben, 2004; Whyte, 2013; Agamben, 2011). For this reason, we will no longer talk about either economic or political actors in this chapter, but about economic/political actors. Also, we don't talk about either economic or political management, but about management as politico-economic governance.

Based on Agamben's conceptuality of governance as bipolar machine, we can criticize the current discourse about the sovereignty *of* the market and call for a new sovereignty *over* the market, because it shows that control cannot be found in a unilateral preference of political sovereignty over economic governance or vice versa. In fact, the symmetry between sovereignty and economy in governance as bi-polar machine shows why economic governance may pretend not to make use of norms, but requires such norms on the one hand, and in fact implicitly presupposes such norms in a self-evident and uncritical manner. The concept of management as politico-economic governance in fact provides good reasons for our acceptance of the bipolar machine of sovereignty and economics in which both approaches are integrated in a governance framework for managing corporate social responsibility, and reflection on the presupposed principles and norms is an integral part of the effort to perform social responsible in business life. What is more, management as politico-economic governance can also help to criticize the current calls for a new sovereignty over the market, because they may unconsciously subscribe to the state of exception in which the individual responsibility of managers and their viewpoints is neglected and disciplined in favour of "common" goals.

In sum, although Agamben's genealogy of the concept of governance helps us to analyze current practices of governance, his main contribution is that his conceptuality enables us to take a critical stance. The problem is therefore not that politics should be rehabilitated because such a rehabilitation wouldn't deal with the real problem at stake, namely that each governance framework is characterized by the state of exception. The question then is not how business managers can be limited by political action, but whether the politics of managers, whether it is found in political CSR or in the political limitation of firms by political institutions, can ever be seen as a suitable governance model.

13　Philosophical Reflections on Management as Politico-economic Governance of the Business Operations

At the same time, we may argue that something radically changed in our current society, which is threatened by global warming. On the one hand, management of corporate social responsibility with regard to sustainable development can be seen as a business approach to integrate grand challenges like global warming in the business operations (Dahlsrud, 2008). On the other hand, the urgency of this challenge requires that immediate action is taken by all actors in society, including business managers. The current political context, in which inaction is made excusable because of the complexity of the problem (the difficulty of global politics, scientific uncertainty about calculations of future climate impacts, etc.), and which facilitates the delay of actual climate action at our convenience, is no longer possible (Gardiner, 2006). On the contrary, we need all the creativity and innovative potential to come up with new solutions of global warming, like geo-engineering, etc. Does this mean that we have to rehabilitate management as politico-economic governance, that is, as sovereign power and economic management by economic institutions?

We can argue against such a rehabilitation if we take the nature of grand challenges like global warming serious. We have to acknowledge that there is no sovereignty, no general principle, norm or law that can guide us in the solution of these challenges. While the performance of corporate social responsible behaviour presupposes that we know what is right and wrong in business life, grand challenges like global warming can be considered as wicked problems as we have seen (Section 7). If the key characteristic of grand challenges like global warming is that the distinction between good and bad behaviour is difficult because of their complexity, it is impossible to identify sovereign laws, norms, or principles that can help us to unequivocally distinguish good from bad business practices regarding these type of challenges. This is the fundamental problem of the call for an authoritative regime of global warming, because such a regime presupposes that appropriate norms and principles can be identified, while this is highly questionable if we acknowledge the wickedness of global warming. For instance, it only makes sense to introduce an authoritative regime if we know which behaviour is appropriate, and especially in case of wicked problems like global warming, we don't know which behaviour is appropriate. We have no familiarity with future generations that live on Earth in about 1000 years, we don't know their values and stakes or anything else that can guide our current behaviour. In other words, if we take our epistemic insufficiency regarding the future impacts of our current interventions serious, we don't know which norm or principle could guide our politics of climate change.

Not only political government is limited in case of grand challenges, but also management as governance of the business operations. Business management and control practices are dependent on sovereign principles and norms, while precisely these norms fail in the case of grand challenges which involve a variety of ideas and values frames of different stakeholders. So even if we want to conceptualize management as politico-economic governance because of the urgency of global warming, we have to acknowledge our epistemic insufficiency with regard to both the proper norms and principles (sovereign governance) and the proper management of the problems based on these norms (economic governance). How to navigate between the extremes of a call for an authoritative politics of climate change, which remains groundless in light of the wickedness of global warming, and a political inactivity that is certainly convenient for firms in the Northern hemisphere, but definitely catastrophic for future generations and people in the global South.

Instead of engaging in a pragmatic strategy to tackle these grand challenges in business life (Ferraro et al., 2015), we engage now in a *philosophical* reflection on the grand challenge of global warming in this section and ask whether such global problems leave room for a state of exception. If we reflect on the *global character* of global warming, we understand that a fundamental state of *inclusion* in this problem situation is at stake. The experience of global warming primarily concerns the experience of the globe as a whole. Or put in more philosophical terms, the experience of the *whole* of being, in which the one who experiences is included (Zwier and Blok, 2017). While in previous times, we may thought that we could externalize waste and emissions to the environment, we currently experience that all waste and emissions we try to externalize return to us as a boomerang, namely in terms of global warming which is therefore inescapable for us. With this, the Earth becomes an *interior* space in which we are *included*, that is, without any possibility of a position outside this *whole*. It provides an experience of the immanence of human existence and its institutions to the world we live in and on which we entirely depend. This opens a new perspective on the state of exception, which is characteristic for current climate governance; the state of exception of climate governance turns out to be embedded in a fundamental state of inclusion in this problem. So, even if we acknowledge that management as governance of the business operations is characterized by a state of exception, we may argue that such an exception is embedded in a state of inclusion. What is at stake in wicked problems like global warming is an *intimacy* of actors in the interior space of planet Earth.

A more proper orientation for climate governance by economic-political actors emerges if we ask: what is it, in which we are included? We can argue that planet Earth itself could function as sovereign principle or norm that should guide our climate governance. On the one hand, we can identify the Earth as sovereign principle for our existence, to the extent that human existence emerges, unfolds and expands based on the pre-existence of the Earth, and threatens to go back into the Earth at the end of this era in which humanity is threatened by global warming (Blok, 2016). The Earth can be seen as sovereign in the literal sense of the word. It is the highest (or better, lowest), whose height itself is no longer dependent on or relative to something else: it concerns the absolute (Nancy, 2007). The unique situation of planet Earth that is threatened by global warming unsettles us – we experience our full dependency on the carrying capacity of the Earth for the first time – and calls us to sustain this Earth as supportive ground for human existence.[11] This call is normative, since the Earth as supportive ground operates as norm or regulative idea that guides behaviour. This norm is "open" for revision, as opposed to general or universally valid, to the extent that the application of this norm remains always a finite or limited one compared to the wickedness of the problem, remains always questionable, adjustable and improvable. This means that any norm always remains situational – only valid in a limited way and for a specific purpose and time frame, while we have to remain principally critical towards the applicability of such a norm or principle in light of this wickedness of the problem at stake. Such an "open" norm precludes every effort to establish an authoritative regime, while it at the same time prevents political inaction.

Management as governance of the business operations is guided by this open norm as well; managers engages in corporate social responsibility with regard to sustainable development to address grand challenges like global warming, while it acknowledges the situational character of all management interventions. This means that managers not only constitute a meaningful world for the business operations (third dimension of our philosophy of management), but in their actions, they are responsive to the Earth as normative principle (second dimension of our philosophy of management). It provides a concept of management as politico-economic governance that doesn't claim any universal or general validity of its interventions because of the epistemic insufficiency of economic/political actors regarding the wickedness of problems like global warming.

Based on these considerations, we propose a concept of business management as politico-economic governance as constitution of a meaningful world for the business operations, in which planet Earth itself operates as sovereign dimension for corporate social responsibility with regard to sustainable development. This notion of business management acknowledges the ultimate dependency of economic/political actors on the biophysical capacities and limitations of planet Earth. We propose four characteristics of management as politico-economic governance as fourth dimension of our philosophy of management, that can help economic/political actors to navigate between an authoritarian politics of global warming and political inactivity.

1. If management as politico-economic governance concerns the Earth as a whole, and this whole constitutes an interior space in which any state of exception is embedded, it is characterized by a *state of inclusion*. Contrary to any ex-ceptional position, business managers are radically involved in the governance of this interior space. This inclusion extends management as participation (first dimension of our philosophy of management) from the world of the business operations (third dimension of our philosophy of management) to the Earth as world of society. This state of inclusion does not only highlight the dependency of the world of the business operations on the world of society as supportive ground for their public and private operations, but also their responsibility when it comes to sustaining the Earth as such a supportive ground. Contrary to the state of exception that favours the generality and universality of norms and principles over the singularity of actors, the state of inclusion highlights the intimate involvement of the business managers in the Earth as interior space of the world of society in management.[12]

2. This type of management as politico-economic governance is not only conditioned by the constitution of a meaningful world (third dimension of our philosophy of management), as if it consists in economic governance without any sovereignty. This would suggest that the governance of planet Earth as *oikos* of human existence is primarily in the hands of human management and control to provide for the needs of human life. But in fact, also human efforts to constitute a meaningful world for the business operations are always

already dependent on the Earth as supportive ground. In this sense, management as constitution of meaning (Section 10) is always already Earthbound, that is, primarily conditioned by grand challenges like global warming that unsettle actors and call them to sustain the planet, here and now, in order to subsist as dimension beyond our human control.

3. Because of the situational character of management as politico-economic governance (characteristic 1) in response to the normative dimension of planet Earth (characteristic2), managers acknowledge the principal fallibility of their interventions in light of our epistemic insufficiency with regard to this normative dimension. It is this fallibility of management as politico-economic governance – the negativity, struggle, and difficulties inherent in management – that was already conceived by theologians of the Middle Ages (Mondzain, 2007) and that we already encountered in Xenophon's work (Section 4) and in management as resistance and responsive action (second dimension of our philosophy of management). This fallibility is not only due to the situational character of management but may also be due to the instability and volatility of planet Earth itself, as is indicated in the structural possibility of earthquakes, volcano's, and tsunamis.

4. Management of corporate social responsibility with regard to sustainable development can be seen as *acclamation* or corporate laudation of the normative dimension of planet Earth by the actual execution of responsible business practices in which the Earth functions as normative principle that enforces social responsible behaviour in business life. In the acclamation of the normative dimension of planet Earth, social responsible action and behaviour of managers is *glorified* (Agamben, 2007).

Conclusion

In this chapter, we critically reflected on a fourth contested area in management, namely management as governance of the business operations. We questioned the focus on *planning, organization,* and *control* of management in case of grand challenges like global warming. Our critical engagement with economic and political responses to the call for more corporate social responsibility with regard to sustainable development in Section 11 and with Agamben's analysis of the relation of economics and politics in economic/political actors in Section 12 enabled us to argue for a concept of management as politico-economic governance, which is characterized by a state of inclusion, rather than a state of exception. We subsequently developed four characteristics of management as politico-economic governance as fourth dimension of our philosophy of management in Section 13.

Notes

1 On the one hand, this would require an in-depth engagement with Agamben's philosophy as a whole, which is beyond the scope of this study. On the other hand, it is questionable what would be the added value of such an account, as Agamben himself never reflected on the business environment as particular context of application of his conceptuality.

2 In our conscious selective reading of Agamben's genealogy of the concept of governance, we follow the strategy of eminent colleagues like Jessica Whyte (2013). For a critical introduction in Agamben's work, see de la Durantaye (2009).

3 One can question whether such a strict dichotomy can ever be encountered in real life and whether both spheres are not always intertwined, as we will argue in the next section with the help of Agamben's genealogy of the concept of governance. Nonetheless, we explore this dichotomy in this section because, on the one hand, it helps to contrast the traditional Aristotelian concept of the duality of governance with its modern conceptualization in the network society and, on the other hand, because contemporary debates on CSR still rely on these distinctions as we will see.

4 Another way to frame the current context is by referring to Zygmunt Bauman's concept of liquid modernity, which indicates the fluidity of social positions of social actors in the current age (Bauman, 2002).

5 In fact, Agamben is ambiguous in this. Sometimes, he suggests that economic governance can exist independently because it is not dependent on sovereign power (Agamben, 2011: 17–18) – it is an-archic power – while he at the same time argues that governance is dependent on such sovereign power (Agamben, 2011: 5), as we will see in the next section. If we take the idea of governance as bi-polar machine of sovereign political and economic power serious, we have to acknowledge their mutual dependency. This implies that they always co-exist and cannot exist independently.

6 It is clear that Agamben himself did not apply his categories in the context of contemporary management practices. If we pursue this way in this chapter, we depart from a strict interpretation of his work and apply his categories for our own purposes.

7 To the extent that *oikonomia* concerns the origin of economy according to Agamben's genealogy of economy and government, as the subtitle of *The Kingdom and the Glory* suggests, we are legitimized to conceptualize *oikonomia* as economy and management. This is also confirmed in Agamben's interviews in which he directly connects his understanding of *oikonomia* with *economic management* (Agamben, 2007).

8 While Agamben associates the state of exception with sovereign power in his early work, in *The Kingdom and the Glory*, he seems to associate it with economic power as well. "The paradigm of government and of the state of exception coincide in the idea of an *oikonomia*, an administrative praxis that governs the course of things, adapting at each turn, in its salvific intent, to the nature of the concrete situation against which it has to measure itself" (Agamben, 2011: 50). This does not mean that both coincide. While the state of exception is clearly related to universal rules and norms that imply inclusion and exclusion practices, as Agamben has shown convincingly, this cannot be said of economic governance. *Oikonomia* concerns the administrative action, which can be performed without a set of rules or principles, as is the result of situational and pragmatic consideration on a case to case basis (Whyte, 2013). According to Aristotle, economy concerns the administration of the household with respect to the satisfaction of needs. The political

domain of living the good life limits economy and thanks to this limitation, a rational or virtuous economy is possible which does not degenerate. Without such a limitation by politics, economy would degenerate and end in the limitless accumulation of wealth. Agamben points in another direction. Even if economy is limited by the political domain, it does not result in the good life because of the state of exception it is dependent upon. While sovereign power neglects the singularity of human existence in favour of the generality of rules and principles, economic power can be seen as the actual disciplining power, which is at stake in the economic execution of inclusion and exclusion practices. In this respect, we can also speak of an economics of exception.

9 Contrary to the state of exception of sovereign governance, which founds a politics of inclusion and exclusion, Agamben proposes to develop a notion of politics beyond sovereign law and based on his notion of bare life. For Agamben, the reduction of the singularity of human existence to bare life in light of totalitarian claims by universal laws shows a non-relation between law and life and opens a new perspective on politics. While politics is always seen within the context of the law – whether it is constitutive power that establishes the law or is contaminated by the law – Agamben explores the possibility to move beyond the connection of politics and law and to connect it with bare life in his project (Agamben, 2005: 88; Humphreys, 2006: 683–684). The further elaboration of this notion of politics is beyond the scope of this study.

10 Agamben's criticism of a strict distinction between political and economic governance makes clear that the "state" of exception can be considered as "economics" of exception as well. In this respect, he anticipated criticisms like the one uttered by Hardt and Negri: "The political is not an autonomous domain but one completely immersed in economic and legal structures" (Hardt and Negri, 2009: 5). For Agamben, the state of exception is connected with governance as bi-polar machine of both sovereignty and economic governance. It may be the case that Agamben, because he associates the state of exception both with political and economic governance, doesn't pay full attention to other problems, which can be associated with economic governance. Although Negri and Hardt misunderstood Agamben, as if he associated the state of exception only with sovereign governance, they hint in this direction when they say that by focussing on the sovereign exception, "economic and legal structures of power tend to be pushed back into the shadows" (Hardt and Negri, 2009: 4).

11 With this, we do not want to imply yet that the Earth has a call on human existence to act in an ethical way, as is sometimes suggested in the literature (Blok, 2015). We leave this question aside for the moment and highlight the normative dimension of the Earth, whether this Earth positively or negatively calls for our taking actual responsibility in our actions and behaviour.

12 With this intimacy, we don't have a complete coalescence of man and Earth in mind in which no-self is left (see Section 10), but an intimacy which acknowledges the res-cendence of the spacio-temporal infinity of the Earth beyond our human involvement, an asymmetric relation between the world of the business operations and the Earth as world of society at the same time. The articulation of this intimate asymmetry is beyond the scope of this study.

4 Management as Non-reductive Stakeholder Engagement

In the chapter 1, we critically reflected on management as the assignment of tasks and roles to human resources in order to establish and govern the functioning order of the business. As management first and foremost have to engage in *collaboration* with internal and external *stakeholders* with different and even conflicting visions and value frames, we questioned whether managers can easily manage these human resources by assigning tasks and roles (Section 7). We raised the question what implications the wickedness of the grand challenges of our time and our epistemic insufficiency to manage these challenges have for our conceptualization of the management of human resources inside and outside the firm. In this chapter, we take this contested area of management as the point of departure to philosophically reflect on the nature of management as the engagement and collaboration with internal and external stakeholders.

Contrary to the previous chapter, we do not engage in an historical analysis but take contemporary debates on cross-sector partnerships (CSPs) and multi-stakeholder alliances (MSAs) in management science as the point of departure. As we already saw in the previous chapter, because the primary responsibility for economic, socio-cultural, and environmental aspects is allocated to different players in society, it is argued that the balancing of *people, planet,* and *profit* in sustainable business development presupposes the active involvement of and partnership with society (Hens and Nath, 2003). From the firm perspective, stakeholder engagement, partnership, and collaboration are seen as important prerequisites for responsible business practices. Partnering with a diversity of stakeholders not only enhances learning and the emergence of new insights (Jehn et al., 1999). It also enhances the wealth-creating capacity of a firm (Post et al., 2002; Harrison et al., 2010) by avoiding negative outcomes of business practices and promoting an excellent firm reputation (Graves and Waddock, 1994; Gray and Stites, 2013). More important in the context of the management of corporate social responsibility with regard to sustainable development, however, is that stakeholder engagement, partnership, and collaboration encourage more

DOI: 10.4324/9781003231875-4

responsible or ethical business practices (Wood, 2002). In particular, in case the inequality amongst stakeholders is potentially enhanced by business practices, or in case of uncertainty with regard to the future impact of new products and services, collaboration and partnership for responsible business is required (von Schomberg, 2013). By involving stakeholders in CSPs and MSAs who are possibly affected by these practices, ethical decision-making by managers and democratic participation of stakeholders in these decision-making processes are enhanced and secured (Belucci et al., 2002). The growing number of CSPs and MSAs in recent years shows that the private sector is actually partnering with stakeholders in order to solve sustainable challenges (Eweje, 2007).

In Section 14, we set the scene by introducing contemporary debates on CSPs and MSAs in management science. We reflect on the concept of identity, unity, and difference in the management of these type of collaborations. We ask how to reach unity within these collaborations with multiple internal and external stakeholders and respect fundamental differences between multiple stakeholders at the same time. We articulate three specific questions with regard to unity, identity, and difference in CSPs, based on an analysis of the Selsky and Parker and Seitanidi and Crane framework of partnership implementation. In Section 15, we articulate four characteristics of the metaphysical concepts of identity, unity, and difference that are operational in stakeholder management. This will provide a philosophical perspective to assess the metaphysics of the management of stakeholders, collaborations, and partnerships in Section 16. In this effort, we focus on the question how differences between partners are exactly bridged in management and what the role of identity and difference is in the process of partnership implementation. Moreover, we show the limitations of these concepts in the case of managing wicked problems like global warming.

Because this conceptuality of partnership and collaboration turns out to be inappropriate in case of the management of wicked problems like global warming, we subsequently reflect on a non-metaphysical concept of partnership and collaboration. We develop a concept of management as non-reductive stakeholder engagement, collaboration, and partnership in which fundamental differences are acknowledged and appreciated. Management as non-reductive stakeholder engagement involves a shift from the cognitive level of primarily understanding other stakeholders, to the behavioural level of actual ethical behaviour in response to their call on the manager to take social responsibility in the business operations. We further explore and apply this notion of the management of stakeholders in order to conceptualize in a positive way an ethical approach to stakeholder engagement, collaboration, and partnership in management practices (Section 17). With this, we engage in a philosophical reflection on the concept of management as non-reductive stakeholder engagement as a fifth critical dimension of our philosophy of management. In the conclusion of this chapter, we illustrate the advantages of management as non-reductive stakeholder engagement by outlining the partnership stages of an ethical approach to stakeholder engagement, collaboration, and partnership in management practices.

14 Identify, Unity, and Difference in CSPs and Collaborations

Managing CSPs and Collaborations

In a recent review of partnerships for sustainable development, CSPs are defined as "collaborative arrangements in which actors from two or more spheres of society (state, market and civil society) are involved in a non-hierarchical process, and through which these actors strive for a sustainability goal" (Van Huijstee et al., 2007). Profit- and non-profit organizations start cross-sector collaborations when they experience that they cannot solve these problems on their own and are not willing to merge their activities into a new organization in order to solve these problems (Bryson et al., 2006).

Although these collaborations amongst profit- and non-profit organizations appear under a variety of names – public–private partnerships, global action networks, CSPs to address social issues, etc. – and can be categorized in various typologies, the problems addressed by these partnerships are comparable (Van Huijstee et al., 2007): complex public problems like climate change, desertification, the loss of biodiversity, etc., which cannot be solved by the public or private sector alone. Although empirical evidence for the impact of CSPs on sustainable development is still lacking, it is widely assumed that the establishment of CSPs is a desirable management interventions to address complex problems like sustainable development. By "linking and sharing of information, resources, activities, and capabilities", it is expected that CSPs "achieve jointly an outcome that could not be achieved by organizations in one sector alone" (Bryson et al., 2006).

At the same time, it is acknowledged that CSPs cannot solve all public problems because of their "wicked" nature (Section 7). The complexity of wicked problems like global warming is partly related to the multiple stakeholders involved in managing these problems. It is assumed that many stakeholders have differing ideas about what the "real" problem is (Kreuter et al., 2004) and that the solution to the problem is based on "judgments" of multiple stakeholders, which can differ widely and are not (always) based on shared values (Batie, 2008). These differences are due to differences with regard to the *content* of the wicked problem; for instance, the problem of the definition of global warming and its solution in the business context will be framed differently by different stakeholders (Lewicki et al., 2003). Moreover, some actors are more powerful than others in defining the problem and its solution. Although various authors highlight the importance of sharing power by empowering weaker or disadvantaged stakeholders (Ansell and Gash, 2008), it is expected that power imbalances are especially prominent in the management of wicked problems simply because of the different value frames of the different stakeholders involved (Bryson et al., 2006). Differences can also be due to different agendas and divergent motives of profit and non-profit organizations (Yaziji and Doh, 2009). While non-profit organizations are mainly motivated by altruistic motives, for instance (Milne and Iyer, 1996), profit organizations are often solely self-interested (Iyer, 2003). Furthermore, profit and non-profit organizations have divergent approaches to value creation; business managers will naturally focus on economic value creation by producing and selling products and services, while non-governmental organizations (NGOs) for instance will focus on social value creation by advocating social norms and values (Yaziji and Doh, 2009). Finally, profit and non-profit organizations have different identities (Brickson, 2007).

Because of these sector-specific differences – besides the complexity of problems like global warming itself – actual partnerships to solve wicked problems are vulnerable to failure. Therefore, the literature focuses on the management of the initial conditions affecting CSP formation and the ways CSPs try to understand and overcome their differences and align partners in order to enhance successful collaboration. An example is the experience of sector failure to solve complex social problems such as public health or poverty, and initial agreements amongst partners on the problem definition. One of the reasons for this is that agreements on the problem definition can help clarify the interest's partners have in solving the problem. In the literature, therefore, both acknowledgement of the interdependency of partners and recognition of the self-interest of each partner in solving the problem are seen as necessary conditions for successful partnership formation (Logsdon, 1991; Bryson et al., 2006). Recent research is focusing for instance on management of business involvement (Reed and Reed, 2009) and consensus-building in general (Rondinelli and London, 2003), and value frame fusion in particular (le Ber and Branzei, 2010). Although several authors have contributed to the question how to manage participatory and partnership processes in complex problems (Guston, 1999; Stirling and Mayer, 2001; Burgess et al., 2007), most of the management literature on collaboration and partnership shows a tendency towards convergence, consonance, complementarity, or at least compromise between partners (Croteau and Hicks, 2003; Nowell, 2010; Cuppen, 2012), that is, an implicit ideal of alignment, unity, and harmony in the management of these partnerships.

This ideal of unity and harmony seems to be paradoxical. On the one hand, this unity or harmony is conceived as a necessary condition for effective CSP collaboration. On the other hand, this ideal seems to be out of reach in the case of wicked problems like global warming, in which multiple stakeholders with *different* judgments and *different* values are involved. The question is therefore: how can management reach unity within CSPs and respect the fundamental differences between multiple stakeholders at the same time? There are at least three reasons why an answer to this question is not obvious.

Although the literature on the management of partnership and collaboration acknowledges the importance of "complementary differences" (le Ber and Branzei, 2010) and "tensions, fluidity and paradox" between partners (Hardy et al., 2005), it is unclear how exactly the concepts of identity and difference are understood in the CSP literature. The hypotheses we want to explore in this chapter is that a *metaphysical* concept of identity, unity, and difference is self-evidently assumed in the literature on the management of stakeholders in partnerships and collaborations. In the history of western philosophy, the identity of an entity is understood as a general characteristic – for example, *animal rationale* – that various entities – for example, human beings – have in common. This generality is found in a unifying principle *(idea, eidos)* in the light of which different entities synthesize to and appear *as* the same (identity). It is, however, questionable whether these metaphysical concepts of identity and difference are applicable in the case of CSPs for wicked problems like global warming. According to the French philosopher Emmanuel Levinas, the metaphysical concept of identity is the result of a reduction of difference to identity, in which the fundamental differences between actors is neglected and even violated (Section 15). The first reason why the management of stakeholders in collaborations and partnerships is not self-evident is that current notions originate from the metaphysical tradition; it explains why current concepts of inclusion and partnership often show a tendency towards consensus and alignment and cannot deal with fundamental differences amongst stakeholders during the inclusion and collaboration processes. Because the ideals of partnership and inclusion are difficult to realize in practice (Hansen, 2006), this raises the question how the management of stakeholders can acknowledge and appreciate differences amongst partners during the partnership.

The tendency towards consensus and alignment does not imply that all differences amongst stakeholders are eliminated. Several authors have indicated the importance of controversy and constructive conflict in collaboration and partnership, because these enable learning and gaining new insights in emerging technologies (Rip, 1986; Cuppen, 2012). However, although the importance of variety and disparity amongst the ideas and values of stakeholders is stressed, the cognitive distance amongst stakeholders should not be too large. In the case of radically different perspectives on the problem and its solution, for instance, the suggestion is to "include people who can bridge disparate perspectives or claims" (Cuppen, 2012, p. 31). Also, in the case of the appreciation of different values and ideas in constructive conflict, the constructivity of conflict and controversy is dependent on the possibility of bridging and aligning disparate perspectives or claims in the end. This means that differences are appreciated, although in light of a common ground or unifying principle, they are seen as complementary differences that can be bridged or aligned by management. Think of a NGO for public health that is collaborating with representatives of the food industry (Blok et al., 2015). These actors find common ground in their efforts to contribute to public health and collaborate notwithstanding their different value frames and interests; they agree to disagree for the remaining issues. In case it is difficult to find such shared objectives – for instance, in the case of a stock listed multinational enterprise (MNE) that is collaborating with an NGO that fundamentally questions the political-economic ideology behind markets – these stakeholders will be excluded from the collaboration. Lezaun and Soneryd, for instance, report on stakeholder meetings on genetic modification (GM), from which so-called extra-ordinary actors were systematically excluded in order to involve the general public (Lezaun and Soneryd, 2007). The second reason why the notion of partnership and collaboration in management practices is not self-evident, is that even if differences amongst stakeholders are acknowledged and appreciated, the inclusion of different but complementary stakeholders and the exclusion of fundamentally different stakeholders seems to be presupposed.

This brings us to a third and final reason why the notion of partnership and collaboration in management practices is not self-evident. The tendency towards consensus and alignment neglects the role of conflict and difference in the constitution of the identity of actors. Chantal Mouffe argues that every identification of an "us" necessarily entails a demarcation from a "them":

> [T]here is always the possibility of this relation us/them becoming one of friend/enemy. This happens when the others, who up to now had been considered as simply different, start to be perceived as putting into question our identity and threatening our existence. From that moment on, any form of us/them relation, be it religious, ethnic or economic, becomes the locus of an antagonism. (Mouffe, 2009: 550–551)

The tendency towards consensus and alignment in the notion of inclusion and partnership is not self-evident, because this tendency neglects the role of fundamental differences in the constitution of actors' identity. The self or identity of actors comes out in the confrontation with fundamentally different actors, which implies that stakeholders will never achieve alignment and harmony in the management of inclusion and partnership practices (Blok, 2014). The self-evident concept of partnership and inclusion cannot account for the role of conflict and difference in the constitution of the identity of stakeholders (Brand et al., 2020; Popa et al., 2020).

These three reasons to question the self-evidence of the concept of partnership and collaboration in stakeholder management lead to the question how managers can reach unity within collaborations and partnerships and respect fundamental differences between multiple stakeholders at the same time. This leads to a philosophical reflection on the nature of unity, identity, and difference in CSPs for wicked problems like global warming in the next subsection.

Managing the Process of Partnership Implementation: Three Questions with Regard to Unity, Identity, and Difference in the Process of Partnership Formation and Implementation

In an influential review article on the design and implementation of cross-sector collaborations, John Bryson and colleagues provide an overview of the initial conditions affecting collaboration formation and the process of collaboration. Here, the experience of sector failure to solve public problems like global warming is seen as a driver for CSP formation:

> Public policy makers are most likely to try cross-sector collaboration when they believe the separate efforts of different sectors to address a public problem have failed or are likely to fail, and the actual or potential failures cannot be fixed by the sectors acting alone. (Bryson et al., 2006: 46; Van Huijstee et al., 2007).

Besides the experience of the dependency on other sectors, initial agreements amongst partners on the problem definition are also seen as an initial condition of CSP formation (Gray, 1989; Westley and Vredenburg, 1997; Selsky and Parker, 2005). One of the reasons for this is that agreements on the problem definition can help to clarify the interest partners have in solving the problem. In the literature therefore, both the acknowledgement of the *interdependency* of cross-sector partners and the recognition of the *self-interest* of each partner in solving the problem are seen as necessary conditions for CSP formation (Logsdon, 1991; Bryson et al., 2006). Based on the ground-breaking work of Selsky and Parker (2005), Seitanidi and Crane revealed the critical micro-processes within partnership formation in a case-study on the management of CSP implementation (Seitanidi and Crane, 2009). We follow their work for a moment to throw light on three questions with regard to identity, unity, and difference in the management of CSP formation and implementation.

According to Seitanidi and Crane, the first stage of partner selection consist of the following steps: the strategic decision of a firm for "partnership" as the preferred associational form to work on sustainable development, the exploration of possible partners, and the selection of a partner organization based on selection criteria. They describe an additional step in the event of reputational risk, that is, the situation in which potential partners would undermine the reputation, integrity, brand, or, in short, the identity of the firm. If for instance Shell and Greenpeace decide to start a partnership, it is at least conceivable that this partnership would raise questions about the integrity of and motives of both partners. An informal risk assessment is an additional step, which consists in internal and external debates within the firm or NGO and with the potential partners and stakeholders about the concerns the CSP raises and its consequences for their own reputation. In this way, the informal risk assessment considers which potential partners are compatible with the identity of the firm/NGO (Van Huijstee et al., 2007).

The various steps in the selection phase show clearly that Seitanidi and Crane acknowledge the fundamental differences or even conflicts between partners. On the one hand, these differences can lead to the construction of partnerships that enable partners to jointly manage innovative solutions to the wicked problem of global warming. On the other hand, these differences between partners can also undermine the identity of the partnering organizations. Otherwise, it wouldn't make sense to perform an informal risk assessment.

Although an informal risk assessment can help to assess which partners are compatible or not, Seitanidi and Crane do not make clear how we can distinguish between differences between partners which undermine the identity of one of the partnering organizations, and differences which are constructive and lead to innovative solutions. Is it possible to make such a strict distinction between constructive and destructive partnerships, or does every construction presupposes a certain amount of destruction and vice versa? Is for instance the construction of the roundtable on sustainable palm oil by WWF, Unilever, and others a real solution to social problems, if it didn't destruct Unilever's business as usual in a certain way? The first question we face with regard to the management of CSPs is therefore, how to distinguish between differences between partners which are destructive for the identity of the partnering organizations, and differences which are constructive for the unity of the partnership and lead to innovative solutions.

According to Seitanidi and Crane, the second stage of the management of partnership implementation concerns the design of the partnership itself and consists in the following steps: partnership experimentation and adaptation, which involves agreements on partnership objectives and a Memorandum of Understanding. These agreements should be operationalized within the partnership, which involves agreements on the content and processes of the partnership. If for instance the meat industry and an NGO for animal protection co-create a market for animal friendly meat products, they have to agree on the specific characteristics of the product, taking both aspects of economics and animal welfare into account (Bos et al., 2013; Van Huijstee et al., 2007).

We already saw that initial agreements on the problem definition are an initial condition of partnership formation and lead to higher degrees of alignment on common goals (Nowell, 2010); without shared objectives, agreements on the operationalization of the partnership – the commitment of resources, designation of formal leadership, the decision-making structure, etc. – will not succeed and the partnership in general will not get off the ground (Bryson et al., 2006).

Although it is clear that partners have to agree on the problem definition and the shared objectives of the partnership and have to adapt to each other in the design phase, Seitanidi and Crane do not make clear how exactly the differences or even conflicts between multiple stakeholders are bridged in order to reach such a common ground. The second question we face with regard to the management of CSP implementation is, therefore, how exactly partners bridge their differences within the process of partnership implementation.

The final stage of implementation concerns the management of the institutionalization of the partnership. According to Seitanidi and Crane, partnership programs and processes should be embedded in the partnering organizations. The institutionalization is measured by the extent to which partners are able to manage and overcome crises within the partnership, "(a) by accepting the other organization's strengths and also weaknesses as a reality of an integrative relationship and (b) by not avoiding conflict but rather accept disagreements as functional which permits retaining the organization's identity intact" (Seitanidi and Crane, 2009). If for instance the meat industry and the NGO for animal protection, based on their conflicting value systems, disagree with regard to specific animal welfare characteristics of a new animal friendly product brand, they have to *agree to disagree* (GEMI, 2008). Here, we see again that Seitanidi and Crane acknowledge the fundamental differences between partners (encountered during the first phase of partnership implementation), which have to be bridged in order to achieve shared objectives (second phase of partnership implementation). On the one hand, the extent to which CSPs are able to solve such crises – that is, differences and conflicts within the partnership – is an indication of the unity of the partnership. On the other hand, the acceptance of differences between partners helps to retain the partnering organizations' own identity. For Seitanidi and Crane therefore, also constructive partnerships with shared objectives allow for differences or conflicts within the partnership, because they can strengthen the identity of the actors involved.

However, if differences between actors can be seen as destructive for the identity of the partnering organizations – as Seitanidi and Crane revealed with regard to the first phase of partnership implementation – and at the same time as constructive for the identity of the partnering organizations – as they suggest with regard to the third phase of partnership implementation – the question is again how we can distinguish between differences which are destructive for the identity of the partnering organizations, and differences which are constructive for their identity. The third question we face with regard to the management of CSP implementation is therefore, how to distinguish between differences between partners which are constructive and destructive for the identity of the actors involved. While the first question concentrates on differences which are destructive for the identity of the partnering organizations and differences which are constructive for the *unity of the partnership,* the third question focusses on the differences between partners which are constructive for the *identity of the partnering organizations.*

Our short consultation of the partnership literature makes two things clear. On the one hand, the philosophical question about unity, identity, and difference is at the heart of the phenomenon of managing stakeholders in CSPs and collaborations. On the other hand, this question is not taken into account in current research on the way collaborations and partnerships overcome their divergences and align their efforts to solve wicked problems like global warming. In the next section, we will reflect on the concepts of identity, unity, and difference in the metaphysical tradition.

15 Identity, Unity, and Difference in the Philosophical Tradition

In the history of western philosophy, identity is understood as *sameness;* each thing is the same with itself and two things are the same if they share certain qualities. In case of two things sharing the same quality – man and woman share the quality human being for instance – we talk about *qualitative* identity. Two things can be more or less qualitatively identical, dependent on the specificity of the qualities they share. In this respect, two men can be seen as "more" identical than man and woman for instance. In case of *total* qualitative identity, we talk about *numerical* identity. Numerical identity only holds for the sameness of a thing with itself, because a thing is only *total* qualitative identical with itself (Noonan, 2011).

Qualitative identity is traditionally understood in terms of a *genus proximum et differentiam specificam.* Each thing can be defined in terms of a genus under which it falls – animal for instance – and a species which differentiates this type of animal – *animal rationale* for instance – from other types of animals. All entities who share the same quality – *animal rationale* – are qualitative the same in contrast with other entities who do not share these specific qualities (plants for instance). The identity of an entity therefore contains one or more unifying qualities (animal or plant for instance) and one or more differentiating qualities (*rationale* for instance). These qualities are understood as universal terms and form a hierarchy of universals (*animal*), which are applicable on lower levels of universality (*rationale*) and so on, down to the lowest level of universals (*Dutch philosopher* for instance), and, in the end, to individual entities (Vincent Blok as a Dutch philosopher). According to the Aristotelian tradition, these individual entities are the "primary substances" of which universal terms (genus, species etc.) are predicated, "while it is not itself predicated of something else" (Aristotle, 1944: 1028b35); rationality may be a quality of Vincent Blok but Vincent Blok itself cannot be seen as a quality of another primary substance.

Aristotle distinguishes between *essential* qualities of primary substances – that is, qualities which are predicated to the primary substance *per se (Kath 'auto)* like the rationality of human being – and accidental qualities like the tallness or rednosedness of a human being. Essential qualities of primary substances (*eidos*) are not restricted to genera or species. According to Aristotle, *eidos* primarily means the form or gestalt of an entity as it appears in contrast to its materiality (Cohen, 2012). The *eidos* has to be understood therefore as a unifying principle in the light of which *different* things appear *as* the same (identity). The first characteristic of identity and difference in the metaphysical tradition is that identity is understood as an essential quality (genus, *idea, and eidos*), which is a unifying principle in the light of which *different* entities appear *as* the same. The difference between entities who share the same qualitative identity (Socrates and Callias as human beings for instance) is explained by their accidental qualities (tallness, rednosedness, etc.) or by their materiality (see also Leibniz' concept of the *identity of indiscernibles)*. While the qualitative identity of Socrates and Callias is due to the essential quality they share (human being), the difference between them is due to differentiating accidental qualities (Socrates has a red nose and Callias is tall for instance) and their particular materiality.

According to Emmanuel Levinas, these metaphysical concepts of identity and difference are the result of a *reduction* of the other to the same, difference to identity. Because the work of Levinas is notoriously difficult, we restrict ourselves to a schematic presentation of his critique of the metaphysical concepts of identity and difference in this section and explore the applicability of his critique in the context of CSPs in the next section.

In *Totality and Infinity,* Levinas argues: "Western philosophy has most often been an ontology: a reduction of the other to the same by interposition of a middle and neutral term that ensures the comprehension of being" (Levinas, 1969: 43). This middle term – *rationale* for instance – is the unifying principle in the light of which different things synthesize and appear as the same. To what extent do we have to conceive such an interposition of a unifying principle as a *reduction* of the other to the same according to Levinas? "The relation with Being that is enacted as ontology consists in neutralizing the existent in order to comprehend or grasp it. It is hence not a relation with the other as such but the reduction of the other to the same" (Levinas, 1969: 45–46). Because of the primacy of the knowledge of the Being of beings in the metaphysical tradition – *rationale* as differentiating quality of human beings for instance – priority is given to the essential qualities, while the accidental qualities of Socrates and Callias are renounced, just as their particular materiality, that is, the singularity of their bodily existence. The second characteristic of identity and difference in the metaphysical tradition is, that identity is the product of a reduction of the other to the same, difference to identity.

This reduction doesn't mean that differences between primary substances are simply rejected in the metaphysical tradition. In light of the unifying principle (essential quality), the remaining differences are understood as accidental or *secondary* qualities; they are appreciated only in light of the essential or primary qualities. In this respect, the difference *as* difference is reduced to a difference *within* the same, or in philosophical language, the difference is *interiorized* (Derrida, 1982). The same holds for the singularity of primary substances, which is neutralized and anonymized by the reduction of the other to the same according to Levinas (Levinas, 1969: 45). In order to understand a primary substance like another human being, we traditionally refrain from his or her singularity and conceive him or her in general terms – the other in his or her animality, rationality, etc. Because this singularity of the singular person is understood in general terms, it is precisely this otherness or singularity which is violated. The third characteristic of identity and difference in the metaphysical tradition is, that differences are interiorized and only appreciated in light of a unifying principle (identity).

According to Levinas, the point of departure of this reduction is found in myself. "The relation with the other is here accomplished only through a third term which I find in myself. The ideal of Socratic truth thus rests on the essential self-sufficiency of the same, its identification in ipseity, its egoism" (Levinas, 1969: 44). The unifying principle in the light of which the other appears as the same, is found in myself, for instance in my own identity, value frames, and judgments. I grasp the other by incorporating him or her in my own ideas and concepts, tam, and domesticate the other in terms of the same. In understanding the other by drawing him or her within the borders of my own ideas and concepts, the other (difference) is suppressed, exploited, and dominated by the self (identity) in the philosophical tradition. According to Levinas, the power exercised by the self guarantees sameness over otherness, identity over difference. The fourth characteristic of identity and difference in the metaphysical tradition is, that the power performed by the self guarantees sameness over otherness, identity over difference.

Contrary to the metaphysical tradition, the point of departure of Levinas' philosophy is precisely found in the encounter with the singularity of another person. The confrontation with another person is completely different from an encounter with any other object, organism, or event in the world. I not only see that another person looks like me, acts like me and appear to have consciousness like me. For Levinas, the main difference is that I, in my face-to-face encounter with another person, (a) experience a fundamental difference between myself and the other person which cannot be bridged – that is, the radical exteriority of the other – and (b) experience myself as the one who is called upon to respond to this other. Contrary to the metaphysical tradition, Levinas develops a way of thinking that is characterized by a desire for the other without reducing him, that is, "the personal Other, the you" (Levinas, 1969: 24). We restrict ourselves to this schematic presentation of Levinas' critique of the metaphysical concepts of identity and difference. In the next section, we trace the four characteristics of the metaphysical concepts of identity and difference in the management context of CSP development and implementation.

16 The Metaphysics of Collaboration: Identity, Unity, and Difference in CSPs and Collaboration

The process of partner selection, as we have seen, starts with forging initial agreements on the problem definition and the shared objectives. These agreements are important in partnership implementation but difficult to manage in the case of wicked problems (Section 7). According to a famous article by Hardy et al., who analyzed the role of discourse and conversation in the management of effective collaborations, agreements on the problem definition, and the shared objectives are the result of constructing a collective identity, that is, a unifying principle which is meaningful to and shared by the actors involved and is able to engage them to solve social problems: "the discursive construction of a collective identity enables participants to construct themselves, the problem, and the solution as part of a collaborative framework in which the potential for joint action is both significant and beneficial" (Hardy et al., 2005: 62–63). The construction of a collective identity has two advantages according to their research. On the one hand, it forge agreements on the problem definition and the shared objectives of the partnership. On the other hand, the potential benefits of the partnership for the partnering organizations become clear, that is, the interest partners have in solving the problem.

According to Hardy and colleagues, collective identities are constructed in two specific types of conversations amongst partners. First of all, conversations that connect partners to a *common issue* – AIDS, sustainable development, poverty alleviation, etc. – produce generalized membership ties. These conversations involve the diagnosis of a shared issue or problem and the prognosis of a possible solution of the problem, that is, a common goal or shared objective. In our example of the partnership between the meat industry and the NGO for animal protection, this shared objective can be found in a new market for animal friendly meat products for instance. Secondly, the construction of collective identities involves conversations that connect partners in a direct way to each other, for instance because of a common history of collaboration or position in the network, because of the status or authority of a specific partner etc. These conversations produce particularized membership ties. Both types of conversation are important in the construction of a collective identity (Hardy et al., 2005).[1]

The concept of a collective identity which is produced by generalized and particularized membership ties shows that the identity of the partnership is understood as the unity of two distinct actors which can be seen as the "primary substances" of the partnership and are connected or *tied* together in a unity. Although these actors are seen as members of the partnership who share a *common* or *collective* identity, the unity of the partnership cannot be understood as a physical unity like a merger; CSP's concern collaborations between actors without merging their activities into a new organization. The unity of the partnership concerns a *unifying principle* – stop the violation of animals in the meat industry for instance – in the light of which different actors show themselves *as* the same, *as* unity. The collective identity of the partnership is understood here in line with the metaphysical tradition, that is, as a unifying principle in the light of which primary substances – the actors involved in the partnership – appear *as* the same.

There are two specific ways in which different actors show themselves *as* the same. (1) The generalized membership ties produce a *commonality* amongst different actors, a *shared* problem definition, and/or *shared* objectives for instance. (2) The particularized membership ties produce a *community* amongst different actors, a spatial or temporal proximity like the *same* home base, or the *same* field of action (animal production and animal welfare for instance). Mediated by these two types of identity – commonality and community – different actors become intertwined and form a synthesis.[2] The identity of the partnership is understood here as the unity that different actors have in *common* in light of a unifying principle; the commonality of shared objectives and/or the community of spatial-temporal proximate actors. It is this concept of the unity of the partnership as the synthesis of different partners in the light of a unifying principle (commonality/community), which is presupposed in all efforts of CSPs to overcome their differences and converge or align their efforts.

If we realize, however, that CSPs deal with wicked problems, which are characterized by *different* judgments and *different* values of multiple stakeholders, it is questionable whether this unity of different partners can ever be expected. In this respect, various researchers on CSPs conclude that conflicts are "pervasive and likely unavoidable in cross-sector partnerships" (le Ber and Branzei, 2010: 169). In a recent case-study on value frame fusion in CSPs by Le Ber and Branzei, the point of departure is exactly the fact that differences amongst multiple stakeholders are unavoidable and, therefore, that the ideal of a unifying synthesis of different partners is out of reach.[3] Because the importance of agreements on shared problem definitions and shared objectives is acknowledged by Le Ber and Branzei too, the question of their work is how CSPs can find a common ground (identity) and respect the differences between partners at the same time. We follow the framework of Le Ber and Branzei for a moment to see how identity and difference are conceived in their work.

According to Le Ber and Branzei, the management of CSP formation starts with the way social problems and their solutions are understood by the individual partnering organizations. Because it is difficult to find a "common ground" amongst these different actors, the management of partnership formation is seen as an iterative process of revising and adjusting the individual and fundamentally *different* conceptions of the problem and its solution in relation to the other individual actors involved. In our example of an animal friendly product brand for instance, the NGO originally saw the meat industry as "part of the problem", but acknowledged later on that a new market for animal friendly meat products could be seen as "part of the solution" of the problem. To this end, both the NGO and the industry had to adjust their conception of the problem and its solution in relation to the other. The new product brand of animal friendly meat had to meet both the objectives of the industry (focus on animal welfare attributes which can be communicated to consumers, a maximum of 20% above the mainstream product price etc.) and the NGO (significant increase of welfare in the meat supply chain) (Bos et al., 2013). In such an iterative process, different partners manage to find a "common ground", that is, areas where the problem definition and the objectives of the *different* actors *overwrite* or *overlap* each other, without the necessity to embrace the judgments or values of the other actors completely (le Ber and Branzei, 2010).

How are the concepts of identity and difference understood in the framework of Le Ber and Branzei? For Le Ber and Branzei partners do not construct a collective identity but rather look for overlap between their individual identities. The point of departure is therefore found in myself as a primary substance who is interested in collaborating with other actors. In the iterative process of value frame fusion, my essential qualities are the starting point of the process of value frame fusion and these essential qualities are analyzed, compared, and reconciled in relation to the essential qualities of other actors. In this process, it becomes clear that some essential qualities overlap with those of others, while others do not. These overlaps between the *different* identities of partners are in fact *shared* essential qualities. With this, it becomes clear that the unity of the partnership is also here understood as a synthesis – or better "symbiosis" – of different actors in the light of a unifying principle, that is, the essential qualities that different actors have in common (common ground). Because the identities of the different actors do not have to overwrite or overlap each other completely, the unity of the partnership captures the commonality between the identities of the partners involved – their shared essential qualities – while allowing for their differences, that is, essential qualities of the individual partners which do not overlap with each other. We can conclude that on the one hand, the metaphysical concept of the unity of the partnerships we discussed before is also presupposed in the iterative process of finding common ground in the framework of Le Ber and Branzei. On the other hand, although partners try to overcome their differences and manage to converge or align their efforts in order to find a common ground of shared essential qualities, their (remaining) differences are at the same time respected in this framework.

More important than the advantages of Le Ber's framework is, however, that we receive an indication of how this unity of different partners is achieved in CSPs. Le Ber and Branzei distinguish four phases in this iterative process of finding common ground. First, the *different* interpretations of the social problem and its solution are acknowledged and *negotiated* by the partners. Secondly, actors' experiment with the *elasticity* of their own problem definition and objective in order to assess whether it may include the problem definition or the goals of other actors involved. This elasticity presupposes the willingness of the different actors to challenge their own understanding of the problem and its solution, and to embrace their partner's conception of the problem: "The willingness and ability to see each other's point of view builds forward momentum simply by creating a sense of connection" (le Ber and Branzei, 2010: 182). The ability to embrace the other's understanding of the problem definition and its solution is called frame plasticity, that is, the ability to give up aspects of your own understanding of the problem definition and to embrace aspects of the other's conception of the problem, without identifying yourself completely with the other. In the fourth phase of this iterative process of finding common ground, the remaining differences between partners are understood and appreciated as *complementary* differences, that is, as differences which can contribute to solving the social problem by generating synergetic or complementary effects. "Frame fusion partners reach common ground by coming to appreciate their (complementary) differences rather than espousing and/or enacting a similar frame" (le Ber and Branzei, 2010: 177).

The process of frame fusion can be depicted in the following way (Figure 4.1):

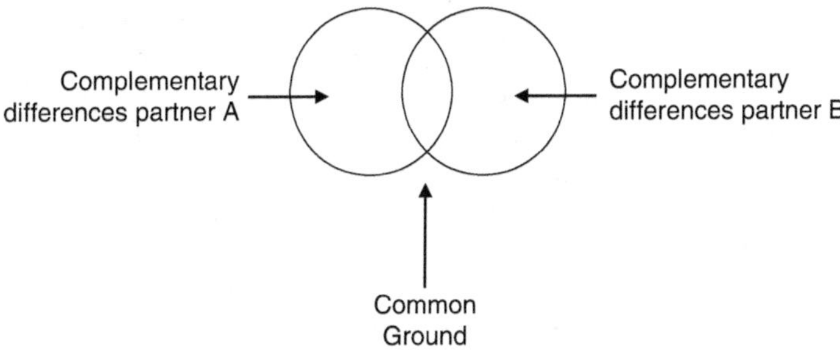

Figure 4.1 Process of frame fusion in CSPs.

The iterative process of finding common ground shows that the actors have to give up parts of their *own* essential qualities and that they have to embrace parts of the *other's* essential qualities in the process of negotiation, elasticity, plasticity, and fusion. This means that the common ground is not a neutral overlap between the identities of different actors but is the product of a reduction of the otherness of the individual partners – their different essential qualities – to the same. In this iterative process of value frame fusion, the essential qualities which are shared by the individual partners increases while the remaining differences between them are acknowledged as *complementary* differences.

We can conclude that differences are reduced to the same in managing the process of value frame fusion. In this respect, we encounter the second characteristic of the metaphysical concept of identity and difference – identity is the product of the reduction of the other to the same, difference to identity – in the partnership literature, that is, the ideal of unity and harmony. At the same time, we may conclude that Levinas' critique of the metaphysical tradition isn't applicable on the process of value frame fusion, because the remaining differences between actors are acknowledged as complementary differences. Contrary to Levinas, we may even claim that precisely these complementary differences contribute to solving social problems by generating synergetic or complementary effects.

And yet, this reduction of difference to identity in management practices is not harmless. This becomes clear if we realize that the differences between the essential qualities of multiple stakeholders are seen here as *complementary* differences. It is senseless to speak about *complementary* differences without any reference to a common ground (identity), and therefore primacy is given to the essential qualities multiple actors have in common. Only in the light of this common ground, differences between essential qualities of partners are appreciated as *complementary* in achieving this common goal of the partnership. These differences may be seen as essential qualities of the individual partners, but are reduced to accidental qualities of the partnership.[4] Here, we encounter the third characteristic of the metaphysical concept of identity and difference in the partnership literature; the differences between partners are only appreciated *in the light of* a common ground (identity), which means that these differences are essentially reduced to the same in order to be able to comprehend and grasp the other's viewpoint and to appreciate his or her viewpoint as complementary difference.

What is more, the reduction of difference to identity in the CSP formation is led by the individual actors involved. This becomes clear if we realize that CSP formation is characterized by power imbalances. While Le Ber and Branzei presuppose that partners are voluntarily involved in finding common ground without any "push or pull" of one of the partners (le Ber and Branzei, 2010), Hardy and colleagues show the violent character of this reduction. In their analysis, Hardy and colleagues point at political processes involved in defining the problem and the objective of the partnership. Political processes are important, because the specific formulation of the problem definition already determines what potential solutions are involved and who are legitimate partners in realizing these solutions. If we conceive the problem of sustainable development for instance in such a way that it affords a systems change, a wholly different solution is at stake than if it is defined at a product level and only involves the substitution of unsustainable resources. This example shows that partners have an interest in the specific way the problem is defined, because it has consequences for the shared objective of the partnership and with this, for the investments of resources to solve the problem.

For Hardy and colleagues, it is clear that some partners are more powerful than others in defining the problem and the shared objectives of the partnership, that is, that partnership formation is not a voluntary process without any push and pull. It is conceivable that power imbalances are especially at stake in the case of wicked problems, exactly because of the different problem definitions and different values of partners. These power imbalances can be seen as a prime source of conflicts between partners (Bryson et al., 2006) but also as their solution. When partners have difficulty to find a common ground with regard to the problem definition and/or its solution, power imbalances, and negotiation processes between partners will lead to the prevalence of the problem definition of the powerful partner over that of the weaker partner. In the light of this negotiated problem definition, the differences between the partners can be respected and accepted as an "agreement to not agree" or as *complementary* differences.[5] The point of departure is therefore not only found in my identity (essential quality) as an individual actor (primary substance), which is voluntarily aligned with the identity of other actors in the process of value frame fusion, but this alignment is the product of efforts of individual partners to dominate the process of finding a common ground of shared essential qualities.

If conflicts and fundamental differences are persistent during the first two phases of CSP implementation (Bryson et al., 2006), power imbalances will lead to the exclusion of "extreme" or "radical" perspectives by the powerful partner (Hardy et al., 2005; Gray and Hay, 1986). In this respect, we can understand why radical stakeholders like Greenpeace or People for the Ethical Treatment of Animals (PETA) are excluded by MNEs like Unilever, Nestlé, and Shell: fundamental differences between actors are excluded and only complementary differences are taken into account in CSP formation. The reduction of the other to the same in CSP formation is therefore not or at least not only characterized by the willingness of both partners to challenge their own identity and embrace the other's perspective on the problem and its solution, as Le Ber and Branzei suggest, but by the (political) will of the partners to master and control the other in CSP formation. Only by the inclusion of complementary differences and the exclusion of radical differences is the unity and harmony of CSPs guaranteed. With this, we encounter the fourth characteristic of the metaphysical concept of identity and difference in the partnership literature, that is, that the point of departure of value frame fusion is found in essential qualities of myself as primary substance and that the power performed by myself guarantees sameness over otherness, difference over identity. In both "voluntary" and "forced" partnerships, common ground is found by using the reductive powers of the actors involved. Through these reductive powers, actors give up the fundamental difference between themselves and the other partners in order to achieve unity (partner inclusion) or they maintain their identity in confrontation with the other to achieve unity (partner exclusion). Only by this inclusion and exclusion of partners can the unity of the partnership be guaranteed.

With the analysis of the process of managing CSP development and implementation, we encountered the four characteristics of the metaphysical concept of identity and difference in the partnership literature: (1) The unity of partnerships is understood as the synthesis of different actors in the light of a unifying principle, which is found in an essential quality they share (commonality, community, common ground, etc.). (2) This unity and harmony of the partnership is the product of the reduction of the otherness of the individual partners to the same, difference to identity. (3) This reduction doesn't mean that all differences between partners are excluded. The differences between individual partners are appreciated in the light of a common ground, which means that the difference *as* difference is essentially interiorized and reduced to the same. (4) The unity of the partnership is guaranteed by the power of the individual actors involved in partnership formation, that is, by the inclusion of complementary and the exclusion of fundamental differences. If actors are able to find such a common ground, the differences between their judgments and values are interiorized as *complementary* differences. If actors are not able to find such a common ground and conflicts remain, fundamental different actors are excluded from the partnership by the more powerful actors involved.

Accordingly, we can conclude that a very specific concept of identity, unity and difference is presupposed in the CSP literature, and that the tendency towards unity and harmony in the CSP literature is rooted in its adherence to the metaphysical tradition. Based on our analysis of the partnership literature and the four characteristics of the concepts of identity and difference which are presupposed in the CSP literature with regard to identity, unity and difference in the process of managing the CSP formation, we are now able to answer the three questions developed in Section 14.

The first question we raised was about the differences between partners and the unity of the partnership; how to distinguish between differences between partners which are destructive for the identity of the partnering organizations and differences which are constructive for the unity of the partnership and lead to sustainable solutions? The unity of the partnership is the product of the reduction of the other to the same, difference to identity, as we have seen. There are two ways in which this unity is constituted. The reduction can result in a common ground, in which the differences between the partners are interiorized as complementary differences. These complementary differences between partners are conceived as drivers for innovative solutions within the partnership. If actors are however not able to find common ground and conflicts remain, the differences between actors undermine the unity of the partnership. In that case, the unity of the partnership is guaranteed by the exclusion of "radical" different partners; only complementary differences between partners are seen as constructive for the unity of the partnership and therefore, as drivers for finding sustainable solutions within the partnership (answer question 1).

The second question was how exactly partners bridge their differences within the process of partnership implementation. As we have seen, the unity of the partnership is constituted and guaranteed by the reductive power of the actors involved. Differences between partners are bridged by the reduction of the other to the same, difference to identity. This identity is found in a unifying principle (commonality, community, common ground), in the light of which the differences between partners are interiorized. What kind of differences between actors are bridged or exorcized in order to find common ground within the partnership, is in the end determined by the power of the actors involved in partnership formation (answer question 2)?

The third question was about differences between partners and the identity of the partnering organizations: how to distinguish between differences between partners which are constructive and destructive for the identity of the partnering organizations. It is important to realize that in a way, all partnerships are destructive for the identity of the partnering organizations. The concepts of frame elasticity and frame plasticity already show that actors should be able to give up aspects of their own identity and embrace aspects of the other actors without identifying themselves completely with the other. This destruction of their own identity is however not problematic if a common ground is found. In the light of this common ground, the differences between partners can be seen as complementary differences which lead to innovative solutions to social problems. These differences are not destructive for the identity of the partnering organizations but "retain organization's identity" intact. If the problem definitions and core values of other actors threaten to undermine the organization's identity, they will use their power to assimilate or exclude these actors from the partnership in order to find common ground. Power imbalances and negotiation processes between partners will lead to the prevalence of the problem definition and values of the powerful partner over those of the weaker partner. This power to assimilate or exclude potential partners can be seen as destructive for the identity of the (weaker) actors involved (answer question 3).

The critical question we have to ask, however, is whether these metaphysical concepts of identity, unity and difference are suitable in the case of managing wicked problems like global warming. If multiple stakeholders are involved with different or even conflicting judgments and values, it is questionable whether the ideal of the unity of the partnership – a common ground of shared problem definitions, common goals or a collective identity – can ever be reached within the partnership.[6] Again, if multiple stakeholders are involved in the solution of wicked problems, it is questionable whether the reduction of these *differences* to identity – common ground – and to *complementary* differences is possible without the destruction of the identity of the partners involved. Finally, if such stakeholders are involved, it is questionable whether it is desirable to deal with complementary differences within the partnership only and to exclude extreme or radical perspectives on the problem and its solution.

In the case of managing wicked problems like global warming, we are in need of (disruptive) innovative solutions. Innovation seems to flourish in an environment of open innovation, in which the interaction with *other* or *different* stakeholders is seen as a resource of competitive advantage (Chesbrough, 2003)[7]; only the *diversity* of problem definitions and values leads to creative and innovative solutions. It is questionable whether it is sufficient to deal with "complementary" differences only in order to find innovative solutions to wicked problems like sustainable development, or that "radically" different stakeholder should be involved as well.

Do we have to conclude then that CSPs are impossible or insufficient in the case of wicked problems like global warming, because these kinds of partnerships all show a tendency towards convergence and harmony and cannot take the wickedness of the problem and the fundamental differences between stakeholders into account?

Hardy et al. do not embrace this conclusion. They acknowledge "people's preference for coherence" and a "tendency towards convergence", but believe that "a number of factors can mitigate this tendency towards convergence" (Hardy et al., 2005: 68). They argue for the production of "private constructions", that is, the construction of the actors' own identity (problem definitions, interest and core values). According to their argument, effective collaboration between partners is facilitated by a tension between the tendencies towards convergence (commonality, community, collective identity of essential qualities) and towards divergence (private constructions of a private identity of essential qualities of the actors involved).

The question is, however, how the tendency towards convergence is related to the tendency towards divergence. Hardy et al. seem to make a strict distinction between the collective identity of the partnership (shared essential qualities of the partnership) on the one hand and the private identity of the partners (private essential qualities of the individual partners), which are not shared. There are two problems with this position. If the mission of an NGO is to stop the pollution of the environment in Asia, for instance, we may expect this mission to be part not only of the private construction of the NGO, but of the shared objectives of the CSP too. In other words, it is for this NGO insufficient when this essential quality is only a private construction and it should be part of the collective identity as well. Otherwise, it wouldn't make sense for the NGO to join the CSP.[8] The first problem is therefore that a strict distinction between the essential qualities which constitute the collective identity of the partnership and the essential qualities which constitute the private identity of the partnering organizations cannot be made in the case of wicked problems like global warming. At the same time, it is precisely this essential quality of the NGO which may be in conflict with the problem definition and values of the other partners involved in the partnership. From the perspective of the partnership, these conflicting essential qualities have to be seen then as part of the private construction of the NGO. Indeed, the success of CSPs is guaranteed by a shared problem definition and shared objectives, as we have seen (Section 14), which means that conflicting essential qualities have to be excluded from the partnership. But this exclusion of conflicting essential qualities from the partnership and their inclusion in the private identity of the actors involved means, that this private identity actually turns out to be an accidental quality and is limited to complementary differences between partners. Why? On the one hand, if these qualities were really essential for the NGO, they should have been part of the collective identity of the partnership in which they are involved. On the other hand, if these essential qualities really concern fundamental differences between (potential) partners – think, for example, of Greenpeace and Shell or PETA and the meat industry – these private identities are unacceptable for the other actors involved. The second problem is therefore that even if we accept the need to acknowledge the private identity (difference) of partners, only *complementary* or *in-essential* differences between partners will be acceptable for the powerful actors involved. In this respect, it is not only likely that the "people's preference for convergence" and "tendency towards convergence" are rooted in the metaphysical tradition, but also that the "ongoing circulation and interplay of common and private constructions", which mitigates the tendency towards convergence according to Hardy and colleagues, is preceded by the inclusion of complementary different partners and the exclusion of radical different partners.

Although Hardy and colleagues give valuable suggestions on how to mitigate the tendency towards convergence – raising mutual awareness of the different conceptions of the problem definition and the objectives of the partnering organizations, a steady flow of new partners over time etc. (Hardy et al., 2005) – our question whether the metaphysical concepts of identity and difference are suitable in the case of wicked problems like global warming in general, and the question about how to maintain one's own identity (difference) and share objectives with other partners at the same time (identity), remain unanswered.

It is however not necessary to conclude that CSPs are impossible or insufficient in the case of wicked problems like global warming, because of their tendency towards convergence and harmony. As soon as we have realized that the meaning of concepts like partnership and collaboration is essentially determined by the metaphysical tradition, we can question whether the metaphysical concepts of identity and difference are appropriate in the case of CSPs for wicked problems like global warming.

Philosophers like Levinas can inspire us to question the metaphysical concepts of identity and difference. He not only pointed at the metaphysical origin of these concepts, but his attempt was also to "destruct" the metaphysical meaning of these concepts and to develop a non-metaphysical concept of identity and difference. For him, the relationship with the other is characterized by a fundamental difference which cannot be bridged. The other stands before me and is radically separated from me and irreducible, but this does not mean that I do not have a relationship with him. The other calls for our response to him in a non-reductive way, that is, calls for our ethical behaviour. In other words, in my face-to-face encounter with the Other, I experience myself as the one who is called upon to respond to the Other. The irreducible Other calls for our response in a non-reductive way, that is, calls for our embracing of the Other while leaving him intact at the same time. Precisely this responsiveness to the call of the Other can be conceived as collaboration and partnership, in which fundamental differences are acknowledged and appreciated. This concept of partnership and collaboration involves a shift from the cognitive level of primarily understanding the other, to the behavioural level of actual ethical behaviour in response to the call of the other.

In the next section, we develop a non-metaphysical concept of partnership and collaboration in which the fundamental and even conflicting differences between partners are embraced and the search for sustainable solutions to wicked problems like global warming is encouraged.

17 Towards and Ethics of Non-reductive Stakeholder Engagement, Collaboration, and Partnership in Management Practices

In this section, we explore four characteristics of a non-reductive and ethical concept of stakeholder engagement, collaboration, and partnership, which allow for the acknowledgement and appreciation of fundamental differences in stakeholder management: (1) focus on the social–ethical relationship with other stakeholders, rather than on the cognitive understanding of the demands and needs of the actors involved; (2) focus on the performance of ethical behaviour in response to the call or need of other stakeholders, rather than on the cognitive understanding of their demands and needs; (3) focus on the self-destruction and self-constitution of managers' identity in confrontation with other stakeholders, in which the performance of ethical behaviour is embedded; and (4) acknowledgement of the fundamental possibility of failure of managers' responsiveness to the call of other stakeholders.

The Social–Ethical Relationships in Stakeholder Engagement, Collaboration, and Partnerships

In Section 14 we have seen that initial agreements amongst stakeholders on the problem definition and the goals of the collaboration are regarded as a precondition for successful collaboration and partnership, since they help clarify the interests and value frames partners have in solving the problem. We can conceive of this as a cognitive approach to the management of stakeholders, collaboration and partnership, in which the interests, ideas and value frames of stakeholders play a central role.

In a way, this cognitive focus on understanding the interests or "stakes" of other stakeholders is already implied in stakeholder theory itself; firms are not managed only in the best interest of their shareholders, because many other societal actors have an interest or stake in the firm as well, for example, employees and NGOs (Freeman, 1984). In stakeholder theory, the point of departure is to understand the rights and claims of stakeholders who can affect or be affected by the business strategy (Freeman, 1984), and subsequently to balance these interests with sometimes competing interests of the firm. In this respect, stakeholder engagement presupposes that managers understand the interests and value frames of multiple stakeholders (Habermas, 1990, 1993), while their stakeholder engagement can enhance understanding, for instance, in the case of public ignorance about the impact of the business operations. The cognitive approach is also presupposed in the normative approach to stakeholder engagement – the idea that firms should be responsive to the interests and demands of their stakeholders (Donaldson and Preston, 1995; Hendry, 2001) – as well as in most literature on collaboration and partnership, as we have seen in Section 16.

We hypothesize, on the contrary, that as long as our point of departure of managing stakeholders is found in a certain cognitive position – their values, norms, and interests, but also a common problem statement or objective – that can be understood or known, the inclusion of stakeholders is subject to the reduction of the singularity of their interests and demands to the same by assimilating their demands and needs to corporate interests of the manager (self-confirmation) or by his or her submission of the corporate interests to stakeholder demands (self-denial; Section 16). Therefore, first, we reject the primacy of the cognitive approach to stakeholder engagement, collaboration and partnership in management practices and propose an approach in which the primacy of the social–ethical relationship is acknowledged. This concerns a shift from the nature of *stakeholder* engagement – the focus on managing their stake or interest – to the nature of stakeholder *engagement*, that is, the engagement with the demand they represent in management practices.

It involves two shifts in our concept of stakeholder engagement, collaboration and partnership. First, the point of departure of the partnership is no longer found in the manager with his or her interests and value frames that may subsequently turn out to be conflicting with the value frames of other stakeholders. Second, the social relationship no longer primarily consists in the effort to understand the other stakeholders involved in the collaboration. The other stakeholder does not simply represent another viewpoint, interest or value frame which should be taken into account or not by the manager. Instead, the other stakeholder is taken as an absolutely different actor with fundamental different value frames and interests, who can never be fully understood in stakeholder management. This separation between actors suspends all understanding, and institutes a social relationship with other stakeholders which is intrinsically ethical, that is, responsive to their demands and needs.[9] While, in the cognitive approach to stakeholder management, other stakeholders are reduced to the same by the assimilation of other stakeholders (self-confirmation) or by managers' submission to other more dominant stakeholders (self-denial), this ethical approach to stakeholder management is able to respect the fundamental differences of other stakeholders in its focus on the ethical responsiveness of managers to stakeholder demands. The call of other stakeholders is normative without calling for a universal norm, and the ethical dimension of stakeholder engagement, collaboration and partnership in management practices consist in managers' responsiveness to this call of other stakeholders. The ethical approach to stakeholder management implies that primacy is given to the demands of stakeholders who appeal to us to act and behave in a responsible way in our business practices.

The advantage of this shift in our attention from the cognitive understanding of the value frames and viewpoints of other stakeholders to focusing on the social–ethical relationship amongst stakeholders is that the focus is not (or not only) on the cognitive level of agreement on a joint problem definition, common ground or shared objective amongst multiple stakeholders, which is often difficult to achieve in practice (Bryson et al., 2006), but on the social–ethical relationship in which managers become responsive to stakeholder demands and needs.

Performance of Ethical Behaviour in Stakeholder Engagement, Collaborations, and Partnerships

This brings us to a second shift in our conceptualization of stakeholder engagement, collaboration, and partnership in management practices. In Section 14, we have seen that the experience of sector failure and therefore the interdependency of various stakeholders are seen as an initial condition of collaboration and partnership, because it helps to develop a common interest and objective. We can understand this as an *intentional* approach to stakeholder management, as the manager intends to address the failure and engages stakeholders to this end. They first make a moral judgment regarding the problem or failure, then establish moral intent, before their engagement in moral behaviour (Jones, 1991; Blok et al., 2017).

We can, however, turn this process around. It enables us to acknowledge that a shift is needed from the best intentions to respect the demands of other stakeholders, to a focus on the performance of ethical behaviour in response to the call of other stakeholders. Why? We have to acknowledge that the tendency to reduce the other to the same in power relations amongst stakeholders is not something actors can easily put an end to as we have seen in the previous sections (Selsky and Parker, 2005). As Cornwall explains: "Participation as praxis is, after all, rarely a seamless process; rather, it constitutes a terrain of contestation, in which relations of power between different actors, each with their own 'projects', shape and reshape the boundaries of action" (Cornwall, 2008: 276). Owing to this tendency to reduce the other to the same and to exhibit power play, the intention to respect the demands or interests of other stakeholders is insufficient; the fundamental differences of other stakeholders can be better respected in the continuous enactment of managers' responsiveness to stakeholder demands and needs. Only in their responsiveness by performing ethical behaviour towards other stakeholders is the moral intention of the manager real. This idea resonates with the second dimension of our philosophy of management, that is, management as responsive action.

This responsiveness goes beyond simple consequentialism but substitutes the other by putting the stakeholder manager in the place of other stakeholders who bear or represent the negative impact of his or her actions. This performance of ethical behaviour does not necessarily call on universal norms, but calls for action, here and now, and is dependent on the circumstances in which problems emerge and can be addressed. In this respect, the rejection of universal norms and the call for ethical behaviour in response to the call of other stakeholders highlights the importance of the singularity of the circumstances in which ethical issues in management emerge and have to be addressed.

More important than the application of universal norms is, therefore, the demand that managers' ethical responsiveness to other stakeholders should go beyond their own interests and value frames. In this respect, the focus on the behavioural performance of stakeholder management provides a strategy to no longer be involved in the ideal of harmony and alignment amongst multiple stakeholders, but instead to acknowledge fundamental differences amongst multiple stakeholders in managers ethical responsiveness to their demands and needs. A further advantage of such a behavioural approach to partnership and collaboration is that it prevents an "ethics of Narcissus", that is, an approach in which actors' being seen as ethical is stressed, rather than them taking responsibility in their management practices (Roberts, 2001). By focusing on ethical behaviour of the manager, we are not dependent on their best intentions which may turn out to be unethical. On the contrary, in our focus on behaviour, reflection on the limited and biased character of actors' current approaches of complex public problems is enhanced.

Self-destruction and Self-constitution in Stakeholder Engagement, Collaborations, and Partnerships

The shift from managers' intentions to managers' performance of ethical behaviour brings us to a third characteristic of an ethical approach to stakeholder engagement, collaboration, and partnership in management practices. The primary function of the social relationship with other stakeholders is no longer the self-expression of the interests and value frames of managers in order to convince other stakeholders, but to become critical towards themselves, that is, towards their own interests and value frames in response to the other (self-destruction) and to become responsive to the demand of the other stakeholders (self-constitution). In partnerships and collaborations, other stakeholders tell and teach the stakeholder manager the limitations of their interests and value frames and help them to question their self-evidently presupposed value frames and interests; businesses and NGOs can broaden each other's perspective on complex public problems and on the role and responsibility these different stakeholders have in solving the problem. In order to enhance self-criticism and self-constitution in management practices, actors should not only collaborate with different but complementary partners, or partners with relatively low cognitive distance (Section 16), but with fundamentally different stakeholders as well. Precisely these fundamentally different stakeholders ensure diversity and pluriformity amongst multiple stakeholders involved (Fiorino, 1990), enhance and secure social learning (Bandura, 1986), and the emergence of new insights (Jehn et al., 1999).

Self-criticism has two sides. On the one hand, other stakeholders can question corporate actors' ideas and value frames (self-destruction) and, on the other hand, corporate actors can become responsive to the demands and needs of other stakeholders (self-constitution). In such an ethical approach to stakeholder engagement, collaboration, and partnership, the focus is no longer on the interests and value frames of the actors as input in the collaboration and partnership, but on the values and ideas as output of their responsiveness to the demands of other stakeholders during the collaboration.

This focus on the values and ideas as output of managers' responsiveness in the development of previously unimagined solutions (Gray and Stites, 2013) is especially important in the context of innovation. Innovation seems to flourish in an environment of open innovation, in which the interaction with other or different stakeholders is seen as a resource of competitive advantage (Chesbrough, 2003); it is mainly the diversity of problem definitions and values that leads to creative and innovative solutions (Blok, 2014). In this, stakeholders not simply represent another viewpoint, interest, or value frame which should be taken into account. Other stakeholders are taken as absolutely foreign, because there are always other others, for instance, future generations or foreign societies, which may be affected by the future impact of actors' innovations. To the extent that a manager has to be responsive to an infinity of other stakeholders, their responsiveness involves, first, the fundamental acknowledgement of the pluriformity of other viewpoints, interests, and value frames. It is the engagement with a pluriformity of different viewpoints and interests which can increase social learning (Rip, 1986), enhance and secure managers' openness towards other perspectives and other possible solutions of public problems, and benefit from different stakeholders as a resource to finding new opportunities to address public problems (Blok, 2014). Furthermore, collaboration and partnership with fundamentally different stakeholders will help keep open various options for innovation during the process, increase managers' adaptivity to changes in the environment, and accommodate plurality in business practices.

Structural Possibility of Failure in Stakeholder Engagement, Collaborations, and Partnerships

To the extent that managers have to be responsive to an infinity of other stakeholders, manager's responsiveness involves the acknowledgement that this responsiveness to other stakeholders will always fail in light of the infinity of other stakeholders they cannot be responsive to. The other stakeholders show primarily that our own understanding of the grand challenges of our time is always limited and biased by our own interests and value frames, that our knowledge is always insufficient to predict the future impact and the consequences of our business operations. This acknowledgement of our epistemic insufficiency (Section 7) implies a shift from immunization strategies to prevent stakeholder criticism of management practices and to be only seen as responsive, towards a vulnerability strategy in which stakeholder criticism is enhanced. This is the fourth characteristic of an ethical approach to stakeholder engagement, collaboration and partnership in management practices.

In this concept of stakeholder management, other stakeholders primarily represent the complexity of public problems, such as public health or global warming, and the fundamental uncertainty of the future impact of managers' interventions and business operations to address these challenges. It is the complexity of public problems and the structural possibility of failure of managers' responsiveness to stakeholders' demands which calls for stakeholder engagement, collaboration and partnership to solve these problems. On the one hand, this engagement in partnerships and collaborations precisely engages stakeholders in order to define the right impact of management policies, to prevent innovation lock-in and path dependency (Stirling, 2007, 2008), enhance corrigibility (Collingridge, 1980), and accommodate plurality in business strategies. However, owing to the fundamental uncertainty and possible failure of all approaches to public problems, stakeholder management consists, on the other hand, in the performance of ethical behaviour in order to deal with these problems, although there is still the possibility of failure (Blok and Lemmens, 2015).

The advantage of acknowledging the fundamental possibility of failure of managers' responsiveness to the demands of an infinity of other stakeholders is that it prevents overly easy solutions and acknowledges that alignment and harmony amongst stakeholders is difficult to achieve in the case of wicked problems such as global warming. On the one hand, we cannot propose definite solutions if we do not have a definite problem description. On the other hand, all proposed solutions remain finite and provisional compared with the complexity and depth of the public problem itself. We can never reduce complex public problems to a finite set of particular problems, nor say that these problems can definitely be solved, that is, that sustainable development or public health is fully achieved. The advantage of an ethical approach to stakeholder engagement, collaboration and partnership in management practices is that the complexity of public problems is represented by the infinity of other stakeholders involved in partnership and collaboration, each with their own and legitimate value frames, and even ideologies, with regard to such public problems.

Conclusion

In this chapter, we critically reflected on a fifth contested area in management, namely people management in the business operations. We questioned the nature of people management in case of grand challenges like global warming. Our critical engagement with the metaphysical concept of identity, unity and difference in stakeholder engagement, collaboration and partnership in management processes in Sections 14–16 enabled us to argue for a concept of management as non-reductive stakeholder engagement as fifth dimension of our philosophy of management, that is able to acknowledge and appreciate fundamental differences amongst stakeholders. We subsequently developed four characteristics of management as non-reductive stakeholder engagement, collaboration, and partnership in management practices, as summarized in Table 4.1.

These four characteristics of a non-reductive and ethical approach to stakeholder engagement, collaboration and participation have several implications for management practices in CSPs, multi-stakeholder engagement, etc. We explore these implications in the remainder of this chapter.

In Section 14, we discussed the critical micro-processes within partnership formation. According to Seitanidi and Crane, the first stage of partnership implementation consists of the following steps: the strategic decision of a firm for partnership as the preferred associational form to work on complex public problems (Utting and Zammit, 2009); the exploration of possible partners; and the selection of partner organizations based on selection criteria. They describe an additional step in the event of reputational risk, the situation in which potential partners came to undermine the reputation, integrity, or brand of the firm.

From the perspective of the cognitive approach to stakeholder management, partnership selection should consider the cognitive distance amongst

Table 4.1 Reductive and cognitive versus non-reductive and ethical approaches to stakeholder engagement, collaboration, and partnership in management practices

Reductive–Cognitive Approach to Stakeholder Engagement, Participation, and Partnership in Management Practices	*Non-reductive-ethical Approach to Stakeholder Engagement, Collaboration, and Partnership in Management Practices*
1. Cognitive focus on the interests, viewpoints, and value frames of stakeholders. 2. Focus on managers' *intention* to respect the demands of other stakeholders. 3. Focus on the identity (mission, interests, core values) of the manager as *input* of collaboration and partnership practices, i.e. as input to *convince* other stakeholders. 4. Focus on the prevention of stakeholder criticism (immunization strategy).	1. Focus on the *social-ethical relation* in which managers become ethically responsive to stakeholders' demands. 2. Focus on actual performance of managers' ethical behaviour in response to the demands of other stakeholders. Only in managers' *actual* responsiveness to the demands of other stakeholders are their demands and needs actually acknowledged and appreciated. 3. Focus on the identity (mission, interests, and core values) of the manager as *output* of his or her actual responsiveness to the demands of other stakeholders/complex public problems (self-destruction and self-constitution). 4. Focus on the enhancement of self-criticism by involving fundamentally different stakeholders, because of the structural possibility of the imperfection or failure of managers' responsiveness to other stakeholders/complex public problems (vulnerability strategy).

actors and select bridgeable perspectives or claims of different stakeholders; it excludes unbridgeable perspectives and includes bridgeable perspectives. The ethical approach to stakeholder management would focus on the fundamentally different stakeholders as well, because these "unbridgeable" perspectives and claims, in particular, show the limitations and insufficiency of managers' understanding of public problems, on the one hand, and provide new insights to other possible solutions, on the other. In this respect, the ability of stakeholders to criticize managers – and question the legitimacy of their reputation – is one of the main criteria for partner inclusion according to a non-reductive and ethical approach to stakeholder engagement, collaboration and partnership.

According to Seitanidi and Crane, the second stage of partnership implementation concerns the design of the partnership itself and consists of the following steps: partnership experimentation and adaptation, which involves agreements on partnership objectives and the operationalization of these agreements within the partnership (Section 14). From the perspective of the cognitive approach to collaboration and partnership, the focus should be on the initial agreements on the problem definition, based on the interests and value frames of the different stakeholders involved, in order to achieve higher degrees of alignment on common goals (Le Ber and Branzei, 2010; Nowell, 2010). In an iterative process of revising and adjusting the different conceptions of the problem and its solution, different actors can find areas where the problem definition and the objectives of the different actors overwrite or overlap each other in a process of value frame fusion (Le Ber and Branzei, 2010). The ethical approach to stakeholder engagement, collaboration, and partnership, however, would focus on (1) the social–ethical relationship in which stakeholders become ethically responsive to each other's demands. The operationalization of this social–ethical relationship is (2) primarily found in managers' performance of ethical behaviour in response to the demands of other stakeholders. In this, the focus is not on the initial agreement on the problem definition based on the interests and value frames of the actors involved. Instead, it is based on managers' responsiveness to the demands of other stakeholders in their (face-to-face) encounter.

The final stage of partnership implementation concerns the institutionalization of the partnership. According to Seitanidi and Crane, partnership programs and processes should be embedded in the partnering organizations. The institutionalization is measured by the extent to which partners are able to overcome crises within the partnership, (a) by accepting the other organization's strengths and also weaknesses as a reality of an integrative relationship and (b) by not avoiding conflict but rather accept disagreements as functional which permits retaining the organization's identity intact (Seitanidi and Crane, 2009: 422). The ethical approach to collaboration and partnership in management practices would agree with this third stage of partnership formation, although the institutionalization does not necessarily serve the conservation of an organization's identity, but rather serves the continuous adjustment of their identity because of the structural possibility of the failure of managers' responsiveness to other stakeholders. The focus is no longer on the identity (interests and value frames) of the actors as input in the partnership, but on the values and ideas as output of their mutual responsiveness during the partnership.

In Figure 4.2, we depict the process of partnership formation that integrates the partnership stages of Seitanidi and Crane (2009) with our ethical approach to stakeholder engagement, collaboration and partnership in management practices.

With this, we have opened a new perspective on an ethical and non-reductive stakeholder engagement, collaboration, and partnership in management practices. Contrary to traditional conceptualizations, our

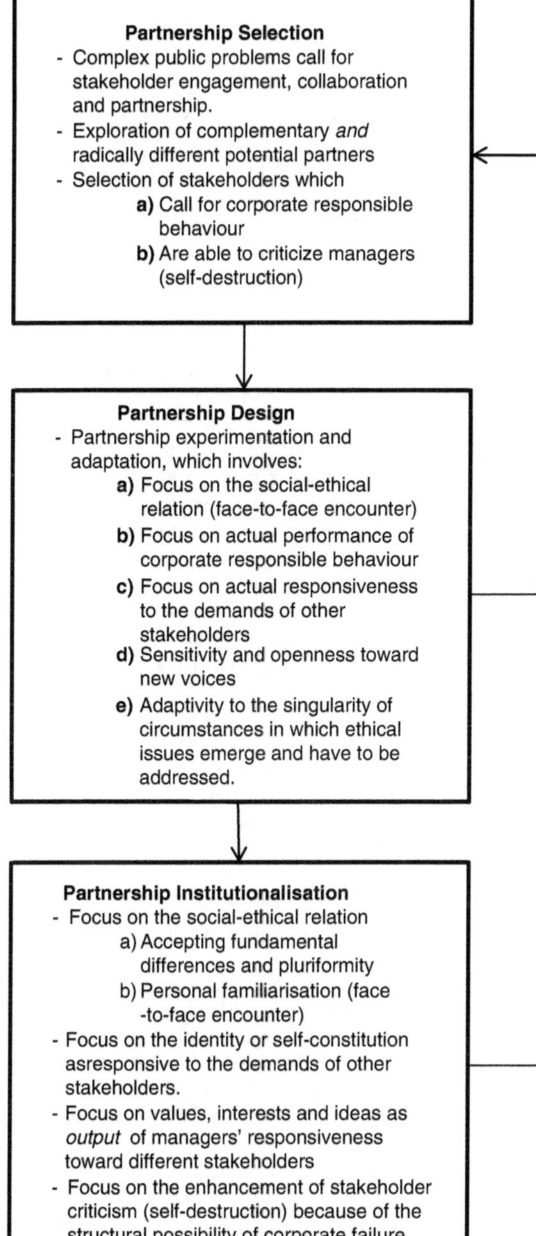

Figure 4.2 Partnership stages of a non-reductive and ethical approach to stakeholder engagement, collaboration and partnership in management practices.

non-reductive and ethical approach to stakeholder engagement, collaboration, and partnership does not presuppose a direct or indirect ideal of harmony and alignment, which is difficult to achieve in the case of the grand challenges of our time, but acknowledges and appreciates the role of difference and constructive conflict without allowing only bridgeable or complementary differences amongst multiple stakeholders. We have shown the fundamental role of different stakeholders in the constitution of managers' identity, in which their ethical behaviour in response to the demands of other stakeholders or complex public problems is embedded.

Notes

1 Although the case study of Seitanidi and Crane does not speak in terms of a collective identity, their partnership selection criteria correspond in general with the generalized partnership ties – a mutual interest like sustainable development, for instance – and the particularized membership ties; previous experience in working with CSPs, covering similar geographical areas, etc.

2 This double origin of the identity of the partnership corresponds with the double – onto-theo-logical – origin of the philosophical question of being (Heidegger, 2006: 37–38). The further elaboration of this connection is beyond the scope of this study.

3 In her article, Le Ber and Branzei speaks in terms of frames. Frames are ways in which specific phenomena – problems, ideas, issues, etc. – are understood and "framed" by various individuals and/or organizations. With regard to the question of this section, we will avoid the terms frame and framing and refer to the way problems and objectives are understood by various partners.

4 There is also a more subtle form of reduction at stake in the process of value frame fusion. The ability to see the other's point of view and to embrace the other's viewpoint presupposes already that I abandon the fundamental – unbridgeable – differences between myself and the other in order to be able to grasp and comprehend him or her.

5 A negative consequence of such a situation can be found in the legitimacy loss of the weaker partner or the blurring of responsibility within the CSP (Van Huijstee et al., 2007).

6 Although Bryson and colleagues acknowledge the risk of conflict within the partnership due to differing aims and expectations, differing strategies, and different attempts to control the collaboration, they see no principal obstacle to developing a common problem definition and shared objectives. Because conflict is common in partnerships, they argue for the use of "resources and tactics to equalize power and manage conflicts effectively" (Bryson et al., 2006: 48). We do not argue against the possibility of managing conflicts but question whether this ideal of the unity of the partnership can ever be guaranteed by power equalization and conflict management in the case of wicked problems like global warming. Le Ber et al. seem to ignore this risk of conflict within partnerships completely. The frame elasticity presupposes the willingness of the partners to challenge their own conception of the problem and its solution, and to embrace their partners' understanding of the problem "without push and pull" (Le Ber & Branzei, 2010). We do not argue against the possibility of embracing the other in CSPs, but raise the question whether

the different (conflicting) judgments and values of multiple stakeholders could also *prevent* such openness towards other partners.

7 See for an example of competitive advantage based on interorganizational collaborations between *for-profit* firms, Wubben et al., 2012).

8 It's for this reason that "mutual interests" is an important criterion for partner selection (Seitanidi and Crane, 2009: 418).

9 With this, the difference between a Habermassian and a Levinassian conceptualization of stakeholder engagement, collaboration, and partnership becomes clear. While both Habermas and Levinas focus on the social relationship amongst actors, Levinas, contrary to Habermas, would reject the Habermassian ideal of understanding the other stakeholders, for instance, in an ideal speech situation (Blok, 2014).

5 Management as Epistemic Insufficient Entrepreneurship

In chapter 1, we critically reflected on management as entrepreneurial action (Section 7). The very nature of grand challenges like global warming turned out to challenge the win-win paradigm of sustainable entrepreneurial action and shows a fundamental tension between the call for sustainable development and entrepreneurial action. This raised the question of what implications the wickedness of the grand challenges of our time and our epistemic insufficiency to manage these challenges have for our conceptualization of management as entrepreneurial action. In this chapter, we take this contested area of management as a point of departure to philosophically reflect on the nature of entrepreneurial action.[1] In this chapter, we use the words manager and entrepreneur interchangeably as our objective is to define the sixth dimension of management as entrepreneurial action.

Like the previous chapter, we take contemporary debates on sustainable entrepreneurship in management science as the point of departure in this chapter. We synthesize theory from entrepreneurship and sustainable development and develop an integrated concept of management as sustainable entrepreneurship as the sixth dimension of our philosophy of management, including the mechanisms by which entrepreneurs can contribute to sustainable development. In Section 18, the role of information in collective actions for sustainable development and the need to reduce information asymmetries in order to engage stakeholders in sustainable entrepreneurial action is explored. Subsequently, we investigate the role of information in entrepreneurship and the need to enhance and secure information asymmetries in sustainable entrepreneurship. In Section 19, a new and integrated theory of sustainable entrepreneurship that overcomes this paradox is proposed. The basic argument is that sustainable development has to be conceptualized as a wicked problem or a sustainability-related ecosystem failure. Because all actors involved in entrepreneurial action are characterized by their epistemic insufficiency regarding the solving of these problems, information asymmetries are maintained as a source of new sustainable business opportunities. Based on the analysis of the paradox of

DOI: 10.4324/9781003231875-5

sustainable entrepreneurship and its solution, we develop three further characteristics of management as epistemic insufficient entrepreneurs as the sixth dimension of our philosophy of management. With this, we open a new perspective on the opportunities and limitations of management as epistemic insufficient entrepreneurship.

18 The Paradox of Sustainable Entrepreneurship

The Role of Information in Collective Actions for Sustainable Development

The point of departure of this section is an economic perspective on entrepreneurship, rather than a moral-based or anthropology-based conception. According to environmental economics, environmental problems can be conceptualized as market failures. Because many natural resources like air and water are not easy to allocate to markets and because it is difficult to hold markets accountable for global phenomena like climate change resulting from increased or changed production and consumption processes, markets fail to ensure the sustainable provision of the natural resources on which economic actors depend (Dorfman, 1993).

It is important to take the conceptualization of environmental problems as the result of market failures into consideration because market failures can also be seen as the source of new entrepreneurial business opportunities. Entrepreneurial opportunities can be defined as "those situations in which new goods, services, raw materials, and organizing methods can be introduced and sold at greater than their cost of production" (Shane and Venkataraman, 2000: 220). Sources of opportunities can be found in changes in supply or demand in the market, for instance, new products or technologies for production or new preferences of customers. Furthermore, they can be found in different levels of awareness of these changes and their solutions by the entrepreneur, for instance, different levels of information about the problem or its solution (Eckhardt and Shane, 2003).

Three key factors seem to enable entrepreneurs to identify superior business opportunities: the active search for opportunities, alertness to opportunities, and prior knowledge of market failures, the industry, or the customer (Baron, 2006). Opportunity recognition involves not only the "alertness to changed conditions or overlooked possibilities" (Kirzner, 1985) – that is, the intellectual capacity and creativity to develop new solutions, new technologies, and new products (Shane, 2003) – but also the active search for new or alternative solutions for existing or anticipated problems (Shane, 2000). The ability to identify superior business opportunities is dependent both on the prior knowledge possessed by the entrepreneur and on how this knowledge or information is processed by the entrepreneur (Gaglio and Katz, 2001). In this respect, entrepreneurship can be seen as the recognition of opportunities in combination with the ability to act upon these opportunities, that is, explore and exploit these opportunities.

Because, on the one hand, environmental problems can be conceptualized as the result of market failures, and, on the other hand, market failures can be seen as sources of new entrepreneurial business opportunities, Dean and McMullen (2007: 57–58) argue:

> Whereas environmental economics concludes that environmental degradation results from the failure of markets and the entrepreneurship literature conclude that opportunities are inherent in market failure, the logical conclusion is that environmentally relevant market failures represent opportunities for simultaneously achieving profitability while reducing environmentally degrading economic behaviours. In other words, some market failures which result in environmental damage provide entrepreneurial opportunities whose exploitation promises profit and improvements in social welfare.

However, if we broaden our perspective on sustainable development, it becomes clear that environmental problems can be considered as wicked problems (Section 7). On the one hand, entrepreneurial action in response to sustainability-related market failures seems to be quite simple, suggesting that sustainable entrepreneurship can eliminate or correct market failures while reducing environmental degradation, pollution, and greenhouse gas emissions (Dean and McMullen, 2007). On the other hand, if we take the biophysical finiteness of planet Earth into account under the condition of economic growth, whether or not as a result of increased world population, it becomes clear that the problem is difficult to pin down and highly complex, just as its solution; environmental problems do not only concern market failures, which can principally be solved by the market when the failure is fixed, as Dean and McMullen seem to assume. On the contrary, they concern an ecosystem failure to provide infinite resources for production and consumption, to provide optimum conditions for sustained production and consumption, and to do justice to intra- and inter-generational equity criteria (Korakandy, 2008). As long as environmental problems are seen as market failures, the solution to these failures is found within the economic paradigm, in which the environment is seen as a subset of human economy, that is, as a resource for production. The wickedness of phenomena like global warming makes clear, however, that the economy is on the contrary a subsystem of the ecosystems of planet Earth (Van den Bergh, 2001) and operates within the limits of the carrying capacity of Earth's life-support system. It is in this respect that environmental problems like global warming, which are even expected to increase because of population growth, do not primarily constitute market failures, but an ecosystem failure to provide infinite resources for economic exchange. Sustainable entrepreneurship therefore has to be understood as the process of exploring and exploiting opportunities that are present in sustainability-related ecosystem failures.

The complexity of environmental problems is also confirmed in the cross-sector partnership (CSP) and multi-stakeholder alliance (MSA) literature that we discussed in the previous chapter. Because the primary responsibility for economic, social, and environmental issues is allocated to different types of actors in society, action by multiple stakeholders is needed in order to address wicked problems like global warming (Section 14). In the context of sustainable entrepreneurship, this means that the exploration and exploitation of new sustainable business opportunities presupposes the active involvement of multiple stakeholders. On the one hand, information from stakeholders can open a window of opportunity, that is, new ideas for sustainable solutions, new forms of green supply and logistics, new substitutions for exhaustible natural resources, new market needs, and so forth (Ayuso et al., 2011; Hart and Sharma, 2004; Noland and Phillips, 2010). In this respect, stakeholder engagement is key in the process of sustainable entrepreneurs' value creation and business model development (Harrison et al., 2010). Because of the complexity of environmental problems and the high uncertainty of the future impact of (un)sustainable innovations – one can think of biotechnology and nanotechnology – the active involvement of many stakeholders can enable a better understanding of these challenges and the risks and uncertainties involved in new sustainable business opportunities (Belucci et al., 2002; Bulkeley and Mol, 2003; Chilvers, 2008). Furthermore, it can help to assess the social-ethical risks related to actual developments in sustainable production and consumption (Adriana, 2009; Anderson and Bateman, 2000; Blok, 2014; Dunphy et al., 2007; Freeman, 1984; Lee, 2009; Molnar and Mulvihill, 2003). In this respect, stakeholder engagement is key to managing ecosystem failures in an entrepreneurial way.

From the previous analysis, we can define sustainable entrepreneurship as the process of exploring and exploiting opportunities that are present in sustainability-related ecosystem failures. Because ecosystem failures cannot be solved by the market alone, sustainable entrepreneurship involves collaboration with multiple stakeholders in their business operations.

However, stakeholders have different, often conflicting, value frames and ideologies with regard to sustainability as we have seen in the previous chapter. They have for instance differing ideas about what the real problem behind sustainable development is, ranging from a market failure to an ecosystem failure, and the solutions they propose are based on multiple viewpoints that can differ widely among stakeholders and are not (always) based on shared values. The active involvement of stakeholders can be hindered by the incompatibility of the value frames of managers in the private sector (i.e. entrepreneurs), NGOs for sustainable development and governmental organizations. Stakeholders should use resources and tactics to equalize power and manage conflicts effectively. Interaction, communication, and sharing information can be crucial here, as this increases consensus among multiple stakeholders and helps to explore win-win situations and to establish agreements. Sharing information and knowledge is also a way for partners to build trust (Andriof and Waddock, 2002; Bryson et al., 2006). Overall, therefore, information sharing increases the level of stakeholder engagement in sustainable entrepreneurial processes and can even be seen as an important predictor of partnership success (Mohr and Spekman, 1994; Burchell and Cook, 2006).

In the context of sustainable entrepreneurship, we can conceptualize information and knowledge sharing in terms of the reduction of information asymmetries. Information asymmetries, as already stated, can be defined as the situation in which at least one actor in a collaboration has more or better information than the other actors (Kirzner, 1973, 1985). Two specific problems arise in relation to information asymmetries. Information asymmetries may result in adverse selection before the collaboration or engagement with stakeholders is established because actors' actual motivation to collaborate remains hidden from other actors. One can think not only of entrepreneurs involved in greenwashing but also of entrepreneurs who are bluffing about the sustainability performance of new technologies that are still under development (Husted, 2007; Van Oosterhout et al., 2006). Information asymmetries may result in moral hazard after the collaboration or engagement with stakeholders is established, because actors' actual performance remains hidden from other actors. One can think of entrepreneurs who do not keep their promise to contribute to sustainable development and are actually involved in industrial pollution, entrepreneurs who mislead their customers and other stakeholders by manipulating software that measures the sustainability of actual performance, but also of stakeholders who, deliberately or otherwise, share information about the collaboration with the entrepreneur's competitors.

The reduction of information asymmetries enables stakeholders to assess the socio-ethical issues related to the business model, thereby helping to prevent moral hazards and adverse selection problems. Furthermore, by the sharing of information, sustainable entrepreneurs enhance and secure the involvement of, and collaboration with, stakeholders (Section 14). The corporate social responsibility literature also acknowledges the importance of reducing information asymmetries (Lopatta et al., 2015). Transparency towards stakeholders is associated with good governance (Christensen and Cheney, 2015) and involves all kinds of practices, ranging from financial disclosure statements and CSR annual reports to stakeholder dialogues and codes of conduct (Floridi, 2010). Ethical codes for instance can be seen as a way to reduce information asymmetries in order to reduce stakeholders' adverse selection problems (Beneish and Chatov, 1993; Ciliberti et al., 2011).

To conclude, if environmental problems have to be conceptualized as wicked problems and involve collaboration and engagement with multiple stakeholders in the development of corporate social responsibility with regard to sustainable development, sustainable entrepreneurs explore and exploit sustainability-related ecosystem failures together with multiple stakeholders. In this respect, sustainable entrepreneurs acknowledge that the market alone cannot resolve ecosystem failures and, therefore, they actively collaborate with multiple stakeholders in collaborative action to address the wicked problem of global warming.

The entrepreneurial action that follows logically from this definition is captured in the first characteristic of management as epistemic entrepreneurship: in their effort to address sustainability-related ecosystem failures, sustainable entrepreneurs enhance collaborative action with multiple market- and non-market-oriented stakeholders by reducing information asymmetries.

The Role of Information in the Entrepreneurial Process

The reduction of information asymmetries is, however, problematic from an entrepreneurial point of view. A fundamental characteristic of entrepreneurship is the ability to identify and pursue business opportunities (Kirzner, 1973; Shane and Venkataraman, 2000), which can be found in market or ecosystem failures as we have seen. These sources of opportunities can be conceived as additional information of which the entrepreneur takes advantage in the development of the business. Opportunities arise from information about market and ecosystem failures and their solution, and, in this respect, entrepreneurial engagement in, and the active search for, new opportunities is an active search for appropriate information (Shane, 2003). It involves entrepreneurial alertness to information about demand conditions (customer needs, customer tastes, and so on) and supply possibilities (new technologies, newly found resources, and so on), but also overlooked possibilities resulting from emerging market and ecosystem failures (Kirzner, 1985); it concerns the intellectual capacity and creativity to develop new solutions, new technologies, and new products based on this information (Shane, 2003).

The crucial role of information in sustainable entrepreneurship development shows that it is the main source of competitive advantage (Conner and Prahalad, 1996). Entrepreneurs' competitive advantage is based on information asymmetries, that is, additional knowledge that enables them to identify business opportunities in the market, while others do not. This additional or "prior" knowledge (McMullen and Shepherd, 2006) may consist in the ability to "see where a good can be sold at a price higher than that for which it can be bought" (Kirzner, 1973: 14; 1985). In this case, information asymmetries result from market participants' ignorance or imperfect knowledge with regard to existing information, and new business opportunities "arise out of the entrepreneur's alertness to [these] information asymmetries existing in the economy" (Dutta and Crossan, 2005: 431). Information asymmetries may also be related to market and ecosystem failures that create market gaps that can be filled by entrepreneurs; new business opportunities arise then in entrepreneurs' efforts to develop markets for preserved environmental resources (Dean and McMullen, 2007). Finally, information asymmetries may be created by the development of new information or new knowledge. This information provides opportunities for new or alternative solutions for existing or anticipated ecosystem failures.

The importance of information asymmetries as a source of competitive advantage means that, from an entrepreneurial perspective, sustainable entrepreneurs cannot reduce information asymmetries unlimitedly in favour of information symmetries among multiple stakeholders. The reduction of information asymmetries might create vulnerability by revealing the firm's core competencies to other actors (Bigliardi and Galati, 2013). This can affect the entrepreneur's ability to compete, and this could have a negative influence on its competitive advantage (Islam, 2012). Regarding economic actors, therefore, withholding information from other stakeholders is acceptable in order to enable entrepreneurs to achieve competitive advantage (Nayyar, 1990), whereas such practices would not be acceptable in the public or political domain for instance (Dahl, 1997).

To conclude, if entrepreneurship has to be conceptualized as the ability to take advantage of information asymmetries, sustainable entrepreneurial action does not only consist in the enhancement of collaborative action with multiple stakeholders by reducing information asymmetries (characteristic 1). On the contrary, the second characteristic of management as sustainable entrepreneurship is: in their effort to address sustainability-related ecosystem failures, sustainable entrepreneurs maintain and enhance information asymmetries in order to achieve and secure competitive advantage.

The analysis of sustainable development as an ecosystem failure and entrepreneurial practices confronts us with the paradox of sustainable entrepreneurship, which becomes concrete in the first and second characteristics we formulated. The reduction of information asymmetries during the sustainable entrepreneurial process results in the integration of sustainable development within the management practice. However, this reduction of information asymmetries undermines the entrepreneurial process at the same time, that is, the ability of the entrepreneur to enhance and secure competitive advantage. This paradox is depicted in Table 5.1.

Table 5.1 The paradox of sustainable entrepreneurship

	Sustainable Entrepreneurial Value Creation	Collaboration for Sustainable Value Creation
Reducing information asymmetries	Needed to explore and exploit opportunities that are present in sustainability-related market and ecosystem failures; may cause the loss of core competencies, knowledge, or information	Needed to enhance collaborative action with multiple stakeholders to address sustainability-related market and ecosystem failures; may cause the loss of competitive advantage
Maintaining information asymmetries	Needed to enhance and secure competitive advantage; may limit access to new knowledge and information about sustainability-related market and ecosystem failures and their solution	Needed to secure and enhance competitive advantage; may hinder the engagement of, and collaboration with, multiple stakeholders

In the next section, we take advantage of the paradox of sustainable entrepreneurship in order to build an integrated theory of sustainable entrepreneurship in which this paradox is resolved by the introduction of our epistemic insufficiency regarding wicked problems like global warming in the conceptualization of sustainable entrepreneurship (Lewis, 2000; Poole and Van de Ven, 1989; Smith, 2014).

19 Towards an Integrated Theory of Management as Epistemic Insufficient Entrepreneurship

Information Asymmetry as Epistemic Insufficiency

How can the paradox of sustainable entrepreneurship be resolved? There seem to be at least two strategies available: a radical preference for information symmetry over information asymmetry in sustainable entrepreneurship, which seems to be Dean and McMullen's position, or a radical preference for information asymmetry over information symmetry, which requires a new and integrated theory of sustainable entrepreneurship. Let us focus first on the first solution and see its advantages and disadvantages.

According to Dean and McMullen (2007), we should not perceive the disequilibrium in the economic system – that is, sustainability as a market or ecosystem failure – to be a state of nature, in which entrepreneurs take advantage on the basis of existing and created information asymmetries. "The environmental and welfare economics literature recognize not only the ignorance of producers or potential producers, but other barriers that, when overcome, allow the generation of economic rents and the movement of markets towards superior states of equilibrium and efficiency" (Dean and McMullen, 2007: 57). According to these authors, imperfect information is one of these market failures, which, if sustainable entrepreneurs are able to overcome them, can prevent or mitigate environmental degradation (Dean and McMullen, 2007: 67).

This perspective seems to be promising in the case of sustainable entrepreneurship because it allows the entrepreneur to reduce information asymmetries while maintaining his or her role in exploring and exploiting new business opportunities to solve sustainability-related market failures, leading to superior states of equilibrium and efficiency – that is, more perfect levels of competition because of information symmetry – in which environmental issues also are addressed. This strategy solves the paradox of sustainable entrepreneurship by highlighting the reduction of information asymmetries so that sustainable entrepreneurs can address sustainability-related market and ecosystem failures. Is this a suitable solution of the paradox discerned in the previous section?

From a theoretical perspective, information asymmetries and market failures represent a departure from Pareto efficiency, as Dean and McMullen (2007) rightly acknowledge. "Pareto efficiency is often equated with a state of perfect competition in which prices are equal to average total costs and, as a result, economic profits, or rents (profits) above all costs (including a risk-adjusted return to capital), are non-existent" (Dean and McMullen, 2007: 54) thanks to perfect or symmetric information (Scherer and Ross, 1990). Although Dean and McMullen acknowledge that it is questionable whether perfect knowledge and perfect competition can ever be reached in practice, the ideal of sustainable entrepreneurship is that sustainability-related market failures are solved by the reduction of information asymmetries; the solution of these failures will allow sustainable entrepreneurs to develop business models that generate economic rents and that move markets towards superior states of equilibrium and efficiency (Dean and McMullen, 2007).

But this is only one side of the story. The solution of market failures will indeed contribute to superior states of equilibrium and efficiency (information symmetry as a solution for market failures), but, with this, it will no longer generate economic rents after the market failure is solved. Indeed, the more perfect the knowledge (information symmetry), the more perfect the competition, and the more perfect the competition, the lower the economic return of sustainable entrepreneurs, and the lower the competitive advantage of sustainable entrepreneurs. This concept of sustainable entrepreneurship focuses, in other words, indeed on the solution of sustainability-related market failures by the reduction of information asymmetries, but the price it has to pay for this achievement is the denial of entrepreneurial potential, which requires levels of information asymmetry to be maintained. It is precisely for this reason that entrepreneurs in fact maintain information asymmetries in practice in order to benefit economically from the opportunities provided by sustainability-related market and ecosystem failures.

The first solution to the paradox of sustainable entrepreneurship does in fact not solve the paradox but prefers one aspect of the concept (sustainable development) at the expense of the other aspect (entrepreneurial practices). What this solution in fact introduces is a duality between sustainable development on the one hand and entrepreneurial practice on the other in sustainable entrepreneurship, in which sustainable development is preferred at the expense of entrepreneurial practice (reduction of information asymmetries). Reality, however, shows that the opposite can also happen (maintenance of information asymmetries). The advantage of this concept of sustainable entrepreneurship is that it explains the internal tensions within the concept of sustainable entrepreneurship – the continuous trade-offs between sustainability- and entrepreneurship related interests – and it explains why and how these tensions may result in scandals and cases of fraud (Hahn et al., 2015; Van der Byl and Slawinski, 2015). The disadvantage of this dual concept of sustainable entrepreneurship is that it does not solve the paradox of sustainable entrepreneurship. Negatively speaking, we learn from this dual concept of sustainable entrepreneurship that, in order to remain entrepreneurial, sustainable entrepreneurs should try to overcome ecosystem failures without any ideal of competitive equilibrium, because information symmetry would involve the self-denial or self-destruction of the entrepreneurial potential to explore and exploit new business opportunities.

In fact, reality meets this requirement of sustainable entrepreneurship because information is often imperfect and incomplete and even made imperfect by entrepreneurs. In general, one can already question whether the reduction of information asymmetries, for instance, the enhancement of transparency about business models and innovation practices, in fact promotes corporate responsiveness towards stakeholders (Christensen and Cornelissen 2015; Blok et al., 2019). Crilly et al. (2012) found that, in the case of information asymmetries between firms and their stakeholders, managers' responses to stakeholder pressures may consist in an intentional decoupling of firm policies and actual practices in favour of their own interests. Especially because entrepreneurs deal with multiple stakeholders with different and often opposing value frames, ambiguity seems to be a better strategy than transparency in order to serve one's own interests while being open to multiple stakeholders without offending them (Eisenberg, 1984; Christensen and Cheney, 2015). Information asymmetries are not only enhanced and secured in order to be seen as responsible, rather than being responsible (Robert, 2001), but are also sometimes enforced by privacy laws and regulations regarding the disclosure of competitive information.

In open innovation practices also, the paradox of information sharing and information protection can be recognized (Bogers, 2011). Sometimes, firms discourage or restrict their employees from collaborating with stakeholders (Flipse, 2012; Blok et al., 2015) in order to prevent knowledge leakages (Mohamed et al., 2006). Notwithstanding the expected benefits of open innovation, the risk of negative knowledge leakage and, with this, the loss of competitive advantage, is significant for most firms (Gould, 2012). Sometimes, entrepreneurs even increase information asymmetries to claim features of their innovations that are not (yet) justified, such as technical features or sustainability impacts in order to attract investments, or social features or impacts of new products in order to attract stakeholder support (Millar et al., 2012). We therefore reject the preference of information symmetries to solve the paradox of sustainable entrepreneurship because the reduction of these asymmetries would involve the self-destruction of the entrepreneurial potential to exploit sustainable business opportunities.

Let us therefore turn to the other possible solution of the paradox of sustainable entrepreneurship, which involves a preference of information asymmetry over information symmetry. This approach seems to be more legitimate because environmental problems have to be considered as wicked problems as we have seen, that is, as problems that result not from market failures but from ecosystem failures (Section 7). This means that the asymmetry of information has a permanent and structural character; this implies that the ideal of perfect knowledge can never be reached; the sustainable entrepreneur has to acknowledge and deal with imperfect foresight. For this reason, we can conceptualize information asymmetries in the case of wicked problems in terms of entrepreneurs' epistemic insufficiency regarding sustainability-related ecosystem failures. That is, our knowledge of the solution of environmental problems is principally imperfect and therefore insufficient to distinguish between good and bad strategies to solve these ecosystem failures (Section 7). Climate-smart innovations, for instance, may have unintended consequences or even irreversible consequences that may be harmful for future generations.

Entrepreneurs' epistemic insufficiency regarding sustainability-related ecosystem failures implies that the sustainable entrepreneurial ideal of perfect knowledge and perfect equilibrium in the economic system has to be dropped and that the fact of permanent information asymmetries has to be acknowledged by the entrepreneur. This means, first of all, that, irrespective of the sustainable entrepreneur's epistemic insufficiency regarding these ecosystem failures, information asymmetries can still be seen as a source of new sustainable business opportunities. This means, secondly, that sustainable entrepreneurs can enhance collaborative action with multiple stakeholders by reducing information asymmetries in their development of sustainable business (characteristic 1) because their epistemic insufficiency regarding these ecosystem failures will principally prevent the achievement of information symmetry and enable the entrepreneur to uphold information asymmetries in order to maintain and enhance competitive advantage (characteristic 2).

The epistemic insufficiency of sustainable entrepreneurs, their stakeholders, and their competitors shines another light on the meaning of entrepreneurship. The word entrepreneur comes originally from *entre-* (between) and prendre, *prehendere*, to grasp, to get hold of. What the sustainable entrepreneur grasps and acts upon is the wickedness – or in more philosophical terms, the strangeness or otherness – of sustainability-related ecosystem failures, which can only be "apprehended", with no ability to "know" them or to "predict" their solution. It is this apprehension of sustainability-related ecosystem failures that is the source of new sustainable business opportunities. Hence, the third characteristic of management as epistemic entrepreneurship is: the maintenance of information asymmetries as a source of new sustainable business opportunities is enhanced and secured by the epistemic insufficiency of entrepreneurs and their stakeholders and competitors regarding sustainability-related ecosystem failures, which can be "apprehended" by the sustainable entrepreneur as a source of new sustainable business opportunities.

By reformulating the maintenance of information asymmetries in terms of entrepreneurs' epistemic insufficiency regarding sustainability-related ecosystem failures, we provide a solution for the paradox of sustainable entrepreneurship.

Implications of Entrepreneurs' Epistemic Insufficiency for an Integrated Concept of Sustainable Entrepreneurship

Entrepreneurs' epistemic insufficiency regarding sustainability-related ecosystem failures has some additional consequences for an integrated concept of sustainable entrepreneurship. First of all, it makes clear why it is crucial to involve and engage multiple stakeholders in the sustainable entrepreneurial process, as we have seen in the previous chapter.

The critical stance of stakeholders towards the exploration and exploitation of sustainable business opportunities is crucial because sustainable entrepreneurs' epistemic insufficiency makes the development of new business opportunities a highly risky and uncertain endeavour. This risk is not necessarily problematic from an entrepreneurial perspective, because risk-taking is traditionally seen as one of the main characteristics of entrepreneurship. Knight (1921) distinguishes between insurable and uninsurable risk and argues that the entrepreneur takes an uninsurable risk by exploiting business opportunities that are highly uncertain upfront, for instance, investment in new sustainable product development without any guarantee of sufficient returns on investment.

Although Knight's concept of uninsurable risk assumes a general equilibrium of economic systems in which risks occur as a consequence of economic changes and differences in the entrepreneurial ability of different actors within this economic system, we can see risk-taking that results from the entrepreneur's epistemic insufficiency regarding sustainability-related ecosystem failures as a key element of sustainable entrepreneurship. The reason is that sustainability also can be considered as an uninsurable risk. No insurance can cover the risk of limited availability of natural resources like oil and gas for future generations – all opportunities to satisfy the needs of the current generation will change the conditions of the opportunities for future generations – and no insurance can cover the risk of the future negative impacts of new technologies like GMOs, nanotechnology, or synthetic biology for future generations. In this respect, both sustainability and entrepreneurship concern radical uncertainty, and sustainable entrepreneurs deal with this radical uncertainty in their exploration and exploitation of new sustainable business opportunities. This leads to the fourth characteristic of management as epistemic entrepreneurship: in their effort to address sustainability-related ecosystem failures, sustainable entrepreneurs take risks by exploring and exploiting radical, uncertain sustainable business opportunities. The risks and uncertainty involved in sustainable entrepreneurship concern not only the entrepreneurial risk involved in the exploration and exploitation of new business opportunities but also sustainable entrepreneurs' epistemic insufficiency to assess the long-run sustainability of their solution to ecosystem failures.

The difference between the risks taken by the entrepreneur and the risks concerning sustainability-related ecosystem failures is that the uncertainty relating to entrepreneurship is not necessarily problematic – one could argue that the free market decides which entrepreneur will be successful in his or her risk assessment – whereas uncertainty relating to sustainability is in fact problematic if we take into account the urgency to address global warming for instance. Because sustainable entrepreneurs apprehend the sustainability-related ecosystem failures without the ability to "know" them or to "predict" their solution, they acknowledge that the exploration and exploitation of new sustainable business opportunities involve not only entrepreneurial risks but also sustainability-related risks and uncertainties that may decrease, but also may increase sustainability-related ecosystem failures.

This brings us to the second consequence of epistemic insufficiency for an integrated concept of sustainable entrepreneurship. Although sustainable entrepreneurs acknowledge this fundamental uncertainty, for instance, the potential harm they can cause for others (customers, civil society, future generations, and so forth), and, although they will continuously have to recapture their business operations in their struggle against their possible unsustainability for future generations, the acknowledgement of their epistemic insufficiency does not necessarily have to lead to an entrepreneurial attitude characterized by prudence with regard to new innovative technologies for instance. On the contrary, entrepreneurial action is also characterized by fundamental *optimism*, namely the entrepreneur's belief that he or she is able to make the difference in his or her exploitation of new business opportunities. To explain this, one could refer to the concept of self-efficacy, which is often associated with entrepreneurial behaviour. Self-efficacy concerns an actor's belief in his or her own ability to perform well (Bandura, 1997), and entrepreneurial self-efficacy concerns an actor's belief in his or her own entrepreneurial competence to explore and exploit new business opportunities (Ploum et al., 2017; Rauch and Frese, 2007). The entrepreneur believes that he or she is in control in the sense that he or she has the power to change the world in a responsible way, and this experience of power motivates his or her resistance to the status quo. This idea resonates with the second dimension of our philosophy of management: management as resistance and responsive actions.

Interestingly, the concept of self-efficacy has also emerged in the literature on competencies of sustainability professionals. Here, self-efficacy determines the action competence of sustainability professionals (Almers, 2013; Mogenson and Schnack, 2010). Action competence can be defined as the "capability … to involve yourself as a person with other persons in responsible actions and counter-actions for a more humane world" (Schnack, 1996: 15) (we will come back on this subject in Section 21). In the context of sustainable entrepreneurship, self-efficacy means that, because of the epistemic insufficiency regarding sustainability-related ecosystem failures and their solution, sustainable entrepreneurship does not consist in prudence. On the contrary, self-efficacy means that the sustainable entrepreneur is involved in actions to address sustainability-related ecosystem failures and also believes that he or she is capable of addressing these failures. Whereas self-efficacy in the context of the action competence of sustainability professionals means that actors feel themselves responsible for, and capable of, acting in a more sustainable way – a trait that is not necessarily present in entrepreneurial self-efficacy – self-efficacy in the context of sustainable entrepreneurs concerns their belief in their own responsibility and capability for addressing sustainability-related ecosystem failures (Lans et al., 2014; Ploum et al., 2017). Indeed, entrepreneurship originally means an undertaking, that is, the ability to undertake action to address sustainability-related ecosystem failures as we have seen in Section 9. This leads to the fifth characteristic of management as epistemic insufficient entrepreneurship: notwithstanding their epistemic insufficiency and the risks and uncertainties involved in the exploration and exploitation of new sustainable business opportunities, sustainable entrepreneurs feel responsible for, and capable of, addressing sustainability-related ecosystem failures, and act upon these failures on the basis of their sustainable entrepreneurial self-efficacy.

The undertakings of the sustainable entrepreneur are focused primarily on the solution of sustainability-related ecosystem failures, and, in this respect, sustainability is definitely a normative concept. In Section 13, we already encountered this normativity in terms of the Earth's sovereign principle. It does not describe the world as it is but the way it should be and focuses on Earth's sustainability as a life-supporting ecosystem. As we have seen, however, this does not mean that the sustainable entrepreneur embraces pre-given norms in his or her exploration and exploitation of new sustainable business opportunities: neither the norm of economic growth nor the norm of economic degrowth (Jackson, 2011; Schneider et al., 2010; Van Griethuysen, 2010), neither the norm of prudent innovation nor the norm of reckless innovation like geoengineering and so on. If we take entrepreneurs' epistemic insufficiency regarding sustainability-related ecosystem failures seriously, entrepreneurial action cannot consist in the application of pre-fixed norms and values regarding proposed solutions (Section 13). In Section 21, we will explore this paradoxical responsibility of the sustainable entrepreneur in terms of a virtuous competence.

This brings us to a third consequence of the epistemic insufficiency for an integrated concept of sustainable entrepreneurship. In practice, this means that the sustainable entrepreneur is not looking for perfect solutions, which in any event do not exist in the case of wicked problems like global warming, but for satisficing business models that, on the one hand, are satisfactory and sufficient to maintain Earth as a life-supporting ecosystem and, on the other, are always open to future subversions, revisions, and improvements. The sustainable entrepreneur feels responsible for exploring and exploiting such satisficing business models together with multiple stakeholders (fifth dimension of our philosophy of management) but acknowledges the futural status of his or her responsibility in light of the wickedness of sustainability-related ecosystem failures. This leads to the sixth characteristic of management as epistemic insufficient entrepreneurship: sustainable entrepreneurs take responsibility for sustainable actions by engaging in the exploration and exploitation of new sustainable business opportunities together with multiple stakeholders, thereby providing satisficing and open-ended solutions for sustainability-related ecosystem failures.

Conclusion

In this chapter, we critically reflected on the sixth contested area in management, namely management as entrepreneurial action. We first pointed to the paradox of sustainable entrepreneurship in the current conception of sustainable entrepreneurship in the literature. Although at first sight environmental problems seem to provide an additional source of new business opportunities, we raised the question of the consequences of the integration of sustainable development and the opportunity recognition process for the concept of entrepreneurship. The win-win paradigm of sustainable entrepreneurship was challenged by pointing to a tension between processes involved in sustainable development and processes involved in entrepreneurial practices, conceptualized as the paradox of sustainable entrepreneurship. Sustainable entrepreneurship contains a paradox because sustainable development involves the reduction of information asymmetries whereas entrepreneurial practices involve enhanced and secured levels of information asymmetries.

The paradox of sustainable entrepreneurship required us to move beyond the self-evident understanding of entrepreneurial action and to develop an integrated concept of epistemic insufficient entrepreneurship as the sixth dimension of our philosophy of management. We defined management as epistemic insufficient entrepreneurship as the process of exploring and exploiting opportunities present in sustainability-related ecosystem failures. Because ecosystem failures cannot be solved by the market alone, entrepreneurial action involves collaboration with multiple stakeholders in the development of sustainable business models. On the basis of this definition of sustainable entrepreneurship, it is possible to identify the paradox of sustainable entrepreneurship. On the one hand, it was argued that, in order to collaborate with multiple stakeholders to address collectively sustainability-related ecosystem failures, sustainable entrepreneurs should reduce information asymmetries. On the other hand, it was argued that, in order to achieve and secure competitive advantage, sustainable entrepreneurs should maintain and enhance information asymmetries.

A possible solution to the paradox of sustainable entrepreneurship was provided by the preference of information symmetry over information asymmetry in sustainable entrepreneurship. This solution was rejected in this chapter, as it indeed focuses on the reduction of information asymmetries needed to address sustainability-related ecosystem failures, but at the price of its denial of entrepreneurial potential, which requires levels of information asymmetry to be maintained. What this concept of sustainable entrepreneurship introduces is a duality between sustainable development on the one hand and entrepreneurial practice on the other, in which either sustainable development is preferred at the expense of entrepreneurial practice (reduction of information asymmetries) or the other way around (maintenance of information asymmetries).

The first contribution of this chapter is that it articulates a duality in the traditional concept of sustainable entrepreneurship found in the literature, thereby explaining the internal tensions in sustainable entrepreneurial practices – the continuous trade-offs between sustainability- and entrepreneurship-related interests – and why and how these tensions occur in sustainable entrepreneurship. The second contribution of this chapter is that the analysis of this dual concept of sustainable entrepreneurship enables us to criticize the traditional concept of sustainable entrepreneurship. On the one hand, this dual conceptualization of sustainable entrepreneurship does not solve the paradox, but only prefers one aspect (sustainable development) at the expense of the other aspect (entrepreneurial practices). On the other hand, this dual conceptualization of sustainable entrepreneurship shows that, in order to remain entrepreneurial, sustainable entrepreneurs should try to overcome ecosystem failures without any ideal of competitive equilibrium, because high levels of information symmetry would involve the self-denial or self-destruction of their entrepreneurial potential to explore and exploit new business opportunities.

The third contribution of this chapter is that the reflection on sustainable development as a wicked problem enables us to solve the paradox of sustainable entrepreneurship by developing an integrated concept of management as epistemic insufficient entrepreneurship. The basic argument is that sustainable development has to be conceptualized as a wicked problem or a sustainability-related ecosystem failure (Section 7). Because all actors involved in the development of sustainable businesses are characterized by their epistemic insufficiency regarding the resolution of these ecosystem failures, the role of stakeholder information in the sustainable entrepreneurial process changes. On the one hand, the reduction of information asymmetries aims primarily to enable actors to become critical of sustainable entrepreneurs' actual business model; stakeholder information helps to question the limitations of the value frames and interests involved in the actual business model and the possible one-sidedness of the provided solutions as a result of entrepreneurs' epistemic insufficiency. On the other hand, even if this requires the reduction of information asymmetries in collaborative entrepreneurial action, the epistemic insufficiency of sustainable entrepreneurs and their stakeholders guarantees that information asymmetries remain as a source of new sustainable business opportunities.

This resolution of the paradox of sustainable entrepreneurship implies three other characteristics of an integrated concept of management as epistemic insufficient entrepreneurship. First, sustainable entrepreneurs take risks by exploring and exploiting radical, uncertain sustainable business opportunities in sustainable business development. This uncertainty concerns not only the classical entrepreneurial risk involved in the exploration and exploitation of new business opportunities but also the sustainability-related risks that proposed solutions do not, or do not sufficiently, solve sustainability-related ecosystem failures. Second, notwithstanding their epistemic insufficiency and the risks and uncertainties involved in exploring and exploiting new sustainable business opportunities, sustainable entrepreneurs feel responsible for, and capable of, addressing sustainability-related market and ecosystem failures, and act upon these failures in their development of sustainable businesses on the basis of their sustainable entrepreneurial self-efficacy. Third, sustainable entrepreneurs take responsibility for sustainable actions by engaging in the exploration and exploitation of new sustainable business opportunities together with multiple stakeholders, thereby providing satisficing and open-ended business models for sustainability-related market or ecosystem failures. With this, we encountered six characteristics of an integrated concept of epistemic insufficient entrepreneurship as the sixth dimension of our philosophy of management (Table 5.2).

In conclusion, this chapter contributes to our understanding of the role of entrepreneurs in addressing sustainability-related ecosystem failures, that is, sustainable entrepreneurship. By viewing sustainable development as an ecosystem failure, we conceptualize sustainable entrepreneurship as the process of exploring and exploiting, together with multiple stakeholders, the new and innovative business opportunities present in these sustainability-related ecosystem failures. Sustainable entrepreneurs feel responsible for exploring and exploiting new

Table 5.2 Six characteristics of an integrated concept of management as epistemic insufficient entrepreneurship

1. In their effort to address sustainability-related ecosystem failures, sustainable entrepreneurs enhance collaborative action with multiple market- and non-market-oriented stakeholders by reducing information asymmetries.
2. In their effort to address sustainability-related ecosystem failures, sustainable entrepreneurs maintain and enhance information asymmetries in order to achieve and secure competitive advantage.
3. The maintenance of information asymmetries as a source of new sustainable business opportunities is enhanced and secured by the epistemic insufficiency of entrepreneurs and their stakeholders and competitors regarding sustainability-related ecosystem failures, which can be "apprehended" by the sustainable entrepreneur as a source of new sustainable business opportunities.
4. In their effort to address sustainability-related ecosystem failures, sustainable entrepreneurs take risks by exploring and exploiting radical, uncertain sustainable business opportunities. The risks and uncertainty involved in sustainable entrepreneurship concern not only the entrepreneurial risk involved in the exploration and exploitation of new business opportunities but also sustainable entrepreneurs' epistemic insufficiency to assess the long-run sustainability of their solution to ecosystem failures.
5. Notwithstanding their epistemic insufficiency and the risks and uncertainties involved in the exploration and exploitation of new sustainable business opportunities, sustainable entrepreneurs feel responsible for, and capable of, addressing sustainability-related ecosystem failures, and act upon these failures, on the basis of their sustainable entrepreneurial self-efficacy.
6. Sustainable entrepreneurs take responsibility for sustainable actions by engaging in the exploration and exploitation of new sustainable business opportunities together with multiple stakeholders, thereby providing satisficing and solutions for sustainability-related ecosystem failures.

sustainable businesses to address sustainability-related ecosystem failures, and, notwithstanding their acknowledgement of the fundamental risks and uncertainties involved, they feel capable of providing, together with multiple stakeholders, satisficing and open-ended solutions for sustainability-related market or ecosystem failures.

Note

1 Sometimes management is opposed to entrepreneurship because the latter concerns the exploration and exploitation of new business opportunities, while the first maintains the functioning order of existing business operations. To the extent that the entrepreneur has to direct, plan, and control the exploitation of new business opportunities as well and the manager has to exploit new business opportunities as well to survive, we see entrepreneurship as a dimension of business management in line with contemporary definitions (Section 7).

6 Managing for the Common Good: Towards an Integrated Principle of Business Ethics

While it is increasingly acknowledged that firms are not only economic institutions but also moral institutions that contribute to society at large, the starting point of philosophical questions about the ethics of business is often found in an original *disconnect* between business and ethics. It is either found in a theoretical disconnection between business and ethics, which makes business ethics an oxymoron (Collins, 1994), or in a practical disconnection, for example, in the case of manipulation of interest rates of banks, or manipulation of research outcomes about the negative environmental impacts of new products and services. Based on this assumed disconnection, business ethicists argue why and how future business operations should be connected with ethics, for example, by engaging in corporate social responsibility (CSR). In the first instance, the assumption of such an original disconnect seems to be logical, as business traditionally belongs to the private sphere, while ethics belongs to the public sphere. Based on such an original disconnect of business and ethics, then, business ethicists subsequently make a call to connect the two domains. To this end, they apply ethical theory in the particular domain of business, leading to the applied field of business ethics.

As we have elaborated in chapter 1, business management is often understood from the perspective of managerial power and mechanisms to control, inspired by scientific management theory. Business management consists in (1) the establishment and governance of a functioning order of the business; (2) the engagement in the business operations via the work done by other people (e.g. employees); and (3) proper asset management and entrepreneurial behaviour to serve the objectives of the business. Looking at these characteristics, it is conceivable why the business ethics literature assumes an original disconnect of business management and ethics, as ethics is definitely beyond the functions of (scientific) management (i.e. planning, organizing, instruction, co-ordination, and control) (Fayol, 1949). These characteristics of business do not have an intrinsic normative component, that is, they are amoral and therefore outside the scope of moral considerations (Carr, 1968). And if they have a normative component, then only in a negative sense,

DOI: 10.4324/9781003231875-6

for example, they are unethical and should be remedied by ethics. For instance, the establishment and governance of a functioning order of the business lead to bureaucracies in which the moral impulse of individual managers and professionals is neglected and can be criticized for this reason (Section 8) (Bauman, 1989). Furthermore, current practices of people management assume the withdrawal of managers from the primary process and their engagement in management and control of the workforce via instrumental control mechanisms. This instrumental approach of human resources is criticized as well (Section 6) (Solomon, 1992). Moreover, current practices of entrepreneurial behaviour focus on the self-interested and amoral entrepreneur who focuses only on profit maximization, in which ethical considerations are absent and even legitimately violated in favour of shareholder interests, and can be criticized for this reason (Freeman, 1984). In other words, given this conceptualization of business management, it is conceivable why the business ethics literature calls for the inclusion of deontological, utilitarian, or virtue ethical considerations in business management in general, and for ethical remedies of the self-interested and unethical nature of business management in particular.

This criticism has lead for instance to deontological, utilitarian, and virtue ethical conceptions of business ethics. Irrespective of their fruitfulness, the original disconnect between business and ethics raises the question of *what* it precisely is in business management, that it is originally *separated* from ethics and only becomes ethical by the *application* of ethical theory to business management practices. In this study, we encountered several counterexamples that help us at least to substantiate this question. According to Xenophon, for instance, the aim of business is not only to increase profits but also to evoke public admiration, which requires that the business operations both serve private and public interests in an integrated way and that private profits are partly spent to serve society (chapter 1). For Xenophon, then, business and ethics are not originally separated but integrated and embedded in the very nature of business management itself. In a similar vein, according to the concept of management as politico-economic governance, the aim of business is not only to increase profit but also to respond to the normative dimension of planet Earth which is threatened by global warming (chapter 2). And according to the concept of management as non-reductive stakeholder engagement, the socio-ethical relation with stakeholders is an integral part of the business operations (chapter 3).

If business management practices can be conceptualized in such a way that they are intrinsically related to ethics, we may be able to circumvent the assumption of an original disconnect between business and ethics. What is more, we may even find a new argument against free-market ideologists like Milton Friedman who argues that the only responsibility of the private sphere is to increase profits, while staying within the "rules

Table 6.1 Six dimensions of the nature of business management

1. Management as participation
2. Management as resistance and responsive action
3. Management as constitution of meaning
4. Management as politico-economic governance
5. Management as non-reductive stakeholder engagement
6. Management as epistemic insufficient entrepreneurship

of the game" provided by the public sphere, that is, the basic rules of society as they are embodied in law and ethical custom (Friedman, 1970). If business and ethics are intrinsically related, it is no longer possible to exclude ethics from the business operations.

In order to explore the possibility of such an integrated principle of business ethics, we have to first ask for the nature of business management and its intrinsic relation to ethics. Second, we have to ask what consequences this connection has for our understanding of business ethics. Negatively put, if business management is *intrinsically* connected with ethics, this ethics of business cannot be found in ethical theory that remains *external* to it and is then *applied* on the case of business. Positively said, if business management is intrinsically connected with ethics, we have to reflect on the nature of business management itself to find the building blocks for such ethics of business.

The first question is answered in the previous chapters, leading to a philosophy of management with six dimensions of the nature of business management (Table 6.1).

We build on the six dimensions of business management to explore a principle of business ethics. By showing the intrinsic relation between business management and ethics, we reject the free market ideological claim that ethical responsibility has to be excluded from business management. By applying management theory on ethical considerations, we at the same time move beyond applied ethical approaches in business ethics and instead can embed ethics in the nature of business management. With this approach, we explore a new integrated principle of the ethical responsibility of business management.

The chapter is structured as follows: in Section 20, we ask which of the six dimensions of the philosophy of management potentially hinder or enhance business ethical management practices. We apply these dimensions of the philosophy of management on ethical issues in business management to define a principle of business ethics. In Section 21, we ask for the individual competencies of managers that enable them to engage in business ethical practices and explore the concept of individual virtuous competence. In Section 22, we ask for the institutional conditions that enable managers to engage in business ethical practices and explore the concept of performative codes of conduct.

20 Towards an Integrated Principle of Business Ethics

Management as Participation

The starting point for our reflections on the principle of business ethics that builds upon our philosophy of management can be found in the first dimension: management as *participation* in the primary process of the business operations. While managerial practices are often characterized by a *loss of participation* – for example, a withdrawal from the primary process of the business operations in favour of an externalized position to manage and control this process – we argued for management as *participation* in the primary process of the business operations. Participation enables the business manager to develop the necessary *know-how* to manage the primary process that produces the products and services of the business, to teach and coach his or her employees, and to appreciate the work that is accomplished under his or her supervision.

Participation of business managers in the primary process may counter their tendency to withdraw from the primary process to control the workforce via instrumental control mechanisms, in which the moral impulse of individual managers and professionals are neglected. Participation enables managers to take situational factors into account as well as the individual conditions, strengths, and weaknesses of the employees involved. Because of his or her involvement in the primary process, he or she can easily consult and learn from his or her employees and can decide to adjust the business operations, for instance, in case of emerging problems. In short, because participation in the business operations replaces indirect and instrumental contact for direct and personal contact, it enables business managers to act upon their moral impulses and/or the moral impulses of their employees in collective action.

But irrespective of its advantage, to facilitate business ethical management practices, participation is not in itself ethical. Participation constitutes the know-how of the business manager and this knowledge how to make products and services may be embedded in the manager's *ethos* how to live the good life, but this is not necessarily the case. Business managers who are participating in the primary process may take their moral impulses into account in managing the business operations but can also neglect their moral intuitions, for instance, in favour of their private interests. We can also think of a business manager who is involved in the primary process of the business but leads his or her employees in an autocratic way – for example, engages in a leadership style that gives full decision power and authority to the manager without consulting his or her employees. We can therefore conclude that participation is a necessary condition for ethical business operations, as it enables business managers to act upon their moral impulses and to act upon the moral impulse of other stakeholders involved in or affected by the business operations, but not yet sufficient condition for business ethical management practices.

Management as Resistance and Responsive Action

We turn therefore to the second dimension of our philosophy of management: management as *resistance* to the problems or failures that the manager encounters in the world as it currently is, and as *responsive action* to address these failures. While managerial practices are often characterized by managerial power to *control* the business, we argued that managerial practices are primarily initiated by *problems* or (market) *failures* that the manager encounters in the world. Business management consists in *resistance* against the world as it currently is and in a new beginning or acting out to change the world to address these problems or failures in the world, for example, a new or product or service in response to these problems (Section 9).

We can argue that the idea of resistance contains a moral moment as morality concerns the norms and values that determine what is "right" and "wrong", and the problems or failures are definitely something "wrong" that the manager is resistant to. If the starting point of business management is found in resistance against problems and in acting out to address these problems, we can frame this resistance and acting out in moral terms. CSR is a normative concept because it does not describe the world as it is, but as it *should* be. In this case, the business manager's resistance is inspired by his or her assessment of child labour or environmental pollution as something which is morally wrong, while his or her acting out is inspired by the judgment that cleaner production and consumption as something that is morally right. With this we encounter a particular meaning of responsibility – current business practices are *held responsible* for a non-sustainable society – while the acting out of the business manager can be conceived as *taking responsibility* for addressing these problems and failures in the world.

Although managerial resistance can be ethically motivated in this respect, it is questionable whether we can build a business ethics based on the concept of business management as resistance and responsive action. Managerial resistance can be found in a morally problematic situation like climate change, but also in amoral problems or failures – for example, the market introduction of the cell phone to address the problem of "connectivity". The morality involved in the assessment of problems and failures in the world of society may therefore be seen as a necessary condition for business ethical resistance, but it is certainly not a sufficient condition.

The same holds for business management as acting out in response to failures encountered in the world of society. Business management consists in the decision to change the world of society by introducing new or changed products or services that address these failures. This decision to change the world does not accept the status quo and results in an acting out, rather than bearing and managing this impulse, and consists in a new beginning – for example, the introduction of new or changed products or services that address the failures that the business manager experiences. With this, the manager *takes responsibility* to address the failures that he or she encounters. Managerial action can be found in more socially responsible products and services, but also in amoral business opportunities.

Management as Constitution of Meaning

We therefore turn now to the third dimension of our philosophy of management as constitution of meaning. Because management consists in the establishment and governance of a functioning *order* of the business, we argued that the primary performance of the business manager consists in the articulation of an organizing principle in light of which the natural and human resources involved in the primary process of the business constitute a meaningful order that enables the business manager to address the problems or failures in the world that he or she experiences. In the first instance, we conceive the articulation of a meaningful order from the perspective of its utility, that is, as a functioning order of the business that enables the manager to act appropriately in times of setback or unforeseen circumstances that threaten the survival of the firm, for instance, in stormy weather. Next to this instrumental meaning of the functioning order of the business, which can be associated with self-evident conceptualizations of management that we rejected in this study, we encountered a conceptualization of management as the constitution of a meaningful world for the business operations (Section 10). The order of the business is not only a *functioning* order but also a *meaningful* order for the business operations. This meaningful order evokes public admiration because the world of business is responsive to problems or failures in the world of society. We can think of managers embracing sustainability as a normative principle in light of which the business operations are (re)designed and constitute such a meaningful world for the business operations in response to global warming as ecosystem failure in the world of society.

On the one hand, this meaningful world is articulated by the acting out of the business manager, who articulates such a meaningful world for the business operations in which all natural and human resources have their proper place, role and task and are arranged in such a way that they enable him to produce new or changed products and services, that is, to participate in the primary process. On the other hand, it is in his or her participation in the primary process, that is, in his or her active engagement in the business operations, that this meaningful world emerges as a world for sustainable business. In this respect, both the acting out of the business manager and his or her actual participation in the business operations are interconnected and interdependent in the articulation of a meaningful world for the business operations. We therefore frame this particular performance of business management as an articulation of a meaningful world for the execution of the business operations, that enables the business manager to address the problems or failures that he or she experiences in the world of society.

What is the moral dimension of the constitution of a meaningful world for business operations? The manager constitutes a meaningful world for the proper execution of the business operations, for instance, a meaningful world for sustainable businesses that enables the business manager to address problems or failures in the world of society. The normative dimension of the constitution of a meaningful world consists in the fact that this world is *responsive* to the world of society. The world of society can be seen as a normative principle that guides the articulation of a meaningful world for business operations to address the problems or failures in the world of society. This production of a meaningful world for the business operations is not so much embedded in the *know-how* to make the products and services of the firm, but in his or her practical knowledge on how to live the good life, that is, in the *ethos* of the business manager. This *ethos* can, for instance, be recognized in a sustainable entrepreneur who never wanted to start a business but took his or her responsibility to engage in entrepreneurial action in order to address a morally problematic situation, for example, sustainability-related ecosystem failures. The problem is, however, that this normative principle of the world of the business operations can be found in sustainability, fairness, justice, etc. as ideal characteristics of the world of society, but is often found in the private world of the self of the business manager; egoism and self-interest as guiding principle of the business operations, as is common in free-market idealism. With this, we encounter the same situation as with the previous two dimensions we discussed, namely that business management as an articulation of a meaningful world to address the problems and failures in the world is definitely a necessary condition for business ethical management practices, but not yet sufficient condition.

Management as Politico-Economic Governance

Such a sufficient condition for business ethical management practices may be found if we further reflect on the fourth dimension of our philosophy of management: management as politico-economic governance. As we have seen in chapter 3, politico-economic governance in times of global warming involves the Earth as a sovereign but open principle or norm for the business operations (Section 13), and this open principle can also inform the constitution of meaning in a normative way. This means that managers do not only constitute a meaningful world for the business operations (Section 10) but also, in this effort, are responsive to the Earth as a normative principle. Based on these considerations, we proposed a concept of business management as politico-economic governance of the business operations. Management constitutes a meaningful world for the business operations, in which planet Earth itself operates as a sovereign dimension for CSR with regard to grand challenges like global warming. Is this normative principle that operates in management as politico-economic governance a *sufficient* condition for business ethical practices?

On the one hand, the idea that the business manager is a moral subject that articulates guiding norms and principles for business operations can be seen as a condition of business ethical practices. On the other hand, it is the articulation of norms and principles which can be criticized from an ethical perspective. Whether we conceive the articulation of norms and principles as a state of exception like Agamben (Section 12) or as a reduction of the other to the same as Levinas (Section 15), the focus on norms and principles neglects and instrumentalizes the moral impulse of the manager. It is precisely the "narcissistic preoccupation with the self" of the business manager and his or her self-interests (Robert, 2001: 109), that neglects the moral impulse and moral intension of individual managers and their employees and constitute a system of instrumental management and control. The same holds for his or her preoccupation with norms and principles that constitutes bureaucratic governance structures (Section 1). Why? If the business manager articulates a normative principle that establishes and governs a functioning order of the business, it is precisely such a unifying principle that neglects the singularity of the individual employee or manager and his or her value frames and norms in favour of common corporate goals. If it turns out that all acting out is determined by the bi-polar machine of economy and sovereignty, as we have seen in chapter 3, it is questionable whether management as politico-economic governance is a *sufficient* condition for business ethical practices.

Should we then not simply *reject* management as politico-economic governance from an ethical perspective? In chapter 3, we followed another strategy. We argued that the articulation of guiding norms and principles for the business operations is a necessary condition for business ethical practices but that these norms or principles have to be found in grand challenges like global warming, which unsettle managers and call them to sustain the planet. As these grand challenges are wicked problems, there is no universal norm or principle available to address these problems. On the one hand, this leads to the fundamental acceptance of "open" and "revisable" norms and principles. On the other hand, this leads to the acknowledgement of the fallibility of managers' interventions in light of their epistemic insufficiency with regard to this normative dimension.

In other words, although the acting out of the business manager *intends* to establish and govern a functioning order of the business that is responsive to the Earth as a normative principle, it is not certain whether he or she will succeed or not. On the one hand, this norm is 'open' for revision, as we have seen, to the extent that the application of this norm remains finite compared to the wickedness of the problem, and remains questionable, adjustable, and improvable in light of our epistemic insufficiency regarding the wickedness of problems like global warming (Section 13). Such a principle limitation of the questionability of the norm makes that we never know whether our business operations are ethically good and whether we did the right thing or not. On the other hand, there are always fundamental risks involved in business operations, as well as unforeseen circumstances and the possibility of misfortune, irrespective of the good intentions of the business manager to address problems or failures in the world of society. The radical fallibility and vulnerability of management make that we never know whether our business operations are ethically good and whether we did the right thing or not. With this, we encounter the same situation as with the previous three dimensions we discussed, namely that business management as politico-economic governance is definitely a necessary condition for business ethical management practices, but not yet a sufficient condition.

Management as Non-Reductive Stakeholder Engagement

Because of the fundamental risks, unforeseen circumstances, and the possibility of misfortune, Xenophon already included the propitiation of the Gods as an integral part of business management (Section 4). In our secularized and democratic world, we can replace the call for the blessing of the Gods by the call for public approval that provides the business manager with a social license to operate (Wilburn and Wilburn, 2011). This *acclamation* by society, as we called it in chapter three, can be gained if the acting out of the business manager is not only *responsive* to the Earth as a normative principle but in this, is also responsive to the concerns and needs of society, next to his or her effort to make a profitable business. In the case of business operations that involve significant risks for employees or users, responsiveness may require that business managers become responsive to these concerns in the (re)design and execution of the business operations. In other words, because business management is intrinsically exposed to risk and the possibility of misfortune, the acting out of management to solve problems or failures in the world should at the same time be characterized by its *responsiveness* to stakeholders. On the one hand, only such responsiveness to stakeholders safeguards that the problems and failures in the world of society are not *only* market failures that can be commercially exploited, but *also* moral problems and failures. On the other hand, only in the actual engagement with internal and external stakeholders do managers become responsive to the normative principle that constitutes the world of society. Is management as responsiveness to stakeholder needs and concerns a *sufficient* condition for business ethical practices?

On the one hand, stakeholder engagement, collaboration, and partnership with society can be seen as a condition of business ethical practices (chapter 4). On the other hand, it is precisely the inclusion as participation of stakeholders that we criticized from an ethical perspective in that chapter. Why? If business management involves stakeholders, their participation in the business operations is always participation in a unifying principle or norm in which the singularity of the participants is neglected. They appear *as* workforce, *as* a shareholder, or *as* a stakeholder with interests and values, while the singularity and situatedness of their individual moral impulses are neglected in favour of such common characteristics. Responsiveness to the needs and concerns of internal and external stakeholders faces therefore the risk of reducing the other to the same, difference to identity. There are two ways in which the moral subject is accordingly constituted (chapter 4), namely by assimilating the stakeholders to the normative principles of the business manager (self-confirmation) or by his or her submission to the normative principles of other stakeholders (self-denial). In both cases, the moral impulse and singularity of either the business manager or internal and external stakeholders are neglected. Should we not simply reject management as stakeholder engagement from an ethical perspective? Furthermore, should we not simply reject management as participation from an ethical perspective as well?

To deal with this possible objection, we have to first distinguish between two types of participation. We discuss first the nature of the participation of the business manager in the primary process (the first dimension of our philosophy of management) followed by the nature of the participation of stakeholders in the primary process (the fifth dimension of our philosophy of management). This will enable us to reject the reductive nature of participation in case of the participation of the business manager in the primary process. But by distinguishing between a reductive and non-reductive type of responsiveness to stakeholders in the primary process of the business operations, we can opt for the second one in our concept of business ethical responsiveness to the needs and concerns of stakeholders.

In Section 8, we criticized the loss of participation in current management practices and argued for management as participation in the primary process of the business operations. Earlier in this section, we argued that the participation of the business manager in the primary process is a necessary condition of business ethical practices because it counters the tendency to control the business via instrumental control mechanisms, in which the moral impulse of the individual manager is neglected. Participation in the primary process enables business managers to take situational factors into account and enables them to consult and learn from others as well. The criticism of the reductive nature of participation does not apply here. Participation, on the contrary, enables the business manager to have direct and personal contact with internal and external stakeholders and to act upon his or her moral impulses. In fact, participation enables the manager to act upon his or her moral impulse or that of other stakeholders, and to act upon his or her resistance to the problems or failures in the world of society. Instead of accepting the status quo of current (amoral or unethical) business practices, managers' participation in the primary process enables them to claim a state of exception and to take the sovereign decision to act upon their moral impulses and to actually engage in responsive action. With this positive notion of the state of exception that enables the business manager to move beyond the status quo of amoral business practices and engage in business ethical management practices, we oppose to Giorgio Agamben's negative assessment of the state of exception that we encountered in chapter 3. We agree with the negative aspects of the state of exception, which is in line with our criticism of the reductive type of stakeholder engagement we discussed in chapter 4. But we distinguish another type of exception that is ethically significant, namely resistance against the status quo and taking responsibility for the grand challenges of our time by acting out to change the world. Only by his or her participation in the primary process of the business, the manager takes responsibility to address the problems or failures in the world of society.

This first type of participation is self-referential, that is, embedded in the manager's abilities and capacities, in his or her ego or self (Section 8). All acting out of the business manager remains embedded in the ego or self of the manager as the centre of his or her participation in the business operations. But this self-referentiality does not imply that the manager is the moral subject of his or her acting out to address problems or failures in the world. First, although the business manager may be seen as a primary actor who engages in his or her acting out in the business operations, this acting out is only accomplished in the actual execution and fulfilment of the tasks and duties that are accordingly assigned to him. In this respect, the business manager is not only the moral subject of his or her acting out but also its object. This means that the meaningful arrangement of the business operations is not constituted once and for all, but is constituted only in the actual execution of the maintenance of this meaningful world by the responsive action of the manager (Section 10). Second, although the business manager may be seen as a primary actor who engages in his or her acting out as new beginning of the business, this acting out is only accomplished or achieved in collaboration with other stakeholders (employees, suppliers, etc.). In this respect, the business manager's acting out is at the same time responsive to the needs and concerns of other stakeholders.[1] Third, if the self of the business manager is characterized by a relational term – that is, participation in the primary process – we can argue that the self of this relation is not given *prior* to the relation (Section 8); only the managers' actual participation in the business operations and acting out to address the problems and failures in the world of society constitutes his or her self or ego, namely his or her *know-how*. In fact, management as participation means that the self of the manager, the problems or failures in the world of society which he or she tries to address in his or her primary process, and the world for the business operations to address these problems and failures that he or she articulates, are co-constitutive. This concept of business management as participation is not yet contaminated by the negative connotations of participation we discussed before. On the contrary, business management as participation enables the business manager to act upon his or her moral impulses. In this respect, we can reject the criticism of participation in the case of the participation of the business manager in the primary process and highlight its ethical significance for business ethical management practices.

But we have to distinguish between this positive type of participation of the business manager in the primary process (first dimension of our philosophy of management) and a second type of participation of internal and external *stakeholders* in the business operations. We have seen that the criticism of participation still holds for this second type of participation, which is at stake in management as stakeholder engagement. Normally, this second type of participation is understood from the perspective of stakeholder theory, according to which business managers have to become responsive to the interests or "stakes" of employees, NGOs, suppliers, etc., next to the shareholders of the firm (Freeman, 1984). As discussed in chapter 4, as long as the point of departure of the participation of stakeholders in the business operations is found in a cognitive "position" of stakeholders – the values, norms, and interests of various stakeholders – that can be understood or known by the business manager, participation may be criticized; it reduces the singularity of the interests and demands of other stakeholders to the same by assimilating their concerns and needs to the interests of the business manager (self-confirmation) or by the submission of the interests of the business manager to their demands and needs (self-denial). This reductive nature of stakeholder engagement, collaboration, and partnership can be recognized in both theory and practice.

For this reason, in chapter 4, we developed the fifth dimension of our philosophy of management, that is, management as non-reductive stakeholder engagement. We rejected the cognitive approach of stakeholder engagement and developed an approach in which the primacy of the *social-ethical relation* between a business manager's acting out to address problems or failures in the world of society, and internal and external stakeholders with their own concerns and needs regarding these problems is at stake. The point of departure of business ethics is then found in the business manager and his or her resistance to problems or failures in the world of society. In his or her resistance, the manager is not primarily responsive to the stakes, values, or viewpoints of internal and external stakeholders that should be taken into account. Stakeholders are taken as absolutely different societal actors with fundamentally different value frames and interests that can never be fully understood by managers. This separation between the business manager and internal and external stakeholders suspends all participation and institutes a social relation with employees, NGOs, etc., which is intrinsically ethical, that is, *responsive* to their demands and needs regarding the problems or failures in the world of society and regarding the proposed solutions by the business manager. While in the cognitive approach of business manager's responsiveness to stakeholders, other societal actors are reduced to the same by the assimilation of internal and external stakeholders to the interests of the business manager (self-confirmation) or by business manager's submission to the interests of other more dominant stakeholders (self-denial), the ethical approach of business manager's responsiveness to stakeholder engagement can respect the fundamental differences between the business manager and other internal and external stakeholders, while he or she is responsive to their demands and needs regarding the problems or failures in the world of society and his or her proposed solution of these problems. This responsiveness of ethical business management implies that primacy is given to the demands of internal and external stakeholders who appeal to the business manager to act and behave in a responsible way in addressing the problems and failures in the world of society. Based on this distinction between a reductive and non-reductive type of stakeholder engagement in the business operations, we can reject the first and embrace the second type of responsiveness to stakeholders to define a necessary and sufficient condition for business ethical business operations. While the starting point of business ethics is found in the *participation* of the business manager in the primary process, his or her actual resistance and acting out in the business operations is at the same time *responsive* to the concerns and needs of other stakeholders regarding the problems and failures in the world of society in his or her actual engagement in the social-ethical relation with these stakeholders.

Management as Epistemic Insufficient Entrepreneurship

As we now provided a principle of business ethics and clarified the meaning of participation and responsiveness that characterize the five conditions of business ethical management practices, we have to consider a final possible criticism. In current society, many firms claim to act in a corporate social responsible (CSR) way. Large firms publish annual CSR reports in addition to their financial reports, many firms have an explicit CSR strategy and a CSR department or an ethical advisory board. Likewise many start-ups actually engage in the transition towards cleaner production and consumption. As we are at the same time confronted with all kinds of moral scandals in firms with extensive CSR activities – think for instance about the manipulation of interest rates like in case of Rabobank, lobbying against new regulations for healthy food production by large food firms in the EU, or significant contributions to environmental pollution like in case of Shell or Exon Mobile – we may ask how society can distinguish between business ethical management practices according to the five conditions we discerned so far, and non-business ethical management practices. This question not only emerges because the first four conditions of business ethical management practices are necessary but not sufficient conditions as we have seen. Even if we consider the fifth condition of business ethical management practices based on the social-ethical relation with stakeholders as a necessary and sufficient condition, it is not easy to distinguish between a responsive and a non-responsive action based on actual business performance.

An example can make this problem clear. Due to lifestyle diseases like obesity and Type II Diabetes, European food firms engage in innovations for healthy food. They increasingly bring new products on the market with less sugar, fat, and salt, or otherwise change their recipes in order to make more healthy food products. When asked for their motives to engage in responsible innovations for healthy food, they both provide economic and moral reasons. On the one hand, they argue that they engage in healthier product development because they feel responsible for the emergence of lifestyle diseases in the Western world and because they have the power to change the market. On the other hand, they argue that they are operating in a competitive market and have to make a profit, which limits their ability to further reduce sugar, fat, and salt levels in their products (Garst et al., 2018). The problem here is that we cannot distinguish between a food firm that is purely economically driven and engages in healthy food production due to the increased market for such products, and a food firm that is responsive to the needs and concerns of society and for this reason, engages in business ethical management practices. What appears as business ethical management practices may be in fact an instance of greenwashing.

An additional complicating issue is that responsiveness to the needs and concerns of stakeholders is not straightforward. First, if the problem or failure in the world of society is, for instance, highly complex like climate change, many different viewpoints and value frames of different stakeholders are at stake. In such contexts of complex or "wicked" problems (Section 7), it is not clear what business ethics should entail and what not. Furthermore, even if we know what responsive action should entail, it is unclear whether business ethical action and behaviour will always go hand in hand with un-ethical decisions, as the 'success' of every solution remains incalculable and exposed to risks and the possibility of misfortune. Responsiveness to internal and external stakeholders may help to mitigate the risks of negative impacts of the business operations, and to get societal approval for the business operations but risk reduction and societal approval does not lift the fundamental uncertainty of future impacts and the possibility of misfortune. Finally, if the resistance and acting out of business management is embedded in the self or ego of the business manager, his or her actual performance is incalculable and unpredictable. His or her decision to change the world does not accept the status quo and consists in a new beginning which is incalculable in light of the status quo – think for instance of the incalculable nature of disruptive innovations or blue ocean strategies that overthrow the market's equilibrium – and is always boundless to the extent that it breaks through this status quo. It is also unpredictable because the outcome of his or her decision to change the world can only be described with the benefit of hindsight. Think, for instance, of the strength of Rabobank's CSR performance that diminishes in light of the later Libor scandal in which they were involved, or Exon Mobile's support of sustainability research that shrivels in light of their public communication against the human factor in climate change. This incalculability and unpredictability of business management implies that also ethical business management remains incalculable and unpredictable. These issues show that actual business ethical management practices are in fact undecidable, as they may always turn out to be questionable with the benefit of hindsight. Our responsiveness to the ethical unacceptability of child labour may, for instance, have at the same time detrimental consequences for their livelihood.

This undecidability between amoral or un-ethical and ethical business management cannot be solved and shows why business ethics is a *struggle* that the business manager engages in, rather than something that he or she can claim to have or possess already as a characteristic. Not in the *awareness* of moral problems or failures in the world of society or the *intention* to address these problems does the responsiveness of business management consist, but in the actual exploration and exploitation of new emerging business opportunities to address these problems and failures in the world of society. Here, the sixth dimension of our philosophy of management – management as epistemic insufficient entrepreneurship – can provide a necessary condition for ethical business operations. On the one hand, only in the actual engagement in the *exploration* of radical uncertain business opportunities, the business manager discloses his or her *ethos* as knowledge how to live the good life. On the other hand, only in the actual *exploitation* of radical uncertain business opportunities, the business manager discloses to what extent he or she is *responsive* to the concerns and needs of other stakeholders. Only in the entrepreneurial struggle, the concerns and needs of other stakeholders are *acknowledged*. Although this entrepreneurial struggle does not guarantee ethical behaviour, the manager feels responsible for and capable of addressing problems and failures based on his or her entrepreneurial self-efficacy (Section 19).

Because only the actual engagement with the exploration and exploitation of ethical business opportunities disclose the *ethos* of the business manager in his or her responsive action, we propose that business ethical management practices should bear the *traces* of a business manager's struggle in his or her acting out to address problems and failures in the world of society. By traces, we do not mean the ideas or values of stakeholders that are adopted by the business manager. This would involve the reductive type of participation of stakeholders in the primary process that we rejected in the previous section. Instead, we stipulate that the business operations bear the traces of this struggle. Such a trace can, for instance, be found in a deliberate change of the production process in response to actual engagement with stakeholder's demands for fair or healthy food and comes at the expense of the profitability of the business. It can also be found in a proactive decision to engage in services to society (e.g. investments in public health, science and education beyond its potential to contribute to the employability and profitability for the business). It can also be found in a change of the business strategy in response to stakeholders' demand to remedy structural injustices in global food and health problems (Tempels et al., 2020). To be clear, this entrepreneurial struggle does not consist in a *participation* of stakeholders in the business operations, as the moral force of the concerns and demands of stakeholders – for example, the world of society – always exceeds and transcends the responsive actions of the manager – for example, the world for the business operations that enables the business to address the problems and failures in the world of society. Entrepreneurial struggle, on the one hand, means that the world for the business operations bears the traces of the world of society it operates in. Business in society then means that the world for the business is constituted in such a way that its operations are responsive to problems or failures in the world of society and the concerns and needs of internal and external stakeholders concerning these problems and their proposed solution. On the other hand, entrepreneurial struggle does not consist in a final solution of the problem or failure in the world of society, but in satisficing solutions, as the world of business and the world of society never coincide. The failures in the world of society remain wicked and the epistemic insufficiency of the manager to address these failures completely constitutes the two co-existing but fundamentally different worlds of business and society. The world for the business operations and the world of society only meet in the trace of business ethical management practices that are responsive to the concerns and needs of society.

Conclusion: The Integrated Principle of Business Ethics

Contrary to the assumption of an original disconnect between the fields of business and ethics that calls for a connection in business ethical practices, the point of departure of this section was found in an intrinsic relation between business management and ethics. Contrary to the application of ethical theory in the field of business management, we asked what is the nature of business management, that can be seen as intrinsically related to ethics. By reflecting on the six dimensions of the philosophy of management, we provided an integrated principle of business ethics that is intrinsically related to the nature of business management. This principle of an integrated business ethics provides a new argument to reject the free market ideological claim that ethical responsibility should be excluded from business management. It also enables us to move beyond applied ethical approaches in business ethics by providing a principle of business ethics that is embedded in the nature of business management itself.

We articulated six conditions of business ethics in this section (Table 6.2), based on the six dimensions of the philosophy of management. While the first four conditions are necessary but not yet sufficient conditions for business ethical management practices, the fifth condition adds a necessary and sufficient condition.

We further reflected on the nature of the participation of the business manager and internal and external stakeholders in the primary process of the business operations. We highlighted the ethical significance of the participation of business managers in the primary process, as it enables them to reject the status quo of current (amoral or unethical) business practices, to act upon his or her moral impulse and to claim a state of exception that substantiates his or her resistance to the world as it currently is and his or her acting out to address the problems and failures in the world of society. We also highlighted the ethical significance of non-reductive responsiveness of business management to internal and external stakeholders, as it establishes an ethical relationship between business management's acting out to become responsive to the problems and failures in the world of society, and the concerns and needs of internal and external stakeholders regarding these problems and failures.

Table 6.2 Six conditions of the integrated principle of business ethics

1. Business manager's *participation* in business operations constitutes their *know-how* to address problems and failures in the world of society. Participatory *know-how* is a necessary condition for business ethical practices.
2. Business manager's *resistance* to moral problems in the world of society and *acting out* to address these problems builds the state of exception that is conditional for business ethical practices
3. Business manager's *ethos articulates* a normative principle that establishes and governs a meaningful world for the business operations. This *ethos* as knowing of how to live the good life is a necessary condition for business ethical practices.
4. Business manager's politico-economic governance makes sure that the meaningful world for business operations is at the same time responsive to the world of society.
5. Business manager's non-reductive stakeholder engagement makes sure that the business operations are responsive to concerns and needs of other stakeholders regarding the world of society.
6. Business manager's epistemic insufficient entrepreneurship consists in the entrepreneurial struggle to deal with the problems and failures in the world of society and engages in satisficing solutions.

We have also seen that the six conditions of business ethical management practices cannot be taken as characteristics that businesses can claim to have or possess. Because business ethical management practices are fundamentally undecidable, and only show themselves in the entrepreneurial *struggle* for business ethics in actual action and behaviour, the importance of self-disclosure and acknowledgement of stakeholders in responsive action and behaviour became clear.

21 Key Requirements of Business Managers: Individual Virtuous Competence

In the previous section, we have seen that management involves particular knowledge, skills, and virtues, for instance, the capability to act in a risky and uncertain environment with imperfect foresight. In this section, we focus on the key requirements of business managers that enable them to engage in business ethical practices.

To deal with the particular challenges related to wicked problems like global warming, rather than the "tamed" problems which are associated with normal business operations, business managers have to develop the organizational skills, capabilities, and competencies to (re)consider sustainability in all strategic and operational decisions which are made. Organizational skills are derived from practice and experience and concern repetitive behaviours to perform specific tasks developed by an organization (Sanchez et al., 1996), for instance, skills that enable corporate social responsible behaviour. Organizational capabilities combine and reconfigure internal and external skills in such a way that the organization becomes responsive to the changing demands in the environment and creates and produces new products that meet the requirements of the market, for instance, the dynamic capability of understanding, adapting, and responding to the requests of multiple stakeholders (Teece et al., 1997). Organizational competence concerns the coordinated deployment of skills and capabilities in such a way that it helps the manager to achieve his or her strategic goals, for instance, the development and execution of a long-term strategy regarding sustainability, such as Unilever's *Sustainable Living Plan* (Heugens, 2006).

In a case study about the environmental issue management of Unilever, Heugens explored the relationship between individual knowledge and experience of employees and the development of organizational skills, capabilities, and competencies. Not only are organizational skills, capabilities, and competencies embedded in a workforce of employees and managers involved in the execution of these skills and capabilities, but new organizational capabilities and competencies also originate from well-managed individual resources. This concerns the *acquisition* of experiential, reflective, and integrative knowledge by individual employees and the *application* of it at the organizational level (Heugens, 2006; Marcus and Geffen, 1998).

The role of *individual* competencies of managers to engage in CSR with regard to sustainable development is also confirmed in the literature. Managers have to (re)consider sustainability in all decisions they make and actions they undertake at an operational, tactical, and strategic level. According to Dunphy et al. (2007), this implies the need for technical skills to accomplish sustainability tasks, interpersonal skills to interact with, learn from and adapt to stakeholders, management skills in ethics, sustainable decision making, etc. According to Wesselink et al. (2015), dealing with wicked problems like global warming requires specific individual competencies and higher-order thinking skills. These skills, knowledge, and attitudes stem from the individual competencies of managers involved in managing CSR (Wood, 1991).

This raises the question of which individual moral competencies enable the manager to engage in ethical business operations. In Section 7, we introduced research in the field of individual moral competencies: normative competence enables the manager, for instance, to assess and improve the sustainability of socio-ecological systems based on a set of fixed values and principles, and action competence is the capacity to involve oneself as a person in responsible action in this area (Section 7).

We can connect now these findings about normative and action competence with the integrated principle of business ethics that we developed in the previous section. If the business manager's resistance is inspired by his or her assessment of environmental pollution by businesses as something morally wrong, while his or her acting out is inspired by his or her assessment of cleaner production and consumption as something which is morally right, this resistance and acting out of the business manager can be associated with action competence and normative competence.

In this section, we explore the role of these moral competencies in ethical business management. We first introduce the concept of individual competence and then explore the meaning of normative and action competence. The questions of how both these moral competencies have to be understood and how they are related to each other will be raised. We hypothesize that virtue ethics enables us to conceptualize normative competence and action competence as two aspects of one virtuous competence that constitutes the good character of managers and enables them to enhance and secure ethical business operations.

The Concept of Individual Competence

The concept of individual competence has been applied in widely differing ways in different countries (Gonczi, 1994), different disciplines, and different times. This diversity of conceptualizations of the concept is one of the major pitfalls in working with competencies (Biemans et al., 2004). To fully understand what is meant by individual competence, in this section, first a clear conceptualization of the concept is presented.

Gonczi (1994) distinguishes three main conceptualizations of individual competence: behaviouristic, generic, and holistic. Whereas in the behaviouristic conceptualization, competencies are described as discrete behaviours associated with the completion of each small task, in the generic conceptualization, competencies are personal qualities or traits that distinguish average performers from excellent performers (Eraut, 1994).

Many authors warn that the conceptualization of competence in the behaviouristic and generic tradition falls short in addressing the developmental and situated nature of professional practice. The behaviouristic conceptualization results in detailed work descriptions without a connection to the capabilities of a professional to accomplish the task efficiently. The generic approach to individual competence results in a context-independent description of competencies, without a connection to the complexity of the application of these competencies in practical situations (Billett, 1994; Brown et al., 1989; Cheetham and Chivers, 1996). In the context of individual competencies of managers involved in dealing with grand challenges like global warming, it is clear that it is insufficient to judge them on the basis of their performance as measured against certain standards while omitting to include the complexity and dynamics of practical situations in the context of the business operations.

To conceptualize individual competencies for dealing with sustainability, we prefer the holistic approach to competence, because of its close relationship with the context of professional practices. Within the holistic tradition, the concept of competence is defined as follows:

> Competence is the integrated performance-oriented capability of a person or an organization to reach specific achievements. These capabilities consist of clusters of knowledge structures and cognitive, interactive, affective and where necessary psycho-motoric skills, and attitudes and values, which are conditional for carrying out tasks, solving problems and effectively functioning in a certain profession, organization, position and role. (Mulder, 2001: 76)

The holistic approach stresses the situated character of the development of competencies within a (complex) context of professional practices.

Hodkinson and Issitt (1995) have identified two dimensions of the holistic conceptualization of individual competence. The first dimension concerns the integration of knowledge, skills, and attitudes that are meaningful for a practitioner. Individual knowledge refers to the representation of facts, procedures, and principles about a subject, individual skills refer to specific learned activities and individual attitudes refer to a person's feelings and dispositions towards other persons or towards specific topics (Osagie et al., 2016). The second dimension of the holistic conceptualization of competence relates to learning and assessment processes that should be interrelated and take place in relevant practical situations. The importance of these two dimensions is confirmed by our discussion of sustainability as a wicked problem. Managers require specific individual competencies and higher-order thinking skills (Wals and Jickling, 2002), for instance, experiential, reflective, and integrative knowledge and skills (Heugens, 2006). These competencies are developed and employed in their day-to-day decisions and actions on an operational, tactical, and strategic level.

The two dimensions of the holistic conceptualization of competence show two important aspects concerning the capabilities of a manager to fulfil certain tasks, roles or jobs. Namely, the input and output of competencies (Hoffmann, 1999). The input concerns the personal capabilities of a manager, while the output concerns the tasks managers successfully perform. Although the concepts of tasks (output) and personal capabilities (input) can be conceived as two distinctive operationalizations of individual competence (Hoffmann, 1999; Mansfield and Mitchell, 1996), in the holistic conceptualization of competence, these two aspects of individual competence are integrated. A manager is expected to have specific personal competencies which are deployed within the complex and dynamic context and enable him to enhance and secure ethical business practices in an effective way.

The Role of Moral Competence in the Management of Grand Challenges of Our Time

As stated in Section 7, previous research has identified seven competencies required for managing CSR with regard to sustainable development: systems-thinking competence, foresight-thinking competence, strategic management, embracing diversity and inter-disciplinarity, interpersonal competence, normative competence, and action competence (Lans et al., 2014). These competencies can be seen as necessary inputs to manage the wicked problem of global warming as output. In this subsection, we focus on the role of the two moral competencies and ask how both moral competencies have to be understood in case we acknowledge the wickedness of global warming, and how both competencies are related to each other in CSR.

In the literature, normative competence is defined as a competence that enables managers to assess and improve the sustainability of their firm or otherwise of social-ecological systems, based on values and principles (Wiek et al., 2011). Normative competence helps in this respect to ensure that managers are held accountable for the decisions made (Grunwald, 2004; Gibson, 2006). We can assess the role of normative competence if we look at ethical decision-making processes.

According to Jones (1991), ethical decision-making comprises four stages: to recognize a moral issue, to make a moral judgment, to establish moral intent and to engage in moral behaviour. In ethical decision-making, the input is our competence to recognize the moral issue and to make a moral judgment about the right thing to do based on certain ethical norms, and the output is efficient task-fulfilment in response to this moral judgment.

In this study, sustainability is seen as such an ethical norm because it describes the world as it *should* be (Hahn, 2009; Wals, 2010). Sustainable business then functions as a normative principle in light of which the business operations are (re)designed and improved. For Gibson (2006), the normativity of sustainability consists of the integrity of socio-ecological systems. A generic criterion for sustainability is derived from the necessity to maintain and protect the long-term integrity of the ecosystems upon which humans and other organisms depend (Gibson, 2006). Other such sustainability-related norms include democratic governance (Wiek et al., 2011; Mogensen and Schnack, 2010), and intra-generational and intergenerational equity (Wiek et al., 2011). Also, de Haan's (2006) competencies for sustainability imply specific normative measures, such as "striving for a global view", "a global 'we' feeling", etc. In corporate decision-making processes about sustainability, the moral judgment can be based on such norms and on specific measures and moral standards that are derived from these norms.

Important individual influences on ethical decision-making are found in the cognitive moral development of the level of reasoning in the application of moral judgment (Kohlberg, 1969; Rest, 1979; Rest et al., 2000; Fraedrich et al., 1994); in emotional systems that evolve unconsciously based on (early) experiences (Narvaez, 2008); in skills to deal with ethical issues based on training and work experience in general (Trevino and Nelson, 2007); in moral imagination and systems thinking in particular (Werhane, 2002); in personal values such as self-respect, freedom, honesty, etc.; and in the attitude professionals have regarding an ethical issue, whether or not influenced by social or cultural aspects (Heidt, 2001). In the context of business ethics, we can think of the application of universal ethical principles like the socio-ecological system integrity (Gibson, 2006), education for sustainable development (de Haan, 2006; Ellis and Weekes, 2008), environmental values like altruism or self-transcendence rather than egocentrism (de Groot and Steg, 2008; Wall et al., 2007; Clark et al., 2003), and positive attitudes towards the environment (Meinhold and Malkus, 2005; Barr and Gilg, 2006). In short, normative competence comprises the knowledge, skills, and attitudes that enable a manager to recognize moral issues related to the business operations and to make a moral judgment about the right thing to do based on ethical norms.

In this subsection, rather than considering the problems with the reductive nature of universal norms (Section 12) we concentrate on normativity in relation to the grand challenges of our time. If global warming has to be considered a wicked problem (Section 7), this has profound consequences for our conception of normativity. In management practices, for instance, business objectives often compete with sustainability objectives. In a recent study of the individual competencies of CSR managers of multinational enterprises, the ability to strike a balance between idealism, that is, what, from a normative perspective, *should* be achieved to be corporately social responsible – and pragmatism – what, from a business perspective, is *feasible* to achieve given existing market conditions such as consumer preferences, competition, etc. – was stressed (Osagie et al., 2016). But even if a manager accepts the norm that the use of resources today should not constrain the use of resources in the future, it is not clear in advance which use of resources will lead to these constraints and which will not. Do we, for instance, mean that we cannot use fossil fuel anymore to enable future generations to use these resources as well? Or is it possible to use fossil fuels for the current generation while investing in the development of renewable energies for future generations? The problem here is that human needs change over time and their satisfaction develops in different ways. This limits the one-to-one applicability of principles and norms in business life because we should at least know "what" the long-term effect of our actions is to assess whether our acts respect the rights of future generations. In wicked problems like global warming, there are too many unstable and situational factors and complexities that make it at least difficult to apply such principles and norms. In other words, the application of norms in CSR with regard to sustainable development is limited because of the epistemic insufficiency of the manager (Section 7).

Furthermore, an important aspect of the complexity of wicked problems is that multiple stakeholders are involved with differing and often conflicting norms and value frames (chapter 4). In ethical decision making in the context of wicked problems, moral judgment is not easily based on ethical norms, because these norms may differ and even conflict. Establishing norms regarding the wicked problem of global warming requires first of all that a manager is aware of his or her own norms – that is, his or her "moral compass" (Thompson, 2010) or *ethos* how to live the good life (Section 9) – and the norms and values of others (e.g. stakeholders), and can come up with a procedure to develop and establish shared norms with other stakeholders, for instance, via moral imagination (Werhane, 2002). Gibson (2006: 180) speaks about the ability to:

> adopt evaluation and decision criteria and trade-off rules that reflect the full set of core requirements for progress towards sustainability, recognize interdependencies and seek multiple reinforcing gains on all fronts, provide means of specifying the sustainability decision criteria and trade-off rules for specific contexts, through informed choices by the relevant parties (stakeholders).

The first problem is therefore that normative competence does not consist in the one-to-one application of norms and principles in business practices, but involves the "ability to collectively map, specify, apply, reconcile, and negotiate sustainability values, principles, goals, and targets" (Wiek et al., 2011). Or, in terms of chapter 4, the ability to manage the redesign of the business operations in response to the call or needs of other stakeholders (Section 8). The second problem is that the content of these norms and the business operations based on these norms can always be contested in case of wicked problems like global warming. What then does normative competence mean? We need a more open-ended approach to normative competence in which the complexity, instability and situatedness of ethical judgments have to be stressed.

If we conceptualize normative competence from the perspective of wicked problems, we have to put references to norms and principles between brackets. Instead, we have to emphasize that normative *competence* concerns the *ability* to apply, negotiate, and reconcile norms and principles in response to the call or need of other stakeholders. Normative competence does not consist then primarily in the *application* of norms but in the ability to identify and *generate* norms that solve ethical conflicts and are responsive to the call or need of other stake-holders. This process of the development, negotiation, and reconciliation of norms is unique in every situation because of the differences between the norms and interests of multiple stakeholders. The norms and interests of multiple stakeholders have to be weighed and revised over and over again because of changing circumstances or new insights. The role of the manager then is to decide which norms to work within such an "undecidable" situation (Section 20).[2]

But can this normative ability still be seen as a *moral* competence if we conceptualize it in this way? In the next subsection, we introduce a virtue ethics perspective to better understand the normative aspects of both moral competencies.

Virtue Ethics

Virtue ethics assumes that good actions come from good persons and therefore that ethical behaviour will be undertaken by actors with a virtuous character. Virtues are characteristics of a person that enable him or her to lead a good life. These can be found in intellectual virtues like practical wisdom and moral virtues like courage, friendship, modesty, etc. We already encountered a virtue ethics approach in Xenophon's philosophy of management, in which particular virtues of the business manager like self-control, integrity, and modesty are identified (Section 6).

The origin of virtue ethics can be found in the work of Aristotle who developed the vocabulary of virtue ethics: *arête* (virtue), *phronesis* (practical wisdom), and *eudaimonia* (happiness) as the content of good life.[3] The good life can be seen as the general normative basis that is central to virtue ethics, and which is specified in terms of an account of the virtues needed for achieving this good life. Virtue is a character trait or disposition of a person which determines his or her behaviour (Aristotle, 1990: 1105b25–30). An honest person does not act in an honest way because of expected punishment or reward or another ex-ternal cause, but because he or she values honesty or telling the truth in itself. It is quite rare, however, to exercise a virtue perfectly. There are many ways of falling short of this ideal. An important flaw being a lack of practical wisdom (Athanassoulis, 2000; Hursthouse, 1999). To achieve the good life, therefore, we need practical wisdom to decide how we ought to act and behave in a given situation to achieve the good for our life as a whole. While a person lacking practical wisdom may sometimes be too honest in a given situation – think of a young child that is sometimes too honest about his or her feelings for another person, expressing directly what he or she feels – practical wise people *know* which level of honesty is beneficial or harmful in a given situation. In this respect, virtuous actions are conceived as actions in between the extremes of excess (being too honest) and deficiency (being dishonest and misleading) (Aristotle, 1990: 1106a25–b10). In other words, virtue concerns the disposition of a person to do the right thing and virtue in combination with practical wisdom is the ability to actually do this right thing in a given situation (Hursthouse, 1999). Virtues are only fully developed in their deployment in combination with practical wisdom (Aristotle, 1990: 1144b10–20). One can think of professionals like doctors or lawyers who act in the best interest of their clients by doing the right thing in a given situation. Defending a "lost case" by a lawyer, for instance, is not virtuous, just as is giving up a case too easily under the pressure of powerful opponents. The practically wise person has this knowledge of how to act in a given situation, because of his or her experience of (professional) life and because he or she knows what is worthwhile and truly important in life, that is, what amount to a happy (*eudaimon*), good, or virtuous life.[4] For Aristotle, the good life consists in our actual living and acting virtuously, that is, in the actual application of virtues in a way that is practically wise (Aristotle, 1990: 1098b15–20; Kraut, 2014).

We propose that virtue ethics can provide a normative basis for the moral competencies we introduced in this section. The good life (*eudaimonia*) can be seen as a general normative basis for the normative competency, which includes both knowledge about the virtues and the ability to apply these virtues in a given and complex situation (action competence). Before we explore this virtues perspective on normative and action competency any further, in this subsection, we first discuss the general applicability of virtue ethics in the business context, and in the following subsection, we will then discuss the relationship between virtues and competencies.

Following the example of Moore and Beadle (2006), we use MacIntyre's (1985) conceptual framework of virtue ethics to develop our virtue ethics perspective on the normative and action competence for CSR with regard to sustainable development.[5] Elaborating on the work of Aristotle, MacIntyre developed his virtue–goods–practice–institution framework which is well known in the business ethics literature (Moore, 2005; Moore and Beadle, 2006).

The point of departure for MacIntyre's virtue ethics is the practical wisdom of a professional who judges well, and acts effectively to achieve his or her goal. For instance, a professional who knows how stakeholder expectations have to be managed in a particular case or a particular situation. MacIntyre conceptualizes this as a practice in which the practitioner knows what to do in pursuit of a desired end, for instance, a social license to operate. As we conceive management as participation in the primary process (first dimension of our philosophy of management), contrary to the instrumental orientation on management and control in contemporary management theory, we can conceive the manager as such a practitioner.

According to MacIntyre, practices result in goods internal to these practices such as the excellence of a manager that results from his or her increasing experience in professional life and can only be acquired in associated practices – and goods external to these practices such as wealth, fame and power. Internal goods are established by practitioners as a result of cooperative forms of activity, for example, addressing CSR with regard to sustainable development in new product development. These practices are supported by institutions, for instance, a firm like Unilever – which establish external goods such as profit, success, and reputation. From a business point of view, we could say that MacIntyre's central insight is that practices and institutions are two interdependent conditions for managerial behaviour. Managers need institutions in order to produce external goods, and also need practices to produce internal goods.

According to MacIntyre, there is also a tension between practice and institution, because practices tend to pursue goods internal to practice while institutions tend to pursue goods external to practice (Moore and Beadle 2006). The firm in our example may value the external good of profitability more highly than the internal good of the excellence of their workforce. Also, the personal desires of practitioners to pursue goods external to the practice, for instance, a practitioner who is influenced by suppliers to weaken sustainable sourcing strategies, may hinder the pursuit of internal goods. In this respect, both practices and institutions could damage and even destroy the practices with which they are linked. Earlier, we have seen that these tensions can be explained by the *loss* of participation in contemporary management theory and practices. They are solved in our philosophy of management by understanding management as participation and as responsive action, in which the *ethos* of the manager is constituted.

Through the exercise of virtue, professionals involved in a practice are able to withstand these internal and external pressures: "The integrity of a practice causally requires the exercise of the virtues by at least some of the individuals who embody it in their activity" (MacIntyre, 1985: 195). Managers who exercise these virtues are thus key to preventing institutions from corrupting business practices. Here, virtues are conceived as dispositions or "acquired human qualities" that enable managers to achieve the internal goods of a certain practice. Virtues are not practice-specific and help the managers to reach the state of being-well and doing-well, that is, the general aim of a good life based on good character (MacIntyre, 1985).

The virtuous life is however not only an individual matter. MacIntyre distinguishes in fact three levels of the good life. At an individual level, "a virtue is an acquired human quality the possession and exercise of which tends to enable us to achieve those goods which are internal to practices and the lack of which effectively prevents us from achieving any such goods" (MacIntyre, 1985: 191). But this is insufficient because the good life cannot be reduced to excellence in a certain practice but involves the search for the good (MacIntyre, 1985). There is some sort of good life that is naturally good for all human beings and is therefore identical for all human beings at all times (MacAulay and Lawton, 2006). This second level of the good life is still insufficient because it can be understood purely at the individual level, while humans are primarily members of a community that is embedded in a shared moral tradition. According to MacIntyre: "The self has to find its moral identity in and through its membership in communities" (MacIntyre, 1985: 221). In the production of internal goods, the manager is primarily responsive to the community. This community is needed to develop, apply, evaluate and rank internal goods. In this respect, it is *in* a community that virtues are developed. According to Moore (2005), the development of virtues requires collaboration among stakeholders and consequently requires individuals to see stakeholder community building as an important task in relation to working in business organizations. The virtues are exercised in, and partly, executed on behalf of the stakeholder community.

The Relation Between Virtues and Competencies

Before we can answer the question whether a virtue ethics perspective can help us to understand the moral dimensions of the normative and action competence of business managers, we must ask the preliminary question of whether virtues fit the competence perspective that we developed earlier in this section.

The first connection between both concepts is that both the holistic approach to competence as well as virtue ethics stress that the personal capabilities and virtues of a manager are only developed and enhanced within the complexity and dynamics of practice. And, when we have a closer look at the five main characteristics of virtue ethics (Koehn, 1995; Solomon, 1992) and compare them with the concept of competence we developed in this section, it turns out that they closely align with the competence perspective quite well. First of all, both virtues and competence focus on the individual level. Second, both virtues and competencies are not ours by birth, but are developed and learned by practicing (MacIntyre 1985). Both virtues and competencies are developed by witnessing professional behaviour of others, by imitating this behaviour and by reflecting on one's own behaviour (Cheetham and Chivers, 1996). Third, just as competence development and performance depend on the context (Billett, 1994), also the employment of virtues is situational (Murphy, 1991). Fourth, both for virtues and competence, the basis of professional judgements and subsequent actions is found in the character of the professional. In virtue ethics, the input of successful task fulfilment is found in the good character of the decision-maker, while in case of competence it is found in the personal capabilities of a professional (Meara et al., 1996; Billett, 1994; Cramer and Loeber, 2007). Finally, just as the key motivator in virtue ethics is the search for the good life and therefore the aspiration and striving for improvement (Murphy, 1991), the same holds true for the development of competencies. Business managers are increasingly held responsible for their own (competence) development, which motivates them to improve their competencies (Defillippi and Arthur, 1994). We can conclude therefore that there are several overlaps between the concept of virtue and competence; virtues are defined as those cultivated characteristics of an individual that enable a person to attain his or her aspirations regarding the good life in practice (Moore 2005), while competence is defined as the capability of a person that enables him or her to fulfil certain tasks successfully in a (complex) situation.

Are these concepts of virtue and competence, besides having overlapping characteristics, also conceptually linked with each other? Although both concepts have been developed in different academic disciplines – moral philosophy, management development, or education studies – research of MacAulay and Lawton (2006) has shown that in practice they are very similar. Both virtues and competencies concern the character of a person and their application in practice: "Most crucial of all ... is that virtue must have a fundamentally practical application: Without any public demonstration, virtues are effectively meaningless. Thus, like competencies, they exist equally in the realm of action as in the realm of human character" (MacAulay and Lawton, 2006: 708). And because of this, all virtues must have some competence to put the good character into practice (Figure 6.1).

This brings us to the question of whether virtue ethics enables us to conceptualize normative and action competence as two associated virtuous competencies that constitute the good character of competent managers and enables them to enhance and secure corporate social and sustainable business practices.

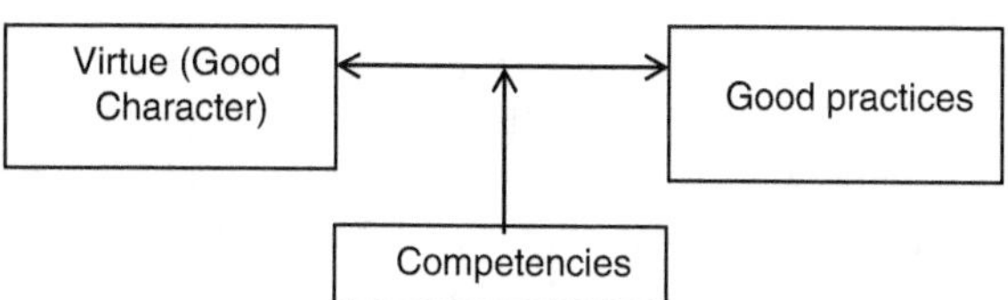

Figure 6.1 General relation between virtues and competencies in order to put good character into practice.

A Virtue Ethical Perspective on Normative and Action Competence

What is the advantage of a virtue ethics perspective on the ethical management of CSR with regard to sustainable development? A virtue ethics perspective acknowledges both the normative aspects of CSR and the complex context and situation in which business ethical decisions are taken. How does sustainable development for instance relate to the good life of an individual? From an Aristotelian perspective, one could argue that the protection of the natural environment is an integral part of the ideal of the good life. In his politics, Aristotle writes:

> Since one should take thought for the health of the [city's] inhabitants, this consists in the location being finely situated ... and second, in using healthy sorts of water, and making this more than an incidental concern; for the things we use most of and most often for the body are what contribute most to health, and the capacity of waters and wind has such a nature. (Aristotle, 1944: 7.11)

Others, like Sandler (2007), argue that we have to extend our concept of the good life to all that is good in the world we live in if we really want to make sense of an environmental virtue ethics. In this way "the good life" and "sustainability" are equated, and as a consequence "... sustainability may well be the primary schema for describing and evaluating what it means to be a good person or good society in today's world" (Vucetich and Nelson, 2010: 542). The good life is the normative basis containing the (environmental) virtues needed for sustainable development: concern for human needs, ecosystem health, and social justice (Vucetich and Nelson, 2010), while practical wisdom enables the manager to apply these virtues in complex contexts and situations to act in a corporately responsible way. In this respect, virtue ethics takes the good character of the manager as the point of departure.

On the one hand, CSR with regard to sustainable development originates from the good character of a manager who is searching for the good life. The good life purely consists in his or her actual living and acting virtuously, that is, in his or her actual social responsible behaviour. This guarantees the disposition of the manager to do the right thing in a given situation. This does not imply, on the other hand, that the good character of manager automatically results in perfectly responsible behaviour. Virtue ethics enables us to explain why ethical business practices sometimes fail, despite even the best intentions of the managers involved. As our consultation of Aristotle already made clear, it is quite rare to realize a virtue perfectly. There are many ways of falling short of this ideal, for example, doing ethically good and making a profit.

Because virtue ethics stresses the good character of the manager who is searching for the good life and acknowledges the possible fallibility or deficiency of his or her efforts to achieve this good life (third dimension of our philosophy of management), the importance of practical wisdom as the ability to find the mean between the extremes of excess and deficiency, for instance, the mean between economic and environmental aspects of CSR decisions with regard to sustainable development – is stressed. In this, the personal and situated aspects are taken into account (Aristotle, 1990: 1106a35–b10). In this respect, virtue ethics better fits the complexity, unstability, and situatedness of ethical managing wicked problems like global warming.

How does sustainability relate to internal goods of a MacIntyrian practice? The good character of the manager consists in his or her aspirations for the good life by producing internal goods, and sustainability can be seen as the contribution of these internal goods to concern for human needs, ecosystem health, and social justice. A virtue ethics perspective therefore enables us to understand the role of normative competence in the production of sustainable internal goods. In this respect, normative competence can be understood as a virtuous competence for CSR with regard to sustainable development and can be defined as the ability to identify, apply and reconcile virtues in the production of sustainable internal goods (CSR), which is embedded in the good character of the manager. This competency enables the manager to engage in the first and third dimensions of the philosophy of management, that is, participation and constitution of meaning. At the same time, the good character of the manager presupposes competence to put his or her virtuousness into practice, that is, the competence to apply these virtues in a given situation. This corresponds with the second and sixth dimensions of our philosophy of management, that is, responsive action and epistemic insufficient entrepreneurship.

This opens a new perspective on action competencies as well. Action competence has been defined as the ability, based on critical thinking and incomplete knowledge, to actively involve oneself in responsible actions to improve the sustainability of social-ecological systems in general and products, processes and procedures in particular (Schnack, 1996; de Haan, 2006). Jensen and Schnack (1997) distinguish four components of action competence: *knowledge and insight* concern knowledge about the problem of sustainability and the ability to think critically about its possible solution; *commitment* relates to the motivation and drives to engage oneself in the solution of sustainability problems; *visions* concern the ability to conceptualize the future state of the world or the good life one wants to pursue; *action experiences* finally stresses the importance of actual involvement in concrete sustainable actions. The advantage of action competence is that it stresses the personal involvement of the manager as participation. It also stresses their resistance against the status quo and involvement in responsive action to solve problems and failures in the world of society. It finally acknowledges the reality of incomplete and situated knowledge, that is, their epistemic insufficiency regarding wicked problems in pursuing sustainable entrepreneurial business opportunities.[6]

From a virtue ethics perspective, action competence can be conceptualized as the practical wisdom to apply the virtues needed for CSR in a particular situation to realize sustainability, followed by appropriate action. This competency enables the manager to engage in the second, fourth, and sixth dimensions of our philosophy of management, that is, responsive action, politico-economic governance, and epistemic insufficient entrepreneurship. This virtuous conceptualization of action competence fosters a more open-ended approach to the ethical management of the grand challenges in which the complexity, unstability, and situatedness of ethical judgements are taken into account (Almers, 2013).

On the one hand, action competence implies that managers are critical about the one-to-one application of principles and norms. They, for example, do not embrace norms like "organic" or "non-GMO" *a priori*, but, as Ellis and Weekes (2008) suggest, should be actively engaged in sustainability problems through independent thinking and their practical wisdom. This holds true for managers who like to challenge established ways of working in a firm and are able to explore new and more sustainable ways of working (Mogensen and Schnack, 2010). This ability to pioneer in order to find new ways to integrate sustainable business practices based on personal engagement with sustainable development is also confirmed in the literature (Osagie et al., 2016).

On the other hand, to overcome weakness of will (*akrasia*) action competence needs a certain kind of moral education and practice. This means that action competence primarily concerns the moral emancipation or transformation from a passive attitude with regard to CSR towards an active, engaged, and virtuous attitude, in which the manager involved in sustainability feels responsible for CSR (Mogensen and Schnack, 2010; Ellis and Weekes, 2008). A virtue ethics perspective helps to understand this moral emancipation (action competence) as the transformation towards a virtuous manager by his or her personal engagement in the production of sustainable internal goods. By engaging oneself in corporate sustainable behaviour (action competence), the manager is personally involved in his or her perfection of the good life (Jensen and Schnack, 1997). At the same time, this perfection of the good life presupposes competence, such as the competence to challenge established ways of working, change the status quo of CSR, explore new and more sustainable ways of working, deal with resistance in his or her application of virtues according to practical wisdom, etc. In this respect, action competence can be understood as a virtuous competence as well.

This does not mean that action competence is a purely subjective conceptualization of sustainable action. On the one hand, because virtues are not available without context and have to be developed in practice, that is, in a context and in interaction with other stakeholders, the determination of the good is not an individual effort but is always responsive to and takes place in collaboration with stakeholders (Moore, 2005). On the other hand, these virtues are based on an account of our human nature. They help us to live well as the kind of beings that we are, and form in the end the normative basis for the social responsibility of our daily practices. The good life can be seen as a normative basis for the normative competence, which includes the ability to identify, apply, and reconcile virtues that enable managers to engage in CSR with regard to sustainable development. In turn, action competency concerns the ability to put these virtues into practice by the personal engagement of the management in the application of these virtues according to their practical wisdom, and together with multiple stakeholders. This aspect of action competence enables the manager to engage in the fifth dimension of our philosophy of management.

As a consequence, the development of good character of the ethical manager is stressed. Managers need the courage to change the status quo of corporate business behaviour and to deal with resistance in their effort to align CSR with his or her personal ideals regarding sustainability. Anyone exercising action competence will judge ethical issues independently and according to their practical wisdom and act accordingly. They are always looking for opportunities to improve the social-ecological efficiency and/or effectivity of systems and they know-how to seize these opportunities in the context of management practice (Osagie et al., 2019; Wesselink et al., 2015).

And here we find an indication regarding the connection between both the normativity and action related aspects of virtuous competence. We defined the normative dimension of virtuous competence as the ability to identify, apply, and reconcile virtues in the production of sustainable internal goods (corporate social responsible behaviour), which is embedded in the good character of the manager. Normative competence enables the business manager to identify the problems or failures in the world based on ethical norms and values. These norms and values define what is right and wrong and enable the business manager to assess problems or failures in the world and to address these problems responsibly. But virtuous competence remains an ideal which is difficult to achieve, if not impossible, because of competing desires, values, and norms. Because of these tensions, managers cannot a priori presume to have good character as the normative aspect of virtuous competence. They require the action-related aspect of virtuous competence in order to *morally engage* themselves in the moral transformation to and internalization of good character by the application of virtues according to

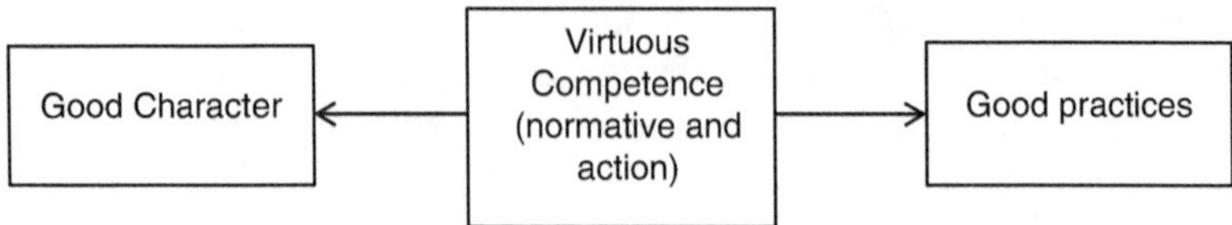

Figure 6.2 Relation between virtuous competence, good character, and good practices.

practical wisdom. This moral engagement enforces one to do the right thing. The action dimension of virtuous competence enables the business manager to end the status quo and to *take* responsibility to address the failure in the world of society. This moral force is not something *given* but is *enforced* by the internalization of the production of social responsible internal goods, that is, by his or her perfection of the good life (which can never be achieved completely). Overall, virtuous competence here is defined as the personal engagement of a manager in the transformation to good character by applying virtues in the production of social responsible internal goods in collaboration with and in response to multiple stakeholders, and by perfecting his or her good character by the internalization of the production of these internal goods (Figure 6.2).

Virtuous Competence for Responsible Business Practices

In this section, we raised the question of how two moral competencies have to be understood and how they are related to each other. After discussing sustainability as a wicked problem, the role of CSR with regard to sustainable development and the genesis of organizational competencies for dealing with CSR, we focussed on competencies at an individual level. It turned out that the holistic approach to competence best fits the wickedness of the grand challenge of global warming, in which the dimension of knowledge, skills, and attitudes on the one hand and their application in relevant practical situations on the other are integrated. A manager is expected to have specific individual competencies which are deployed within the complex and dynamic context of management practices, and this enables him or her to enhance and secure CSR with regard to sustainable development in an effective way.

Subsequently, we reflected on the normativity involved in the concept of sustainability in order to apply, negotiate and reconcile norms and principles based on the judgments of multiple stakeholders. We understood action competence as the moral transformation from a passive attitude with regard to CSR concerning sustainable development towards an active and engaged attitude by the application of these norms in complex situations, in which the manager feels responsible.

Finally, we introduced a virtue ethics perspective on both normative competence and action competence. The advantage of virtue ethics is that it acknowledges the complexity, unstability, and situatedness of corporate decision-making processes in wicked problems like global warming and stresses the necessity to develop virtues in combination with practical wisdom to perform corporate responsible behaviour. We linked both concepts by stressing, first, that both virtue and competence concern the character of a person *and* their application in practice, and second, that the application of virtues in practice presupposes some competence; all virtues must have some competence to put good character into practice. It turned out that in case of grand challenges like global warming, virtues play a central role in competent task-fulfilment.

The virtue ethics perspective enabled us to conceptualize normative competence and action competence as virtuous competences for ethical business practices. The normative aspect of virtuous competence can be defined as the ability to identify, develop, and generate virtues that solve ethical issues together with multiple stakeholders and constitute the good character of the manager as a normative basis for decision-making processes. The action related aspect of virtuous competence is defined as the competence to engage oneself in ethical business practices in which the transformation to good character is initiated, enhanced, and secured by applying virtues in the production of responsible internal goods – CSR – in collaboration with multiple stakeholders, which is embedded in the good character of the manager.

Because virtuous competence remains an ideal which is difficult to achieve, the manager cannot a priori assume being a virtuous manager (normative aspect of virtuous competence) but needs the action-related aspect of virtuous competence to morally engage him- or herself in the transformation to and internalization of good character (action-related aspect of virtuous competence). The relation between the two aspects of virtuous competence consists in the fact that they are two mutually dependent aspects of one virtuous competence. These mutually dependent aspects of virtuous competence are represented in the following definition of virtuous competence for corporate sustainability:

> Virtuous competence is the personal engagement of a manager in the transformation to good character by applying virtues in the production of responsible internal goods together with multiple stakeholders (CSR), and by perfecting his or her good character by the internalization of the production of these responsible internal goods. (Figure 6.2)

It is this individual virtuous competence that enables the business manager to engage in the business ethical practices that we explored in Section 20.

22 Institutionalizing Business Ethics: Performative Corporate Codes

Business ethical practices are not only dependent on the individual virtuous competencies of managers. They are also dependent on the institutionalization of ethics practices in the governance of the business operations. Therefore, we finally ask for concrete governance structures that secure and enhance business ethical practices. Codes of conduct or codes of ethics can be seen as a way to operationalize business ethics within firms. A code of conduct is a set of principles and rules providing a formal framework of responsibilities and proper actions for an individual or a firm. They prescribe or proscribe employee or manager behaviour. Codes of ethics prescribe and proscribe manager behaviour too, although in a different way. They do not concern specific instructions or rules concerning employee or manager behaviour but encourage them to perform ethical characteristics like loyalty, honesty, and integrity. Although there are many differences between codes of conduct and codes of ethics, they can be seen as the terms and conditions of the license to operate of firms: "By adopting its own code, a company can clarify for all parties, internal and external, the standards that govern its conduct and can thereby convey its commitment to responsible practice wherever it operates" (Paine et al., 2005). Nowadays, corporate codes are increasingly seen as successful instruments to increase corporate responsible behaviour and responsible manager behaviour within these firms (Andersen and Skjoett-Larsen, 2009; Mamic, 2005).

Despite their popularity, the adoption of corporate codes does not necessarily lead to more corporate responsible behaviour. Just as corporate codes accepted by over 80% of the publicly traded firms in the US could not prevent the financial crisis (Desjardins, 2011), neither does the adoption of corporate codes automatically accomplish more responsible or accountable behaviour of business managers. This is called the attitude-behaviour gap (O'Driscoll et al., 2013). From a normative ethical perspective, one can argue that corporate codes can undermine individual ethical responsibility and therefore prevent actual responsible behaviour by managers (Section 20). From a descriptive ethical perspective, one can argue that there is only a weak link between corporate codes and CSR (Mathews, 1988; Stevens, 1994; Cassell et al., 1997; Schwartz, 2002; Pater and van Gils, 2003). Some scholars even draw the cynical conclusion that "codes, like laws, tend to keep the honest persons honest and have little impact on those who chose to ignore their precepts or who have never been exposed to their tenets" (Lee and Berleur, 1994).

From a management perspective, one can point to the drawbacks of most corporate codes; they are often vaguely defined, incomplete, not implemented, not independently monitored and/or subject to personal bias of senior managers (Bondy et al., 2007; Dunphy et al., 2007).

Another difficulty concerns the alignment of different codes within networks or supply chains, especially in fields with conflicting interests (Nijhof et al., 2008; Boatright, 2008). Finally, one can point to the minor role of codes compared with the organizational context and culture within which (un)ethical behaviour takes place (Cassell et al., 1997). We are therefore not only in need of a theory of corporate codes that actually enhances and secures actual CSR, but also one that enables the integration of other organizational factors.

In this section, we philosophically reflect on the nature of corporate codes in order to build a new theory of corporate codes that explains (a) why codes often fail to enhance corporate responsible behaviour, (b) how codes can enhance actual CSR, and (c) which other organizational factors can increase the effectivity of corporate codes.[7] Such a concept of codes of conduct can inform the institutionalization of ethical governance of the business operations, which enables the business manager to engage in business ethical practices.

Although many articles have been written which centre on their content and drawbacks in management practice, little work has been done on the nature of codes itself. Contrary to universalist – that is, formal rules and procedures based – conceptualizations of corporate codes, which are already criticized in chapters 3 and 4, and contrary to instrumental conceptualizations, in which corporate codes are instrumental to corporate reputation and strategic competitive advantage, this section hypothesizes that codes have to be understood as performative speech acts, that is, as sentences which do not primarily describe a state of affairs but *do* or *perform* something. A well-known example is the performative sentence: "I name this ship the *Queen Elisabeth*". This sentence does not describe a state of affairs – the name of the ship – but uttered in an appropriate context, this sentence performs the naming of the ship. Based on John Austin's speech act theory, corporate codes will be conceptualized as performative speech acts in this section, in which the behavioural aspect of corporate codes is stressed. A performative concept of corporate codes is characterized by (1) the existential self-performative of the firm identity; (2) this self-performative code is demanded by and responsive to the stakeholders of the firm; (3) because corporate codes are structurally threatened by the possibility of infelicity or failure; (4) a firm's embracing of corporate codes does not only consist in CSR in light of the code, but also in the incessant recapturing of the code in the struggle of firms against the possible incongruence between their ethical principles and their actual responsible behaviour.

In the next subsection, the analysis starts with an introduction of Austin's concept of the performative. Four main characteristics of the performative will be distinguished, which will be applied to the concept of corporate codes in the subsequent subsection. With this, it will become clear how a performative concept of corporate codes, contrary to universalist and instrumentalist conceptualizations, has to be understood. Finally, it will be explored how the first two characteristics of a performative concept of corporate codes enhance CSR, and how the third and fourth characteristic *secure* corporate responsible behaviour. By discussing the advantages of a performative concept of corporate codes, compared with universalist and instrumentalist conceptualizations, it will become clear that a performative concept of corporate codes institutionalize business ethical practices in such a way that they enable the business manager to engage in business ethical practices because the performative involves action and behaviour. At the same time, it will become clear that the effective adoption of a performative concept of corporate codes involves a radical shift of our conceptualizations of the nature, function, and limitation of codes.

John Austin and the Speech Act Theory

The philosopher and founding father of the general theory of speech acts, John Austin, introduced a distinction between two types of sentences, namely constative and performative sentences.[8] His speech act theory explains the ability of language to do other things with words than providing a mere description of reality.

In a constative sentence, a state of affairs is described, asserting that something is the case. The constative sentence – for example, "John and Mary are married" – asserts that John and Marry actually are married. While the primary function of the constative sentence is *to say something* and describe a state of affairs, the performative sentence is primarily a vehicle *to do something* and create something new (Austin, 1961). If someone utters the sentence, "I pronounce you man and wife", he or she definitely does not want to describe the marriage ceremony. With this sentence, he or she actually *performs* the marriage. And when John says, "I do", he is not describing his marriage but he is *indulging* in it.

Originally, Austin thought that the descriptive and performative functions of sentences were mutually exclusive (Austin, 1962). In order to distinguish accordingly between constative and performative sentences, he first of all claimed that constative sentences primarily say something while performative sentences *do* something; the uttering of a performative is, or is part of, the performance of a certain kind of action (Austin, 1962). Austin's second claim was that contrary to constative sentences, performatives cannot claim to be true or false. Constative sentences assert that something is the case and the correctness of these sentences can be tested by assessing whether what is said corresponds with what the world is like. This is impossible in case of performative sentences like, "I name this ship the *Queen Elisabeth*" or "I do". These sentences do not primarily say something but create something new; the ship as Queen Elisabeth, John as a married man. If this last sentence is uttered alone at home or in a context where no registrar is present, the sentence "I do" isn't *false* but disabled, unsatisfactory or inappropriate. Such infelicities, as they are called by Austin, arise if simple rules are broken. For instance, the sentence "I do" only makes sense if the very procedure for marrying actually exists and is accepted by both partners. An infelicity occurs too if the circumstances in which the sentence "I do" is uttered are inappropriate. Uttered alone at home or in a context where not the registrar but the cleaner is present, the act of marrying would not come off. There are also other ways in which infelicities can arise. Performatives like "I do" presuppose certain feelings or intentions with regard to my future wife.[9] If a person says "I do" without these feelings and intentions, he or she is insincere. It is not the case that the person did not actually marry his or her wife, but that he or she married her in an insincere way (Austin, 1961). Although this list of infelicities is not complete and in fact endless according to Austin, it becomes clear that performatives are not truth-evaluable but may be infelicitous.

The third distinction between constatives and performatives is that the latter are normally stated in the first person singular present indicative active; "I do ...", "I name ...", "I bet ...". For Austin, the first person verb differs importantly from the use of other persons and other tenses in constative sentences: "For when we say 'I promise that ...' we do perform an act of promising – we give a promise. What we do *not* do is to report on somebody's performing an act of promising" (Austin, 1961: 242). The third characteristic of the performative is that it is stated in the first person singular and therefore, that the person who performs the speech act is actually *involved* in the performative.

Austin's distinction between constatives and performatives can shed some light on the discussion of oaths and codes on the one hand, and the weak link between corporate codes and actual corporate responsible behaviour on the other. While ethical oaths and codes are normally lumped together as "forms of ethical statements implying a moral imperative" (*Encyclopaedia of Bioethics*, cited in Sulmasy, 1999), Daniel Sulmasy used the distinction between constatives and performatives to distinguish between ethical oaths and codes.

A corporate code can be seen as a written set of rules and regulations that harmonize and standardize employee and management behaviour in order to minimize the risk of misconduct. In the classical view, these rules prescribe ethical behaviour. According to Sulmasy, codes are lists of moral do's and don'ts which are not stated in the first person singular, but in the second or third person. Based on this distinction, Sulmasy distinguishes between codes and oaths, because oaths are performative utterances in which the personhood of the swearer is involved in his or her commitment in future intentions, while codes are not (Sulmasy, 1999).

This distinction is interesting because the constative nature of codes could explain the weak link between corporate codes and actual responsible behaviour of corporations. On the one hand, the increased use of corporate codes does not help because of the constative nature of all codes; the adoption of such codes does not afford a firm directly to *do* something, that is, to accomplish more responsible behaviour. On the other hand, if a professional oath can be understood as a performative oath, then the oath could be seen as a possible solution, which is often signalled in the ethical literature (Sulmasy, 1999; Blok, 2013; de Bruin, 2014); because of the performative nature of ethical oaths, a performative ethical oath would *imply* ethical behaviour and therefore, would be able to bridge the gap between the ethical principles the manager has and their ethical behaviour according to these principles. Is it therefore reasonable to reject at least the primacy of corporate codes in favour of ethical oaths in business?

Unfortunately, the issue at stake is not that simple, that constative codes and performative oaths can easily be distinguished and that one can argue for the latter like Sulmasy seems to claim. First of all, the classical view of corporate codes as rules which prescribe or proscribe behaviour can be criticized. John Dienhart for instance has convincingly shown that codes are rarely sets of rules:

> Many ethical codes begin by citing broad ethical concerns which help define how the profession promotes individual and social welfare. These goals are intended to guide professionals in their interpretation of the rest of the code and to help them make decisions in areas not specifically covered by the code. (Dienhart, 1995: 427–428)

A code is not a set of rules or do's and don'ts but gives guidance and acts as a reference point for managers facing complex ethical questions.

Secondly, the strict distinction between constative and performative sentences can be criticized, as Austin himself already did. With regard to the performance of the performative, he gives various examples of performative sentences with no clear performance; the sentence "I am sorry" can be understood as a performative – just like "I apologize" – but also like the description of one's feelings for instance (Austin, 1961). Furthermore, in constative sentences like "I state that …", a similar act is performed as in performative sentences like "I promise to …". With regard to the non-truth-evaluableness of performatives, Austin states that a performative like a warning, although it cannot claim to be true or false, is in fact comparable with the facts. It is for instance possible to assess whether the warning was in order (Austin, 1961). Also, the third distinction – performatives are stated in the first person singular – has to be rejected because a performative can also be stated in the passive form:

"You are hereby authorized ...". And when a person says, "I order you to shut the door", the sentence is stated in the first person singular and not truth-evaluable, but he or she could perform exactly the same act by the imperative "shut the door" (Austin, 1961). In this respect, the problem of codes, that is, that there is only a weak link between corporate codes and actual responsible behaviour of corporations, cannot be attributed to a strict distinction between constative and performative sentences (contra Sulmasy). And if codes can be conceived as performatives, then performative codes can be seen as a possible solution of the gap between ethical principles, understood as locutionary acts, and actual responsible behaviour according to these principles, understood as illocutionary and perlocutionary acts.

Austin concludes that

> stating something is performing an act just as much as is giving an order or giving a warning; and we see, on the other hand, that, when we give an order or a warning or a piece of advice, there is a question about how this is related to fact which is not perhaps so very different from the kind of question that arises when we discuss how a statement is related to fact. (Austin, 1961: 251)

This general performativity of language is confirmed by social scientists who showed how the language of economics and business does not only explain reality but also *shapes* the reality of institutional designs, management practices, and social norms, thereby performing an act by the *creation* of corresponding behaviour (Ferraro et al., 2005).

Because Austin saw already in an early stage that a strict distinction between constative and performative sentences is not possible, he later developed a new theory about the speech act of all types of utterances; the locutionary, illocutionary, and perlocutionary force of sentences.

The locutionary act of a sentence is the act of "saying something" in a meaningful and grammatically correct way (Austin, 1962: 94); the locutionary act of stating, "I like management" for instance. The illocutionary act of a sentence corresponds with the performative; it concerns the *act* of asserting, questioning, promising, etc. in a linguistic utterance. The speech act of uttering a sentence (locutionary act) can have the form of a question or promise, that is, the performative or illocutionary force of questioning or promising. But the performance of an illocutionary act does not only require the act of a promise or warning by the speaker, but also the "securing of uptake" (Austin, 1962) by the one who perceives or hears the sentence; an illocutionary act like "shut the door" will result, if understood correctly, in someone closing the door. The perlocutionary act concerns this result of the speech act in the hearer as a result of the speech act; closing the window as a result of the speech act "close the window" for instance. The locutionary act of uttering a sentence about the presence of a door which is open, performs the illocutionary act of requesting someone to close the door, and the perlocutionary act of causing somebody to close the door.

With this, the fourth characteristic of the performative occurs.[10] The performative or illocutionary force of a speech act requires that it is *understood* by the hearer; the performativity of a code requires that both the manager representing the firm and the customer of the firm are aware of and understand the code, that is, the performative involves the "securing of uptake". Furthermore, the performative or illocutionary force of a speech act calls for "conventional consequences" of the performative, that is, the performative involves rights, commitments, or obligations related to it (Austin, 1962).

In the next subsection, the four characteristics of the performative which are distinguished in this section are applied – (1) the involvement of action and behaviour, including consequences of the performative like rights and obligations; (2) the possibility of infelicity; (3) the self-involvement in the performative; (4) the securing of uptake – to the concept of corporate codes.

Characteristics of a Performative Concept of Corporate Codes

In the previous section, codes were defined as a set of guiding principles and underlying assumptions which act as a corporate reference point for employees and managers facing complex ethical questions. These codes may include specific measures (i.e. rules) to ensure ethical behaviour, but these rules are embedded in guiding ethical principles. Does the concept of the performative enable us to characterize and understand the nature of corporate codes?

In a famous article on the quest for a code of professional ethics, John Ladd has criticized the connection between ethical principles and codes, because "ethics is basically an open-ended, reflective and critical intellectual activity" which cannot be reduced to rules specifying concrete behaviour (Ladd, 1985: 8; Dienhart, 1995). According to Ladd, codes violate the fundamental ethical principle of *autonomy*: "Ethics must, by its very nature, be self-directed rather than other-directed" (Ladd, 1985: 8). While corporate codes require loyal adherence by managers and result in routinized compliance (Fisher, 2001), Ladd emphasizes the *autonomy* of ethics, that is, the fact that ethical principles are *self-imposed*. We encountered this criticism of routinized compliance already in terms of bureaucratic control in the previous chapters. On the one hand, our concept of management as politico-economic governance moved already beyond the dichotomy between self-imposed and other-imposed principles by the introduction of open norms and principles to which the business manager is primarily responsive (Section 13). On the other hand, the idea of self-imposed ethics resonates with the second dimension of our philosophy of management, that is, management as resistance and responsive action which is existentially embedded in the disposition or *ethos* of the manager (Section 9).

In this section, we follow another strategy. The opposition between ethical principles (self-imposed) and corporate codes (other-imposed) may be lifted if we acknowledge that corporate codes have to be understood as performative speech acts. Considering the self-imposedness of ethical principles, a comparable self-imposedness can be recognized in the performative; self-involvement is characteristic of the performative and therefore a conceptualization of corporate codes as performative speech acts can lift the opposition between self- versus other-imposedness in case of CSR. The self-involvement in the performative provides the first characteristic of a performative concept of corporate codes.

The *self*-involvement in the performative concept of corporate codes shows that acting in accordance with the code not only involves the commitment of a manager towards a future course of action, but primarily involves his or her identity as a person. If a manager for instance *proclaims* professional behaviour according to corporate ethical principles and virtues like loyalty and honesty, he or she not only *intends* to be honest but primarily to be the one who is loyal and honest. In other words, the proclamation of a corporate code cannot be understood instrumentally as a way to punish or reward managerial behaviour but is primarily a *self*-performative of the one this manager wants to be; loyal for instance. This means that the self-performative primarily *articulates* the identity of a manager, which then has consequences for his or her lifestyle, attitude and behaviour towards others. As a loyal and honest man, a professional intends for instance not to betray his or her client and to act in his or her best interest. The self-performative character of codes of conduct shows therefore that they entail an existential moment, in which it is decided what type of person the manager or employee wants to be; it concerns the *identity* as a manager and as a consequence his or her practical commitment, attitudes, and feelings. This idea also resonates with the first dimension of our philosophy of management, that is, management as participation in the primary process ensures that the moral intentions are *real* (Section 8). Therefore, the conceptualization of corporate codes as performative speech acts not only involves the self-imposed *intention* of a person to *do* something, but to *be* the one who is committed to some future course of action and is acting accordingly. The first characteristic of a performative concept of corporate codes is, therefore, that it is an existential self-performative in which a person becomes the manager he or she is expected to want to be.

The self-performative character of corporate codes raises the question of who is the "self" in such a performative concept of codes. The first characteristic of the performative concept of corporate codes seems to be formulated from the perspective of the individual manager, while the corporate level of the code is neglected. In this study, however, a concept of corporate codes is adopted that acknowledges both the institutional level and the individual level of responsibility. On the one hand, codes *condition* and restrain individual management behaviour within firms. On the other hand, it is only through actual management behaviour within firms, that firms acquire the capabilities to apply and enact corporate codes in their business operations. It is through the dynamic interaction between managers and the firm that responsible or accountable behaviour of individual managers and firms is mutually enhanced (Constantinescu and Kaptein, 2014; see the next subsection for this dynamic interaction). For this reason, the first characteristic of a performative concept of corporate codes has to be conceived both at the individual and corporate level.

Corporate identity can be defined as the shared perceptions of the firm's central, distinctive, and enduring qualities by the organizational members (employees and managers), which are embedded in the mission statement and the core values of the firm (Brickson, 2007). The self-involvement in the performative concept of corporate codes does not only concern the identity of the individual manager, but also the corporate identity; the *self*-involvement in corporate codes shows that the promulgation of corporate codes involves the corporate identity, mission statements, and core values of the firm and that this identity is articulated by the first-person perspective of the self-performative code.

The self-performative character of corporate codes raises the further question of whether they have to be taken as subjective or even self-interested norms without universal validity. One of the fiercest criticisms of corporate codes is that there is no universally accepted set of ethical principles (Section 7), and that no one has the moral superiority to impose ethical principles on others. Also, in case of the conceptualization of corporate codes as performative speech acts, the universal validity of ethical principles seems to be abandoned in favour of the self-performative of the identity of the firm that embraces the code. However, although it became clear that codes cannot be understood as universal rules in the previous subsection, and although the firm is *involved* in the self-performative code, the meaning of the performative is not, or at least not completely, dependent on their mission statements and core values. Why?

First of all, Robert Baker has shown that codes develop and grow in response to historical experiences within a profession or firm. Based on historical material, he has shown that ethical codes evolve through three stages: initially conduct is regulated by traditions of practice, which are formalized and rationalized in the second stage by the development of corporate codes.

While adherence to these codes is personal and voluntary in the second stage, they take on an authoritative status in the third stage, capable of enforcing certain behaviour (Baker, 2005). Corporate codes are not universal rules but have to be applied in an ever-changing environment and for this reason, firms revise and adapt their codes and standards continuously (Dienhart, 1995). In this respect, the discussion about the desirability of ethical codes in the banking sector can be understood as a response to the historical experience of the financial crisis, just like the tightening of corporate codes may be the result of stakeholder dialogue of a bank about the ethical acceptability of investments in the weapon industry.

This historical evolvement of corporate codes shows clearly that they:

> develop incrementally, out of disparate precursor documents that were formulated for a variety of purposes as a field grappled with various issues and decided, one-by-one, how best to deal with them. By aggregating these statements of conduct into a single document that strives for a measure of universality and consistency, codifiers help a field to articulate the vision implicit in the standards that a field has already set for itself, so that this vision can be better understood and appreciated by its membership and by the world at large. (Baker, 2005: 34–35)

When a firm promulgates a corporate code, the meaning of this code is not primarily or not only dependent on its intentions with it; it is rather embedded in broader ethical concerns regarding the moral responsibility of firms in society, which are historically determined. Indeed, if a firm embraces a corporate code, it even gets extra weight when it cites such historically determined concerns; by embracing the code of conduct of the Financial Service Council (FSC) for instance, a firm places itself in a tradition of the industry in which their business operations are embedded. This historical embeddedness of corporate codes shows that their meaning is not, or at least not completely, dependent on the intentions or the interests of the firm that embraces them.[11]

A second reason why the conceptualization of corporate codes as performative speech acts is not completely dependent on the intentions and interests of the firm comes up if the securing of uptake, that is, the fourth characteristic of the performative, is considered. Corporate codes operate in a context of stakeholders, in which it has to be *understood* by the stakeholders of the firm. A code which is not stated in a conceivable language is not a code at all (Austin, 1962: 22). The performativity of the corporate code does not only consist in its being understood by the public context of stakeholders but also in its being uttered *for* these stakeholders to enhance and secure actual corporate responsible behaviour.

A firm normally has much more market information than its customers. The firm is therefore able to maximize its own interests at the expense of customers or other stakeholders. Customers therefore face an adverse selection problem, since they are unable to distinguish between self-interested firms and firms that will work in the best interest of their customers (Beneish and Chatov, 1993: 3; Dienhart, 1995: 443). The public character of corporate codes – materialized in publicly available and external audited annual CSR reports for instance – can help to decrease the risk of self-interest, because it enables the public examination of their effectivity by the stakeholders; the external auditors but also the general public are public witnesses of the corporate codes.

The performativity of the code is therefore dependent on the securing of uptake by the stakeholders of the firm, and this prevents a subjective conception of corporate codes. A firm can never completely control the way the self-performative code is perceived by others. Rather, the history of corporate codes can be seen as an incremental development in response to the ever-changing environment (technological, cultural, geographical, etc.).

The securing of uptake provides the second characteristic of a performative concept of corporate codes. The meaning of the self-performative code (first characteristic of a performative concept of corporate codes) is not only dependent on the intentions (mission statements and core values) of the firm but is determined by the public context (securing of uptake) and is articulated in the interaction with these stakeholders. This public context is never completely determinable; in-congruency between the corporate code and actual behaviour is always possible since codes are not univocal and unambiguous and can always miss their mark; codes are often stated in general terms – integrity, honesty but also "the best interest of the customer" for instance – which cover several situations and can raise various expectations. In this respect, the self-performative of the identity, mission statements, and core values of the firm are not only *determined* by the public context, but this public context always *transcends* the firm that embraces a corporate code.

From the perspective of stakeholder theory, the self-performative code can be seen as *demanded* by the stakeholders of the firm (Freeman, 1984). External stakeholders like customers, suppliers, and, in the end, society at large, can not only hold firms to the normative commitments which are stated in the self-performative code. Firms are also responsive to the demands of stakeholders because they represent the societies in which these firms operate. An example is the Dutch Rabobank, an international cooperative bank in the agri-food sector that explicitly tries to be responsive to a broad range of social and non-market demands by their stakeholders. Because the bank is held responsible for unsustainable behaviour of their clients (bad labour conditions, corruption, environmental pollution, etc.), they are expected not to be involved in unsustainable business practices like land grabbing and squeezing smallholders and expected to (financially) contribute to the development of food- and illiteracy programs. To this end, they apply a set of ethical principles and corporate codes to manage their operations responsibly and sustainably (Blok et al., 2013). The self-performative of the corporate identity, mission statements, and core values of the firm (first characteristic of a performative concept of corporate codes) is therefore not only *determined* by their stakeholders (securing of uptake) but also *demanded* by these stakeholders. This idea of the responsiveness of managers to the needs and concerns of stakeholders resonates with the fifth dimension of our philosophy of management. The responsiveness of a firm to these stakeholders enhances and secures its actual corporate responsible behaviour: in their utterance of a self-performative code in front of their stakeholders, firms become the one who is responsive to the demands of their stakeholders and the stakeholders become the one to which these firms are responsive in their corporate code.

This demand does not mean, however, that the success of the corporate code is guaranteed. The performative is not truth-evaluable, as we have seen. An example is the previously mentioned Rabobank that was recently involved in the manipulation of libor interest rates, notwithstanding their broad set of ethical principles and corporate codes.

According to Austin, such infelicities occur when any one of six general rules is broken. These general rules are as follows:

1.   The existence of an accepted procedure, like the procedure at a firm that new employees have to sign the code and/or that all employees have to sign the code every year again, year after year.
2.   The circumstances should be appropriate for the invocation of the procedures involved, for instance, a yearly day of reflection at which all employees discuss the values and norms of the firm, followed by a ceremony in which employees sign the code.
3.   The procedures must be executed correctly.
4.   The procedures must be executed completely, for instance, the correct and complete text of a medical oath.
5.   Congruency must exist between the intentions presupposed by the performative code and the actual intentions of the firm, for instance, the intention to respect fair labour conditions and prevent child labour worldwide.
6.   Congruency between the intentions presupposed by the performative code and actual corporate behaviour, for instance, advising customers in their best interest.

The possibility of the infelicity of the performative shows the third characteristic of a performative concept of corporate codes. Are these rules conceivable as indispensable (although insufficient) conditions for the success of the performative in general and the performative concept of corporate codes in particular? Conditions (a)–(d) can be understood as conditions of the public context in which corporate codes are promulgated and accepted by stakeholders of the firm. Conditions (e) and (f) can guarantee corporate responsible behaviour because they enforce congruency between corporate ethical intentions and actual responsible behaviour of the firm. If this is the case, it can be claimed that a self-performative code, which meets these six conditions or rules, is able to guarantee CSR. The self-performative code then implies corporate responsible behaviour and the six conditions guarantee the congruency between the corporate code and corporate responsible behaviour in general and the trustworthiness and integrity of corporate behaviour in particular.

Nevertheless, Austin is quite ambiguous in his assessment of these conditions, as Jacques Derrida has pointed out (Derrida, 1982). On the one hand, he seems to admit that the possibility of infelicity is a structural characteristic of the performative, which can never be avoided completely (Austin, 1962). On the other hand, this structural risk of failure is not seen as an essential characteristic of the performative, but as "an accidental, exterior one that teaches us nothing about the language phenomenon under consideration" (Derrida, 1982: 323–324). Austin hopes to avoid the structural risk of failure of the performative by invoking the use of "ordinary language" and "ordinary circumstances" (Austin, 1962). But if the possibility of infelicity is a structural possibility of a performative utterance, the possibility of infelicity is *always* there. And if the possibility of infelicity is granted, the risk of failure is not an accident but a structural condition of any corporate code.[12] This acknowledgement of the structural role of risk and failure resonates with the sixth dimension of our philosophy of management, that is, management as epistemic insufficient entrepreneurship.

Here, the structural possibility of infelicity is taken as the third characteristic of corporate codes. It explains how corporate codes can enhance and secure CSR (i.e. actual ethical performance), for instance, by following the six general rules, but also why codes sometimes fail to enhance CSR. This is not or not primarily because the moral impulse of the manager is neglected and instrumentalized in corporate codes, but because of the structural possibility of infelicity of every code.

Is it necessary to draw such a negative conclusion about the fallibility of corporate codes? Various authors have pointed to these fundamental risks of failure of corporate codes (Dienhart, 1995; Mathews, 1988). This infelicity is obvious in the case of a banker who claims to act in the best interest of his or her customers but manipulates interest rates; he or she is faking or cheating and performs therefore an infelicity. But a firm may also fail notwithstanding its good intentions, for instance in case of unintended negative environmental or social impacts of innovative products and services. The normal response to such negative impacts is to develop governance structures like corporate codes, but the problem with these governance mechanisms is that they are retrospective and are less suitable to deal with highly uncertain and dynamic innovation processes (Owen et al., 2013). This means that the code is always fallible and open for reassessment.

However, the fallibility does not have to be conceived merely at an individual level of professionals and top managers within firms. George DeMartino has pointed to the epistemic insufficiency of professionals with regard to complex fields of study like economics (DeMartino, 2011). Their *knowledge* of economic interventions to improve economic development is not only limited, but it is acknowledged that all economic theories are insufficient (Hoffmann, 1999). The economic crisis made clear that economics is a highly complex field of study and that the consequences of economic policies are unpredictable. In other words, the available knowledge is principally insufficient to predict the future and there will always be unintended consequences of economic interventions which can be harmful (DeMartino, 2011). A comparable situation of "imperfect foresight" is at stake in case of complex and uncertain innovations, and may have unintended negative impacts in the future. In an ever-changing environment, one could argue, the possibility of infelicity is *structural*. This structurality of the possibility of infelicity does not imply that a firm cannot claim anymore to act in a responsible way. According to Derrida, this *undecidability* of ethical decisions makes firms and their employees primarily aware of the fundamental uncertainty or imperfect foresight in ethical decision-making processes as we have seen, which unsettles any kind of self-assurance in corporate ethical behaviour (Painter-Morland, 2010).

Negatively speaking, this leads to a relativistic position that suggests that the trustworthiness and integrity of all corporate codes can be questioned because of their structural infelicity; they have no universal validity nor are they necessary. At the same time, this infelicity can be taken in a positive way: the history of corporate codes can be seen as a history of their infelicity, which inspired the incremental development of these codes in response to the ever-changing environment. In this respect, there is no difference between the adjustments of medical oaths because of new legislation with regard to abortion, for instance, the reinforcement of corporate codes in economics and business in response to the economic crisis, and the development of new corporate codes in fields where high negative impacts may be expected in the future, like in case of industrial use of nanotechnology and synthetic biology. The third characteristic of a performative concept of corporate codes is, therefore, that the six rules are an indispensable condition for the self-performative code – they act as a *guidance* which "reminds" firms and their managers of the ethical principles they embraced when they face complex ethical situations (Passmore, 1984) – although they are insufficient to guarantee ethical business practices; the conceptualization of corporate codes as performative speech acts acknowledges that they are structurally threatened by the possibility of failure. The acknowledgement of the structural possibility of failure resonates with the second dimension of our philosophy of management, that is, management as resistance and responsive action.

The question remains, however, whether such a positive assessment of the infelicity of corporate codes implies a relativistic position with regard to ethical issues or not. How can be distinguished between responsible and irresponsible behaviour, if all codes are characterized by this structural possibility of infelicity? Although the structural possibility of the infelicity of corporate codes cannot be denied (third characteristic of a performative concept of corporate codes), the performative provides a way to distinguish between responsible and irresponsible behaviour. To see this, a further reflection on the three characteristics of a performative concept of corporate codes is needed.

Corporate codes are first of all characterized by the self-performative of the corporate identity, mission statements, and core values of the firm. This self-performative code is demanded by the stakeholders and enhances and secures actual corporate responsible behaviour (second characteristic of a performative concept of corporate codes). The structural possibility of the infelicity of codes (third characteristic of a performative concept of corporate codes) made clear that the infelicity primarily concerns the identity and core values of the firm. Austin distinguished between two specific types of infelicity with regard to the identity of actors. The self-performative code is infelicitous if there is incongruency between the performative promulgation of a code by a firm and its actual intentions, that is, the actual mission and core values of the firm, or between these core values and its actual corporate behaviour.

Actual corporate behaviour is however not the result of the corporate code the firm has embraced because the self-performative of the identity, mission statements, and core values of the firm already *implies* and *is* some kind of action and has already behavioural consequences like rights and obligations; a corporate code is a code of *conduct*, that is, it implies already actual behaviour. This idea is confirmed by the debate on performativity in management research, in which performative praxis is seen as the main contributor in making theoretical constructs like codes a social reality (Cabantous and Gond, 2011).[13] To embrace a corporate code is to *declare* something about the firm's future actions and behaviour, but its actual commitment to the code only shows itself in its actual behaviour in accordance with the code in general and with the rights and obligations involved in particular. Because the performative already *involves* some kind of action, the production of the corporate identity by the self/performative code is already accompanied by a second production of the corporate identity as acting and living in light of the code. This idea resonates with the first dimension of our philosophy of management, which highlights participation in the primary process to ensure that moral intentions are real.

With regard to corporate responsible behaviour, there are two possibilities. Either the firm is able to live up to the self-performative code, or the firm fails because it is not able or even not willing to live up to it. The only touchstone the firm has is the question of whether the code is really able to determine and mark the corporate identity, mission statements, and core values of the firm and its corporate behaviour accordingly. This either ... or shows that the second production cannot be seen as an accident or mere result of the first production – the self-performative of the identity, mission statements, and core values of the firm – but is essential for corporate codes. Why? Because of the structural risk of infelicity or failure, a firm only lives up to the code by its actual corporate behaviour in light of the code; only by living and acting in light of the code does the self-performative of the code become *real*. This focus on actual responsible behaviour in business practices resonates with the sixth dimension of our philosophy of management, that is, management as epistemic insufficient entrepreneurship, which bears the *traces* of the world of society it operates in. These traces of the world of society enable stakeholders to *test* whether a firm that embraces a code of conduct actually lives up to these standards.

The testability of CSR, which is implied in the conceptualization of corporate codes as performative speech acts, can also shed some light on the content of the code. The content of the code has to be understood as the behavioural consequences – rights and obligations – of the corporate identity, mission statements, and core values of the firm.

The fourth characteristic of a performative concept of corporate codes is, therefore, that the self-performative is not restricted to the *intention* of firms to commit themselves to some future action, but involves their actual corporate behaviour according to these rights and obligations which are stated in the content of the code. Actual responsible behaviour according to the rights and obligations is the only touchstone the firm and its stakeholders have to distinguish between responsible and irresponsible corporate behaviour.

Is it legitimate to claim, then, that firms that are able to live up to the code by their corporate behaviour in light of the code, in fact perform more responsible behaviour? Because of the *structural* infelicity of every code, their actual living up to the code does not only consist in corporate behaviour in light of the code but also in the incessant appropriation and re-appropriation of the code in their struggle against its possible infelicity. The possible infelicity does not relieve the firm from ethical decision making and corporate responsible behaviour, but makes it aware that corporate responsible behaviour is inseparable from the question whether the firm actually made the right decision, whether its corporate codes are still appropriate and responsive to the demands of the stakeholders. Corporate responsibility does therefore not only consist in actual corporate behaviour according to the content of the code but also in putting its actual behaviour into question. The appropriation and re-appropriation of the corporate code by a firm does not intend to avoid the possibility of infelicity, as Austin's strategy does, but sees the possibility of infelicity precisely as a driver to performatively *produce* actual corporate behaviour in light of the code, that is, to produce corporate responsible behaviour.

Towards a Performative Concept of Corporate Codes in Business

We discussed four characteristics of a performative concept of corporate codes which constitute a theory of corporate codes that enhances and secures their engagement in corporate social responsible behaviour. A performative concept of corporate codes consists (1) in the self-performative of the corporate identity, mission statements, and core values of the firm; (2) this performative code is demanded by and re-sponsive to the stakeholders of the firm; (3) because of the structural possibility of infelicity of corporate codes; the (4) embracing of these codes does not only consist in actual corporate behaviour in light of the code by firms and their managers but also in the incessant recapturing of the code in their struggle against its possible infelicity.

Contrary to an instrumentalist conception of the nature of corporate codes, which conceptualizes codes as instruments to increase the corporate reputation and the strategic competitive advantage of the firm, the perfor-mative concept of corporate codes stresses the self-involvement of the cor-porate identity, mission statements, and core values of the firm in corporate responsible behaviour; the performative code is not only self-imposed in the sense that it involves the corporate *intentions* of firms to commit themselves to some future course of action but also in the sense that it involves the *identity* of the firm that is committed to corporate responsible behaviour. The advantage of the conceptualization of corporate codes as performative speech acts is that this existential moment of the performative is stressed.

The emphasis on this existential moment is particularly important if the criticism of universal ethical principles and norms that we developed in this study are taken into account. According to this criticism, there are no universally accepted principles or norms a firm can commit itself to; these ethical principles are in fact relative to cultural or social differences. But if corporate codes are conceptualized as performative speech acts, precisely this relativity of the code to the corporate identity, mission statements, and core values of the firm is emphasized. Not the universal validity of the content of the code is embraced in corporate codes – the history of corporate codes can be seen as an incremental development of codes in response to the ever-changing environment in general and the infelicity of existing codes in particular – but the existential decision of the firm to live and act in light of the code, here and now.

There is also another advantage of stressing the existential moment in the development and adoption of corporate codes. Based on the work of Hopwood, Cassell et al. (1997) have shown that the *internalization* of corporate codes by individual recipients of these codes will have a positive impact on their individual behaviour. In order to have a positive impact, these principles or norms should be "either directly or indirectly ... internalised by the members of the enterprise and operate as personal controls over attitudes and behaviour" (Hopwood, 1974: 31). The internalization of corporate codes is expected to have a positive impact on individual ethical behaviour of managers in light of the code.

With regard to the content of corporate codes, it is argued in the literature that it should be characterized by clarity, comprehensiveness, and enforceability to be effective (Raiborn and Payne, 1990). On the one hand, a clear and distinct formulation of the content of corporate codes could indeed prevent the ambiguity of their content and provide guidelines for managers within the firm on how to proceed in case of conflicts of interest for instance. On the other hand, the improvement of the clarity and comprehensiveness of its content does not prevent the possible infelicity of corporate codes. Contrary to legalistic or instrumental approaches of the content of corporate codes, in which the content is stated in terms of moral do's and don'ts, the advantage of a performative concept of corporate codes is that it shows the importance of *actual* corporate *behaviour* in light of the code and in accordance with the rights and obligations involved. This actual corporate responsible behaviour is already implied in the self-performative of the corporate identity. The conceptualization of corporate codes as performative speech acts enables therefore the rejection of the classical criticism that codes don't change actual behaviour – codes are too broadly formulated to guide people's behaviour – because the self-performative code already involves some kind of action and has already behavioural consequences like rights and obligations. Only by living and acting in light of the code is the performativity of the code real.

With this, we provide a theory of corporate codes that enables firms to enhance and secure corporate social responsible behaviour; the conceptualization of corporate codes as performative speech acts can enhance corporate social responsible behaviour because a performative code essentially involves action and behaviour. With this, it also becomes clear that a performative concept of corporate codes can bridge classical dichotomies like individualist versus collectivist approaches of moral agency and restrictive versus empowering ethics, and opens a new perspective on the interaction between individual moral learning and development on the one hand and the corporate institutionalization of corporate codes in enhancing and securing corporate responsible behaviour on the other.

This theory explains why corporate codes sometimes fail to enhance and secure corporate responsible behaviour. This structural infelicity of the performative shows that corporate responsible behaviour in light of the code is insufficient to perform corporate social responsible behaviour. The epistemic insufficiency of actors with regard to complex fields of study like economics and business has to be acknowledged. The fundamental uncertainty and high risk in business planning and policy-making and the potential harm these businesses can cause for others – customers, employees, civil society, etc. (DeMartino, 2011) – shows that the introduction of corporate codes cannot solve all problems regarding corporate social responsible behaviour; failure is possible and nothing can guarantee responsible behaviour. Corporate social responsible behaviour does not only consist therefore in the effort of firms to live and act in light of the code but in their incessant recapturing of its content in their struggle against its possible infelicity as well.

The advantage of the conceptualization of corporate codes as performative speech acts is that it acknowledges the fundamental possibility of infelicity, which makes clear that the sole introduction of corporate codes in firms is not sufficient. It should be accompanied by the introduction of formal and informal control systems. These control mechanisms enable the monitoring and evaluation of corporate responsible behaviour in accordance with the code which is promulgated. In addition to the self-control of the firm which is at stake in the self-performative code (guidance), one can also think of formal controls like rules and procedures and informal controls like common customs and values in professional life (Cassell et al., 1997). The introduction of formal and informal controls at firm level not only enhances ethical behaviour by individual managers but also at corporate level.

John Boatright has pointed to the importance of institutional design to ensure ethical behaviour (Boatright, 2008). Institutional design concerns the governance structure, the separation of functions, etc., in which professional behaviour of employees is normally embedded; managers have specific roles and responsibilities and decision-making follows certain procedures for instance. One can also think of interventions like training, monitoring systems, reward systems, ethical officers, recruitment policies, etc. (McDonald and Nijhof, 1999). With this, we integrate other organizational factors like internal and external control in order to enhance and secure corporate responsible behaviour. The conceptualization of corporate codes as performative speech acts shows that corporate codes have to be embedded in the institutional design of firms. These institutional aspects can be conceived as the indispensable (although insufficient) conditions of corporate codes; the existence of accepted procedures, circumstances for the invocation of the procedures, the correct execution of the procedures, etc. are an integral part of the corporate codes, which enables the monitoring and evaluation of corporate responsible behaviour in accordance with the code and in this way, ensures corporate responsible behaviour.

As a consequence, corporate codes have to be seen as a dynamic interaction between individual managers behaviour and the institutional design of corporations (Constantinescu and Kaptein, 2014). The embeddedness of employee behaviour in the institutional design does not only ensure more responsible behaviour at the individual level but also at the corporate level of institutions.

The emphasis on the importance of institutional design as an integral part of corporate codes has an important advantage. It is argued that unethical behaviour of managers is not due to individual moral deficiencies. Jackall for instance argues that the bureaucratic structures of modern organizations encourage unethical behaviour of managers (Jackall, 1988; Roberts, 2001). Although the existential moment in the performative code is stressed in this section, the performance of corporate responsible behaviour should be facilitated by these gestures embedded in the organizational design of the firm.

What are the consequences of the conceptualization of corporate codes as performative speech acts for their adoption in business practices? First, as a consequence of the *self*-performative code, in which a firm becomes corporate responsible, the introduction of corporate codes should be accompanied by policies that enable reflection on what the code means for individual managers, what are the causes of unethical corporate behaviour, and how to establish ethical behaviour in the business operations of the firm (Anderson and Escher, 2010). These opportunities for reflection could be provided by in firm education programs, but also during work team and board discussions for instance (Hill and Rapp, 2014, for a concrete strategy to enhance corporate responsible behaviour in this way). The policies will increase the self-involvement of managers and the internalization of corporate codes.

Because of the structural possibility of the infelicity of corporate codes, due to the complexity, uncertainty, and high risks involved in business and economics, firms and their managers should take these uncertainties into account in their business planning and policy making, resulting in more moderate and safer business strategies. Furthermore, the acknowledgement of their epistemic insufficiency should lead to more caution in corporate activities in high-risk markets. This modesty will not solve the problem of uncertainty and high risk, but enables firms to "manage ethically but imperfectly a problem that cannot be eradicated" (DeMartino, 2011: 187–188).

When the possibility of infelicity, failure, or even insufficiency is stressed in the concept of corporate codes, it becomes clear that it is insufficient to promulgate a code once and for all. In one way or another, firms and their managers have to *repeat* and *re-appropriate* the code again and again by dedicating themselves continuously to its content. In several consultancy firms, for instance, employees have to sign the code of conduct every year again. Policies that enable the reflection on ethical issues could help to appropriate and re-appropriate the corporate code (Painter-Morland 2010). The re-appropriation of the code is however not only an individual affair of managers. In the literature, it is argued that the creation of a collective agreement on the shared principles or codes within the firm is also important (Warren, 1993; Hill and Rapp, 2014).

A performative concept of corporate codes can not only be perceived as a set of principles which are dependent on corporate intentions, but also as *demanded* by the stakeholders of the firm. This *demand*-character of the stakeholders – customers, suppliers, but also civil society – has to be stressed in a performative concept of corporate codes. As a consequence, the re-appropriation of the code cannot be seen as the repetition of the mission and core values of the firm, but as a dynamic product of an ongoing conversation (and negotiation) with these stakeholders. In fact, it is this conversation and negotiation with critical stakeholders that will improve the quality of the code (Garegnani et al., 2013) and will enhance and secure corporate responsible behaviour. They should therefore communicate with stakeholders on a structural basis to assess the applicability of the content of the code in an ever-changing environment and to re-appropriate its content. These conversations help to assess the clarity of the content of corporate codes and their applicability in an ever-changing environment and to enable the re-appropriation of its content if necessary. Furthermore, both in education programs and in professional life, knowledge, attitudes, and skills with regard to learning (Stevens, 1994), reflection (Kjonstad and Willmott, 1995), value attunement (Swanson, 1999), and dealing with the interests of multiple stakeholders should be stimulated and facilitated by policies, governance structures, etc.

The development of these abilities cannot remove the criticism that the interests of multiple stakeholders can conflict with each other. On the one hand, these possible conflicts are acknowledged and mitigated by the capability of firms to deal with multiple stakeholders. On the other hand, the fundamental possibility of the infelicity of corporate codes in economics and business has to be accepted. Just as corporate codes cannot guarantee corporate responsible behaviour, these additional requirements cannot entirely prevent unethical behaviour. Nevertheless, the conceptualization of corporate codes as performative speech acts as described in this section can contribute to more corporate responsible behaviour.

Conclusion

In this chapter, we took the six dimensions of the philosophy of management to develop an integrated principle of business ethics. By showing the intrinsic relation between business management and ethics, we rejected the free market ideological claim that ethical responsibility has to be excluded from business management. In Section 20, we asked which of the six dimensions of the philosophy of management potentially hinder or enhance business ethical management practices. By applying the six dimensions of the philosophy of management on ethical considerations, we moved beyond applied ethical approaches in business ethics and instead, embedded business ethics in the nature of business management. In Section 21, we subsequently asked for the individual competencies of managers that enable them to engage in business ethical practices. We explored the concept of individual virtuous competence that resonates with the philosophy of management we developed in this study, and that enables the business manager to engage in business ethical practices. In Section 22, we finally asked for the institutional conditions that enable managers to engage in business ethical practices. We explored a performative concept of ethical codes and codes of conduct that resonates with the philosophy of management we developed in this study, and that that enables the business manager to engage in business ethical practices.

Notes

1 Hannah Arendt has shown that action originally concerned both aspects, but was later limited to the one ruler or master that is in charge (Arendt, 1958: 189–190). The concept of action we develop in this chapter cannot be confused with Arendt's concept of action, as we orient our concept in the area of the *private* sector, while she oriented her concept of action in the area of the *public* sector. A further comparison between the two notions of action is beyond the scope of this study.

2 In order to deal with multiple stakeholders as indicated here, professionals not only need the moral competencies we discuss in this study, but also the other competencies for sustainability development that are identified in the literature. For this reason, we do not analyse these practices any further but focus on the two moral competencies and their interrelations. For a more extensive description of practices in which the moral competencies and the other competencies for sustainable development are treated, see Wesselink et al. (2015).

3 In fact, also the Presocratics and Plato used the vocabulary of virtues, but Aristotle is normally seen as primary source for thoughts about virtue ethics, probably because of his systematic development of a virtue ethics doctrine.

4 For Aristotle, a virtuous life is insufficient because one needs external goods like power and friends as well (Aristotle, 1990: 1153b15–20). A further elaboration of the different views on *eudaimonia* and the connection with virtues is beyond the scope of this study.

5 We think that the framework of a MacIntyrean approach to business ethics very well fits in the context of wicked problems like sustainable development.

6 On the one hand, one can argue that the four components of action competence make clear that it has a moral component but that this moral component is not fully constitutive of it; it involves critical thinking and reflexivity as well for instance. On the other hand, one can argue that this *self-involvement* in responsible action is constitutive of moral competence. According to philosophers like Levinas, it is primarily this self-involvement as *internalization* of ethical behaviour in the face of the possibility to fail in this and our struggle against it, which constitutes responsible behaviour (see chapter 4). The ethical relevance of personal involvement and internalization of ethical norms and values is also confirmed in the business ethics literature (Cassell et al., 1997). For this reason, in this section, we consider action competence as a *moral* competence, although it also involves non-moral aspects such as critical thinking and reflexivity.

7 There are many possible factors that may explain why codes often fail, like dishonesty, internal pressures, shifting priorities, etc. The identification of these factors is beyond the scope of this section. In this section, only a conceptual explanation for this failure is explored, as opposed to an empirical explanation. It provides a conceptual explanation that should be researched empirically in relation to the other possible explanations in future research.

8 After Austin, many other authors contributed to the conceptualization of the speech act theory, like Grice, Searle, and Strawson. For the purpose of this study, however, a general introduction of the speech act theory based on Austin's work is sufficient.

9 Austin is at least ambiguous here. On the one hand, he claims that the performative does not report inward and spiritual acts (Austin, 1961: 236). On the other hand, the infelicity seems to arise out of the discrepancy between those spiritual acts (intentions) and actual behaviour.

10 Although Austin's later rejection of a strict distinction between constative and performative sentences has to be acknowledged, the concept of the performative is still useful to characterize the typical speech act of corporate codes. For this reason, the use of this concept is continued in this section in order to characterize the nature of corporate codes and codes of conduct (Butler, 1997; Sulmasy, 1999; Briggs, 2001).

11 One can also argue that the development of intentions and interests is historically embedded as well. The further elaboration of this question is beyond the scope of this study.

12 While Austin excludes the structural character of infelicity by stressing the concept of "ordinary language", Derrida asks whether the general possibility of infelicity is necessarily that of *failure*, or an internal and positive condition of its possibility (Derrida, 1982: 325).

13 The main difference between the concept of performativity of these authors and the author of this study is, that according to these authors, individual *actors* within the organization performatively constitute the social reality of theoretical constructs like ethical decision making, while we argue that the promulgation of the code itself is self-performative and constitutes the identity of the actors involved, that is, firms and individual managers (Callon, 1998). The further elaboration of the similarities and differences between a performative concept of corporate codes and the broader discussion of performative praxis in management research and economic sociology is beyond the scope of this study.

7 Conclusion

The problem statement of this study was found in the ubiquity of management in our contemporary society, ranging from self-management to Earth systems management and from business management to social network management, while the systematic study of what we actually mean with the term is relatively absent. In management science, management is self-evidently understood as managerial power and mechanism of control, while in the philosophy of management, the question of what business management is is relatively absent. This leads to the main question of this study: what is (business) management. In order to answer the question of what is business management, we engaged in a *critique* of management, that is, the delineation of what management means. Our objective was not only to provide a delineation of the self-evident conceptualization of management but also to provide a critical concept of management beyond its self-evident conceptualization. Such a philosophy of management can inspire future conceptual and empirical research in this field.

The self-evident conceptualization of management as managerial power and mechanism of control is questioned from two angles in this study. By consulting Xenophon's philosophy of management, we were able to challenge the self-evident orientation on profit maximization and raise the question of how private and public interests can be integrated into business management. Xenophon also enabled us to challenge the external position of the business manager that is disconnected from the primary process of the business and leads to the instrumentalization of management. Finally, Xenophon enabled us to challenge the ideal of managerial control over the business operations and helped us to acknowledge the fundamental role of risk and misfortune involved in business management.

The second critical angle to question the self-evident conceptualization of management was provided by contemporary grand challenges like global warming. The grand challenges of our time pose several challenges for our understanding of business management. By conceptualizing grand challenges like global warming as wicked problems,

DOI: 10.4324/9781003231875-7

we were able to challenge the self-evident orientation of management as governance of the functioning order of the business. Grand challenges like global warming cannot be controlled while our epistemic insufficiency makes it questionable whether management can plan and control its solution. Grand challenges like global warming also disrupt our understanding of management as people management, as the assignment of tasks and roles to human resources is no longer possible and calls our attention to the management of internal and external stakeholders with different and often conflicting value frames. Finally, grand challenges like global warming disrupt our understanding of management as entrepreneurial action that we articulated in terms of the paradox of sustainable entrepreneurship.

These two critical angles enabled us to open up the self-evident conceptualization of business management and articulate six contested areas that call for philosophical reflection. In chapters 2–5, we reflected on these contested areas of business management in order to not only build on but also move beyond contemporary conceptualizations of management as managerial power and mechanism of control. We criticized self-evident practices, such as the loss of participation, the instrumentalization of control systems, the paradigm of process optimization, and profit maximizations, and provided new perspectives on the phenomenon of management. We articulated six corresponding dimensions of the philosophy of management (Table 7.1).

The new dimensions of the philosophy of management we developed in this study can be found in practice as well. They only have a different status as they substantiate our opposition to the dominant concept of management as managerial power and mechanisms of control that is still taught in business schools today, and opens up new perspectives on the phenomenon of management. The normative rather than descriptive

Table 7.1 Contested areas of business management and new critical dimensions of the philosophy of management

Contested Areas of Business Management		Dimensions of the Philosophy of Management
Management for profit	→→→	Management as constituting meaning
Management as managerial power	→→→	Management as participation
Management as mechanism of control	→→→	Management as resistance and responsive action
Management as establishment and governance of a functioning order	→→→	Management as politico-economic governance
People management	→→→	Management as non-reductive stakeholder engagement
Management as entrepreneurial action	→→→	Management as epistemic insufficient entrepreneurship

nature of these new dimensions of management is not at all problematic, as the development of new theories of imagination for management science is necessary to prevent that we remain intellectually imprisoned by the structures of its self-evident conceptualization (Komporozos-Athanasiou and Fotaki, 2015).

With this, we do not so much want to reject the self-evident conceptualization of management completely and replace it with the newly developed conceptuality. For instance, in the last chapter, we introduced a performative concept of codes of conduct that, because of the structural role of infelicities and failure, requires *control* mechanisms. Although we criticized certain forms of control mechanisms and provided a new conceptuality of management as politico-economic governance, we do not want to exclude a priori all forms of control mechanisms to safeguard ethical behaviour. This example serves as an illustration that the philosophy of management should not be conceived only as a rejection of current management theory, but rather as an exploration of this conceptuality of management to open it up for future conceptual and empirical research.

We think that such a reconceptualization is necessary, first of all, in light of the grand challenges of our time. One of the major issues our society faces is global warming, and the acknowledgement of global warming as a wicked problem has consequences for the nature of managing these problems as we have seen. We think that such a reconceptualization is also necessary in light of employee's and professionals' dissatisfaction with current management practices in business life. The critique of management provided in this study aims to substantiate the intuitions of many professionals involved in large organizations and corporations. They experience problems with instrumental management, management by numbers and bureaucratic control as it neglects their professional engagement and responsibility. This study provides the conceptuality to criticize these practices and to find new avenues for future management practices. As a former manager myself, I have to admit that nothing is as difficult as the management of professionals. It is not so much the case that we should get rid of any bureaucracy and managerial control and fully trust the professional responsibility but to find new ways of management together. In this regard, the dimensions of the philosophy of management aim to move beyond strict dichotomies, such as individual-collective, trust-control, and so on, and to develop dimensions of management that acknowledge both the role of individual responsibility and the corporate responsibility that is managed by the business manager.

By engaging both in current debates in management science and philosophical literature, we aimed to safeguard the connection between philosophy and management. By bringing in philosophical theory and conceptuality in connection with contemporary issues in management science, we were able to develop a *philosophy* of management that at the same provides new management *theory* that serves several gaps in the management science literature, for instance, in the field of the political responsibility of firms, the ethics of stakeholder engagement, and the paradox of sustainable entrepreneurship. We do believe that the dimensions of management we developed in chapters 2–5 provide new theoretical insights that do have important advantages and open new perspectives on the nature of business management. With this, we hope this study inspires management theorists and practitioners to engage in the reflections provided in this study and to explore the dimensions in theory and practice in order to empirically substantiate and further develop the insights developed.

In the final chapter, the philosophy of management developed in this study inspired the development of an integrated principle of business ethics with six conditions. Contrary to most literature in business ethics, which starts with an original disconnect between business and ethics and focuses on the *application* of ethical theory in the particular domain of business management, the philosophy of management that we developed in this study enabled us to find our point of departure in the intrinsic relation between business and ethics. Based on the findings of chapters 2–5, we reflected on the nature of business management to reveal the intrinsic relation between business and ethics and developed an integrated principle of business ethics in chapter 6. The advantage of this principle of business ethics is that it is embedded in the nature of management, which enabled us to criticize the free market idea that takes advantage of the disconnection between business and ethics. We provided new theoretical insights in both the individual and institutional level factors that enable business managers to engage in business ethical practices. With this, we hope to have contributed to a new engagement of business with and for society, which is definitely needed in light of the grand challenges of our time.

References

Abor, J., Adjasi, C.K. (2007) "Corporate governance and the small and medium enterprises sector: Theory and implications". *Corporate Governance* 7 (2): 111–122.

Accenture (2010) *A new era of sustainability: UN Global Compact-Accenture CEO study* (accessible via: https://d306pr3pise04h.cloudfront.net/docs/news_events%2F8.1%2FUNGC_Accenture_CEO_Study_2010.pdf).

Adriana, B. (2009) "Environmental supply chain management in tourism: The case of large tour operators". *Journal of Cleaner Production* 17 (16): 1385–1392.

Agamben, G. (1998) *Homo sacer: Sovereign power and bare life.* Stanford: Stanford University Press.

Agamben, G. (2005) *State of exception.* Chicago: University of Chicago Press.

Agamben, G. (2007) "The power and the glory: Giorgio Agamben on economic theology". Transcript of a presentation in Turino on 11 January 2007 (accessible via: http://www.pubtheo.com/page.asp?pid=1566).

Agamben, G. (2009) *What is an apparatus.* Stanford: Stanford University Press.

Agamben, G. (2011) *The kingdom and the glory.* Stanford: Stanford University Press.

Aguinis, H., Glavas, A. (2012) "What we know and don't know about corporate social responsibility: A review and research agenda". *Journal of Management* 38 (4): 932–968.

Almers, E. (2013) "Pathways to action competence for sustainability—six themes". *The Journal of Environmental Education* 44 (2): 116–127.

Anderson, M., Escher, P. (2010) *The MBA oath: Setting a higher standard for business leaders.* New York: Penguin.

Andersen, M., Skjoett-Larsen, T. (2009) "Corporate social responsibility in global supply chains". *Supply Chain Management* 14 (2): 75–86.

Anderson, L., Bateman, T. (2000) "Individual environmental initiative: Championing natural environmental issues in US business organizations". *Academy of Management Journal* 43 (4): 548–570.

Andriof, J., Waddock, S. (2002) "Unfolding stakeholder engagement". In J. Andriof, S. Waddock, B. Husted, R. Sutherland (Eds.) *Unfolding stakeholder thinking: Theory, responsibility and engagement*, Vol. 1. Sheffield: Greenleaf, 19–42.

Ansell, C., Gash, A. (2008) "Collaborative governance in theory and practice". *Journal of Public Administration Research and Theory* 18 (4): 543–571.

Arendt, H. (1958) *The human condition*. Chicago: Chicago University Press.

Aristotle (1933) *Metaphysics*. Loeb classical library. Harvard: Harvard University Press.

Aristotle (1944) *Politics*. Loeb classical library. Harvard: Harvard University Press.

Aristotle (1990) *The Nicomachean ethics*. Loeb classical library. Harvard: Harvard University Press.

Assländer, M.S., Curbach, J. (2017) "Corporate or governmental duties? Corporate citizenship from a governmental perspective". *Business & Society* 56 (4): 617–645.

Athanassoulis, N. (2000) "A response to Harman: Virtue ethics and character traits". *Proceedings of the Aristotelian Society* 100: 215–221.

Austin, J.L. (1961) *Philosophical papers*. London: Oxford University Press.

Austin, J.L. (1962) *How to do things with words*. Oxford: Clarendon Press.

Ayuso, S., Rodríguez, M., García-Castro, R., Arino, M. (2011) "Does stakeholder engagement promote sustainable innovation orientation?" *Industrial Management and Data Systems* 111: 1399–1417.

Bakan, J. (2005) *The corporation: The pathological pursuit of profit and power*. New York: Free Press.

Baker, R. (2005) "A draft model aggregated code of ethics for bioethicists". *The American Journal of Bioethics* 5 (5): 33–41.

Bandura, A. (1986) *Social foundations of thought and action*. Englewood Cliffs, NJ: Prentice Hall.

Bandura, A. (1997) *Self-efficacy: The exercise of control*. New York: Freeman.

Baron, R. (2006) "Opportunity recognition as pattern recognition: How entrepreneurs 'connect the dots' to identify new business opportunities". *Academy of Management Perspectives* 20 (1): 104–119.

Barth, M., Godemann, J., Rieckman, M., Stoltenberg, U. (2007) "Developing key competences for sustainable development in higher education". *International Journal of Sustainability in Higher Education* 8 (4): 416–430.

Barr, S., Gilg, A. (2006) "Sustainable lifestyles: Framing environmental action in and around the home". *Geoforum* 37: 906–920.

Batie, S. S. (2008) "Wicked problems and applied economics". *American Journal of Agricultural Economics* 5: 1176–1191.

Bauman, Z. (1989) *Modernity and the holocaust*. Cambridge: Polity Press.

Bauman, Z. (2002) *Liquid modernity*. Cambridge: Polity Press.

Belucci, S.D., Bütschi, F., Gloede, S., Hennen, L., Klüver, J., Nentwich, M. (2002) "Analytical framework". In S. Joss and S. Belluci (Eds.) *Participatory technology assessment: European perspectives*. London: Centre for the Study of Democracy, 24–48.

Beneish, M., Chatov, R. (1993) "Corporate codes of conduct: Economic determinants and legal implications for independent auditors". *Journal of Accounting and Public Policy* 12 (1): 3–35.

Biemans, H., Nieuwenhuis, L., Poell, R., Mulder, M., Wesselink, R. (2004) "Competence-based VET in the Netherlands: Background and pitfalls". *Journal of Vocational Education & Training* 56 (4): 523–538.

Bigliardi, B., Galati, F. (2013) "Models of adoption of open innovation within the food industry". *Trends in Food Science & Technology* 30 (1): 16–26.

Billett, S. (1994) "Situated learning – A workplace experience". *Australian Journal of Adult and Community Education* 34 (2): 112–130.

Blok, V. (2009) "Communication or confrontation. Heidegger and philosophical method". *Empedocles* 1: 43–57.

Blok, V. (2013) "The power of speech acts: Reflections on a performative concept of ethical oaths in economics and business". *Review of Social Economy* 71 (2): 187–208.

Blok, V. (2014) "Look who's talking: Responsible innovation, the paradox of dialogue and the voice of the other in communication and negotiation processes". *Journal of Responsible Innovation* 1 (2): 171–190.

Blok, V. (2015) "The human glanze, the experience of environmental distress and the 'affordance' of nature: Toward a phenomenology of the ecological crisis". *Journal of Agricultural and Environmental Ethics* 28 (5): 925–938.

Blok, V. (2016) "Thinking the earth after Heidegger: Critical reflections on Meillassoux's and Heidegger's concept of the earth". *Environmental Ethics* 38 (4): 441–462.

Blok, V. (2020a) "The ontology of innovation: On the new, the political-economic dimension and the intrinsic risks involved in innovation processes". In D. Michelfelder and N. Doorn (Eds.) *Routledge handbook of philosophy of engineering*. London: Routledge, 273–285.

Blok, V. (2020b) *Heidegger's concept of philosophical method. Innovating philosophy in the age of global warming*. New York: Routledge.

Blok, V., Hoffmans, L., Wubben, E. (2015) "Stakeholder engagement for responsible innovation in the private sector: Critical issues and management practices". *Journal of Chain and Network Science* 15 (2): 147–164.

Blok, V., Lemmens, P. (2015) "The emerging concept of responsible innovation: Three reasons why it is questionable and calls for a radical transformation of the concept of innovation". In E.J. Koops, J. van den Hoven, H.A. Romijn, T.E. Swierstra, I. Oosterlaken (Eds.) *Responsible innovation 2: Concepts, approaches, and applications*. Dordrecht: Springer, 19–35.

Blok, V., Lubberink, R., Belt, H., van den Ritzer, S., Kruk, H., Danen, G. (2019) "Challenging the ideal of transparency as a process and as an output variable of responsible innovation: The case of 'the circle'". In R. Gianni, J. Pearson, R. Reber (Eds.) *Responsible research and innovation: From concepts to practices*. London: Routledge, 225–244.

Blok, V., Sjauw-Koen-Fa, A., Omta, O. (2013) "Effective stakeholder involvement at the base of the pyramid: The case of Rabobank". *International Food and Agribusiness Management Review* 16 (A): 39–44.

Blok, V., Tempels, T., Pietersma, E., Jansen, L. (2017) "Exploring ethical decision making in responsible innovation: The case of innovations for healthy food". In E.J. Koops, J. van den Hoven, H.A. Romijn, T.E. Swierstra, I. Oosterlaken (Eds.) *Responsible innovation 3*. Dordrecht: Springer, 209–230.

Boatright, J.R. (2008) *Ethics in finance*. Oxford: Blackwell.

Bogers, M. (2011) "The open innovation paradox: Knowledge sharing and protection in R&D collaborations". *European Journal of Innovation Management* 14 (1): 93–117.

Bondy, K., Matten, D., Moon, J. (2007) "Codes of conduct as a tool for sustainable governance in MNCs". In S. Benn and D. Dunphy (Eds.) *Corporate governance and sustainability*. London: Routledge, 165–183.

Bordum, A. (2007) "Managing innovation potential: Revisiting Plato and reading John Dewey as a philosopher of innovation management". *Philosophy of Management* 6 (1): 63–79.

Bos, J., Blok, V., van Tulder, R. (2013) "From confrontation to partnership: The role of a Dutch non-governmental organisation in co-creating a market to address the issue of animal welfare". *International Food and Agribusiness Management Review* 16A: 69–75.

Bowden, H. (2012) "The ethics of management: A stoic perspective". *Philosophy of Management* 11 (2): 29–48.

Brand, T., Blok, V., Verweij, M. (2020) "Stakeholder dialogue as agonistic deliberation: Exploring the role of conflict and self-interest in business-NGO interaction". *Business Ethics Quarterly* 30 (1): 3–30.

Bray, A. (2001) "Why is it that management seems to have no history?". *Philosophy of Management* 1 (1): 21–25.

Brennan, A. (2004) "Biodiversity and agricultural landscapes: Can the wicked policy problem be solved?". *Pacific Conservation Biology* 10 (2): 124–142.

Brickson, S.L. (2007) "Organizational identity orientation: The genesis of the role of the firm and distinct forms of social value". *Academy of Management Review* 32: 864–888.

Briggs, R.S. (2001) *Words in action. Speech act theory and biblical interpretation*. New York: T&T Clark Ltd.

Brown, J.S., Collins, A., Duguid, P. (1989) "Situated cognition and the culture of learning". *Educational Researcher* 18: 32–43.

Bryson, J.M., Crosby, B.C., Middleton Stone, M. (2006) "The design and implementation of cross-sector collaborations: Propositions from the literature". *Public Management Review* 66 (1): 44–55.

Bulkeley, H., Mol, A. (2003) "Participation and environmental governance: Consensus, ambivalence and debate". *Environmental Values* 12 (2): 143–154.

Burchell, J., Cook, J. (2006) "It's good to talk? Examining attitudes towards corporate social responsibility dialogue and engagement processes". *Business Ethics: A European Review* 15 (2): 154–170.

Burgess, J., Stirling, A., Clark, J., Davies, G., Eames, M., Staley, K. (2007) "Deliberative mapping: A novel analytic-deliberative methodology to support contested science-policy decisions". *Public Understanding of Science* 16 (3): 299–322.

Butler, J. (1997) "Sovereign performatives in the contemporary scene of utterance". *Critical Inquiry* 23 (2): 350–377.

Cabantous, L., Gond, J.-P. (2011) "Rational decision making as performative praxis: Explaining rationality's *Eternel Retour*". *Organization Science* 22 (3): 573–586.

Callon, M. (1998) *The laws of the markets*. Oxford: Blackwell Publishers.

Carr, A. (1968) "Is business bluffing ethical?". *Harvard Business Review* 46: 143–153.

Cassell, C. Johnson, P., Smith, K. (1997) "Opening the black box: Corporate Codes of Ethics in Their Organisational Context". *Journal of Business Ethics* 16 (10): 1077–1093.

Castells, M. (2000) *The rise of the network society*. Chichester: Wiley.

Cheetham, G., Chivers, G. (1996) "Towards a holistic model of professional competence". *Journal of European Industrial Training* 20 (5): 20–30.

Chesbrough, H.W. (2003) *Open innovation: The new imperative for creating and profiting from technology*. Boston: Harvard Business School Press

Chilvers, J. (2008) "Environmental risk, uncertainty, and participation: Mapping an emergent epistemic community". *Environment and Planning* 40 (2): 2990–3008.

Christensen, L., Cheney, G. (2015) "Peering into transparency: Challenging ideals, proxies, and organisational practices". *Communication Theory* 25: 70–90.

Christensen, L., Cornelissen, J. (2015) "Organizational transparency as myth and metaphor". *European Journal of Social Theory* 18 (2): 132–149.

Chun, R. (2005) "Ethical character and virtue of organizations: An empirical assessment and strategic implications". *Journal of Business Ethics* 57: 269–284.

Ciliberti, F., de Haan, J., de Groot, G., Pontrandolfo, P. (2011) "CSR codes and the principal-agent problem in supply chains: Four case studies". *Journal of Cleaner Production* 19: 885–894.

Clark, C.F., Kotchen, M.J., Moore, M.R. (2003) "Internal and external influences on pro-environmental behaviour: Participation in a green electricity program". *Journal of Environmental Psychology* 23: 237–246.

Cohen, S.M. (2012) "Aristotle's metaphysics". In E. Zalta (Ed.) *The Stanford encyclopedia of philosophy*.

Collingridge, D. (1980) *The social control of technology*. London: Francis Pinter.

Collins, J.W. (1994) "Is business ethics an oxymoron?" *Business Horizons* 37(5): 1–8 (September–October).

Conner, K., Prahalad, C.K. (1996) "A resource-based theory of the firm: Knowledge versus opportunism". *Organization Science* 7 (5): 477–501.

Constantinescu, M., Kaptein, M. (2015) "Mutually enhancing responsibility: A theoretical exploration of the interaction mechanisms between individual and corporate moral responsibility". *Journal of Business Ethics* 129: 325–339. doi: 10.1007/s10551-014-2161-4.

Cornwall, A. (2008) "Unpacking "participation": Models, meanings and practices". *Community Development Journal* 43 (3): 269–283.

Cramer, J., Loeber, A. (2007) "Learning about corporate social responsibility from a sustainable development perspective: A Dutch experiment". In A.E.J. Wals (Ed.) *Social learning towards a sustainable world*. Wageningen: Wageningen Academic Press, 265–279.

Crilly, D., Zollo, M., Hansen, M. (2012) "Faking it or muddling through? Understanding decoupling in response to stakeholder pressures". *Academy of Management Journal* 55 (6): 1429–1448.

Croteau, D., Hicks, L. (2003) "Coalition framing and the challenge of a consonant frame pyramid: The case of a collaborative response to homelessness". *Social Problems* 50: 251–272.

Cuppen, E. (2012) "Diversity and constructive conflict in stakeholder dialogue: Considerations for design and methods". *Policy Sciences* 45: 23–46.

Dahl, R. (1997) "On deliberative democracy: Citizens panels and Medicare reforms". *Dissent* 44 (3): 54–58.

Dahlsrud, A. (2008) "How corporate social responsibility is defined: An analysis of 37 definitions". *Corporate Social Responsibility and Environmental Management* 15: 1–13.

Dean, T., McMullen, J. (2007) "Toward a theory of sustainable entrepreneurship: Reducing environmental degradation through entrepreneurial action". *Journal of Business Venturing* 22: 50–76.

de Bruin, B. (2014) "Pledging integrity: Oaths as forms of business ethics management". *Journal of Business Ethics* 136: 23–42. doi: 10.1007/s10551-014-2504-1.

Defillippi, R.J., Arthur, M.B. (1994) "The boundaryless career: A competency-based perspective". *Journal of Organizational Behavior* 15 (4): 307–324.

de Groot, J.I.M., Steg, L. (2008) "Value orientations to explain beliefs related to environmental significant behaviour". *Environmental Behaviour* 40: 330–354.

de Haan, G. (2006) "The BLK '21' programme in Germany: A 'Gestaltungskompetenz' based model for education for sustainable development". *Environmental Education Research* 12 (1): 19–32.

de la Durantaye, L. (2009) *Giorgio Agamben: A critical introduction*. Stanford: Stanford University Press.

Deleuze, G. (1992) "Postscript on the societies of control". *October* 59: 3–7.

Deleuze, G. (1997) *Negotiations*. Columbia: Columbia University Press.

DeMartino, G.F. (2011) *The economist's oath*. Oxford: Oxford University Press.

Dentoni, D., Blok, V., Lans, T., Wesselink, R. (2012) "Developing human capital for agri-food firms' multi-stakeholder interactions". *International Food and Agribusiness Management Review* 15 (A): 61–68.

Derrida, J., (1982) *Margins of philosophy*. Chicago: University of Chicago Press.

DesJardins, J. (2011) *An introduction to business ethics*. New York: McGraw-Hill.

Deslandes, G. (2018) "Weak theology and organization studies". *Organization Studies* 41 (1): 1–18.

de Wit, B., Meyer, R. (2010) *Strategy synthesis: Resolving strategy paradoxes to create competitive advantage*. London: Cengage Learning.

Dienhart, J. (1995) "Rationality, ethical codes, and an Egalitarian justification of ethical expertise: Implications for professionals and organisations". *Business Ethics Quarterly* 5 (3): 419–450.

Donaldson, T., Preston, L.E. (1995) "The stakeholder theory of the corporation: concepts, evidence, and implications". *Academy of Management Review* 20 (1): 65–91.

Dorfman, R. (1993) "Some concepts from welfare economics". In R. Dorfman, N. Dorfman (Eds.) *Economics of the environment*. New York: W.W. Norton.

Dunphy, D., Griffiths, A., Benn, S. (2007) *Organizational change for corporate sustainability*. New York: Routledge.

Dutta, D., Crossan, M. (2005) "The nature of entrepreneurial opportunities: Understanding the process using the 4I organizational learning framework". *Entrepreneurship Theory and Practice* 29: 425–449.

Eckhardt, J., Shane, S. (2003) "Opportunities and entrepreneurship". *Journal of Management* 29 (3): 333–349.

Ehrlich, P.R., Ehrlich, A.H. (2009) "The population bomb revisited". *Electronic Journal of Sustainable Development* 1: 63–71.

Eisenberg, E. (1984) "Ambiguity as strategy in organizational communication". *Communication Monographs* 51: 227–242.

Ellis, G., Weekes, T. (2008) "Making sustainability 'real': Using group-enquiry to promote education for sustainable development". *Environmental Education Research* 14 (4): 482–500.

Eraut, M. (1994) *Developing professional knowledge and competence.* London: Falmer Press.

European Commission (2010) *Green paper: Corporate governance in financial institutions and remuneration policies.* Brussels: European Commission.

Eweje, G. (2007) "Strategic partnerships between MNEs and civil society: The post-WSSD perspectives". *Sustainable Development* 15 (1): 15–27.

Fayol, H. (1949) *General and industrial management.* London: Pitman & Sons.

Ferraro, F., Etzion, D., Gehman, J. (2015) "Tackling grand challenges pragmatically: Robust action revisited". *Organization Studies* 36 (3): 363–390.

Ferraro, F., Pfeffer, J., Sutton, R.I. (2005) "Economics language and assumptions: How theories can become self-fulfilling". *Academy of Management Review* 30 (1): 8–24.

Fiedler, F.E., Garcia, J.E. (1987) *New approaches to leadership, cognitive resources and organizational performance.* New York: John Wiley and Sons.

Filatotchev, I., Torns, S., Wright, M. (2006) "The firm's strategic dynamics and corporate governance life-cycle". *International Journal of Managerial Finance* 2 (4): 256–279.

Fiorino, D.J. (1990) "Citizen participation and environmental risk: A survey of institutional mechanisms". *Science Technology and Human Values* 15 (2): 226–243.

Fisher, C. (2001) "'Managers' perceptions of ethical codes: Dialectics and dynamics". *Business Ethics: A European Review* 10 (2): 145–156.

Flinders, M., Wood, M. (2014) "Introduction special issue depoliticisation, governance and the state". *Policy & Politics* 42 (2): 135–149.

Flipse, S. (2012) *Enhancing socially responsible innovation in industry. Practical use for considerations of social and ethical aspects in industrial life sciences & technology.* Ph.D. thesis, Delft University.

Floridi, L. (2010) *Information: A very short introduction.* Oxford: Oxford University Press.

Follett, M.P. (1940) *Dynamic administration: The collected papers of Mary Parker Follett.* London: Pitman.

Fontrodona, J., Melé, D. (2002) "Philosophy as a base for management: An Aristotelian integrative proposal". *Philosophy of Management* 2 (2): 3–9.

Foucault, M. (1979) *Discipline and punish: The birth of the prison.* New York: Vintage.

Foucault, M. (2009) *Security, territory, population. Lectures at the Collège de France 1977-1978.* New York: Picador.

Fraedrich, J., Thorne, D.M., Ferrell, O.C. (1994) "Assessing the application of cognitive moral development to business ethics". *Journal of Business Ethics* 13 (10): 829–838.

Freeman, R.E. (1984) *Strategic management: A stakeholder approach*. Boston: Cambridge University Press.

Friedman, M. "The social responsibility of business is to increase its profits". *The New York Times Magazine*, 13 September 1970.

Gaglio, C., Katz, J. (2001) "The psychological basis of opportunity identification: Entrepreneurial alertness". *Small Business Economics* 16: 95–111.

Gardiner, S.M. (2006) "A perfect moral storm: Climate change, intergenerational ethics and the problem of moral corruption". *Environmental Values* 15 (3): 397–413.

Garegnani, G.M., Merlotti, E.P., Russo, A. (2013) "Scoring firms' codes of ethics: An explorative study of quality drivers". *Journal of Business Ethics*. doi: 10.1007/s10551-013-1968-8.

Garst, J. , Blok, V., Jansen, L., Omta, O. (2018) "Responsibility versus profit: The motives of food firms for healthy product innovation". *Sustainability* 9 (12): 2286. 10.3390/su9122286

Gibson, R. (2006). "Sustainability assessment: Basic components of a practical approach". *Impact Assessment and Project Appraisal* 24: 170–182.

Giddens, A. (2011) *The politics of climate change*. Cambridge: Polity.

Gimbel, S. (2005) "Can corporations be morally responsible? Aristotle, stakeholders and the non-sale of Hershey". *Philosophy of Management* 5 (3): 23–30.

Global Environmental Management Initiative (GEMI) and Environmental Defense Fund (2008) *Guide to successful corporate-NGO partnerships*. 27 (1): 23–37.

Gonczi, A. (1994) *Developing a competent workforce*. Adelaide: National Centre for Vocational Education Research.

Gond, J.P., Kang, N., Moon, J. (2011) "The government of self-regulation: On the comparative dynamics of corporate social responsibility". *Economy and Society* 40 (4): 640–671.

Gould, R. (2012) "Open innovation and stakeholder engagement". *Journal of Technology Management and Innovation* 7 (3): 1–11.

Graves, S.B., Waddock, S.A. (1994) "Institutional owners and corporate social performance". *Academy of Management Journal* 37 (4): 1034–1046.

Gray, B. (1989) "Cross-sectoral partners: Collaborative alliances among business, government, and communities". In C. Huxham (Ed.) *Creating collaborative advantage*. Thousand Oakes: Sage Publications, 57–79.

Gray, B., Hay, T.M. (1986) "Political limits to interorganisational consensus and change". *Journal of Applied Behavioral Science* 22: 95–112.

Gray, B., Stites, J.P. (2013) *Sustainability through partnerships. Capitalizing on collaboration*. London: NBS.

Griseri, P. (2013) *An introduction to the philosophy of management*. Los Angeles/London: Sage.

Grunwald, A. (2004) "Strategic knowledge for sustainable development: The need for reflexivity and learning at the interface between science and society". *International Journal of Functional Informatics and Personalised Medicine* 1 (1–2): 150–167.

Grunwald, A. (2007) "Working towards sustainable development in the face of uncertainty and incomplete knowledge". *Journal of Environmental Policy & Planning* 9 (3): 245–262.

Gulick, L., Urwick, L. (Eds.) (2012) *Papers on the science of administration.* London: Routledge.

Gunningham, N., Kagan, R.A., Thornton, D. (2004) "Social license and environmental protection: Why busineses go beyond compliance". *Law & Social Inquiry* 29 (2): 307–341.

Guston, D.H. (1999) "Evaluating the first US consensus conference: The impact of the citizens' panel on telecommunications and the future of democracy". *Science Technology and Human Values* 24 (4): 451–482.

Habermas, J. (1990) *Moral consciousness and communicative action.* Cambridge: MIT Press.

Habermas, J. (1993) *Justification and application. Remarks on discourse ethics.* Cambridge: MIT Press.

Hahn, R. (2009) "The ethical rational of business for the poor – integrating the concepts bottom of the pyramid, sustainable development, and corporate citizenship". *Journal of Business Ethics* 84: 313–324.

Hahn, T., Pinkse, J., Preuss, L., Figge, F. (2015) "Tensions in corporate sustainability: Towards an integrative framework". *Journal of Business Ethics* 127 (2): 297–316.

Haidt, J. (2001) "The emotional dog and its rational tail: A social intuitionist approach to moral judgment". *Psychological Review* 108 (4): 814–834.

Haines, F. (2011) *The paradox of regulation. What regulation can achieve and what it cannot.* Cheltenham: Edward Elgar.

Hall, J., Daneke, G., Lenox, M. (2010) "Sustainable development and entrepreneurship: Past contributions and future directions". *Journal of Business Venturing* 25 (5): 439–448.

Hansen, J. (2006) "Public participation: Operationalising the public in participatory technology assessment: A framework for comparison applied to three cases". *Science and Public Policy* 33 (8): 571–584.

Harding, G. (1968) "The tragedy of the commons". *Science* 162: 1243–1248.

Hardy, C., Lawrence, T.B., Grant, D. (2005) "Discourse and collaboration: The role of conversations and collective identity". *Academy of Management Review* 30 (1): 58–77.

Harrison, J.S., Bosse, D.A., Phillips, R.A. (2010) "Managing for stakeholders, stakeholder utility functions, and competitive advantage". *Strategic Management Journal* 31 (1): 58–74.

Hart, S., Sharma, S. (2004) "Engaging fringe stakeholders for competitive imagination". *Academy of Management Executive* 18 (1): 23–33.

Hartman, E.M. (2015) "Rationality in management theory and practice: An Aristotelian perspective". *Philosophy of Management* 14 (1): 5–16.

Heidegger, M. (2006) "Der Satz der Identität". *Identität und Differenz.* Gesamtausgabe Band 11, Frankfurt a.M.: Vittorio Klostermann.

Heidt, J. (2001) "The emotional dog and its rational tail: a social intuitionist approach to moral judgment". *Psychological Review* 108 (4): 814–834.

Hendry, J. (2001) "Missing the target: Normative stakeholder theory and the corporate governance debate". *Business Ethics Quarterly* 11 (1): 159–176.

Hens, I., Nath, B. (2003) "The Johannesburg conference". *Environment, Development and Sustainability* 5: 7–39.

Heugens, P.P.M.A.R. (2006) "Environmental issue management: Toward a multi-level theory of environmental management competence". *Business Strategy and the Environment* 15: 363–376.

Hill, R.P., Rapp, J.M. (2014) "Codes of ethical conduct: A bottom-up approach". *Journal of Business Ethics* 123: 621–630.

Hodkinson, P., Issitt, M. (1995) *The challenge of competence: Professionalism through vocational education and training.* London: Cassell.

Hoffmann, T. (1999) "The meanings of competency". *Journal of European Industrial Training* 23 (6): 275–285.

Hopwood, A. (1974) *Accounting and human behaviour.* London: Prentice Hall.

Humphreys, J.H. (2002) "The anabasis and lessons in leadership: Xenophon as a prototypical transformational leader". *Journal of Management Research* 2 (3): 136–146.

Humphreys, S. (2006) "Legalizing lawlessness: On Giorgio Agamben's state of exception". *The European Journal of International Law* 17 (3): 677–687.

Hursthouse, R. (1999) *On virtue ethics.* Oxford: Oxford University Press.

Husted, B. (2007) "Agency, information, and the structure of moral problems in business". *Organization Studies* 28 (2): 177–195.

Huxham, C., Vangen, S. (2005) *Managing to collaborate: The theory and practice of collaborative advantage.* New York: Routledge.

Islam, A. (2012) "Methods of open innovation knowledge sharing risk reduction: A case study". *International Journal of e-Education, e-Business, e-Management and e-Learning* 2 (4): 294–297.

Iyer, E. (2003) "Theory of alliances: Partnership and partner characteristics". *Journal of Nonprofit and Public Sector Marketing* 11 (1): 41–57.

Jackall, R. (1988) *Moral mazes: The world of corporate managers.* Oxford: Oxford University Press.

Jackson, T. (2011) *Prosperity without growth: Economics for a finite planet.* New York: Routledge.

Jamieson, D. (2002). *Morality's progress: Essays on humans, other animals, and the rest of nature.* Oxford: Clarendon Press.

Jehn, K.A., Northcraft, G.B., Neale, M.A. (1999) "Why differences make a difference: A field study of diversity, conflict and performance in workgroups", *Administrative Science Quarterly* 44 (4): 741–763.

Jensen, B.B., Schnack, K. (1997) "The action competence approach in environmental education". *Environmental Education Research* 3 (2): 163–178.

Joldersma, C. (1997) "Participatory policy making: Balancing between divergence and convergence". *European Journal of Work and Organizational Psychology* 6: 207–218.

Jones, M.T. (2009) "Disrobing the emperor: Mainstream CSR research and corporate hegemony". *Management of Environmental Quality: An International Journal* 20 (3): 335–346.

Jones, T. (1991) "Ethical decision making by individuals in organizations: An issue-contingent model". *Academy of Management Review* 16 (2): 366–395.

Kallio, T.J. (2007) "Taboos in corporate social responsibility discourse". *Journal of Business Ethics* 74 (2): 165–175.

Kirzner, I. (1973) *Competition and entrepreneurship.* Chicago: University of Chicago Press.

Kirzner, I. (1985) *Discovery and the capitalist process*. Chicago: University of Chicago Press.

Kjonstad, B., Willmott, H. (1995) "Business ethics: Restrictive or empowering?". *Journal of Business Ethics* 14 (6): 445–464.

Klewitz, J., Hansen, E. (2014) "Sustainability-oriented innovation of SMEs: A systematic review". *Journal of Cleaner Production* 65: 57–75.

Knight, F.H. (1921) *Risk, uncertainty, and profit*. Boston: Houghton Mifflin.

Koehn, D. (1995) "A role for virtue ethics in the analysis of business practice". *Business Ethics Quarterly* 5 (3): 533–539.

Kohlberg, L. (1969) "Stage and sequence: The cognitive development approach to socialization". In D. Goslin (Ed.) *Handbook of socialization theory and research*. Chicago: Rand McNally, 347–380.

Komporozos-Athanasiou, A. and Fotaki, M., (2015) "A theory of imagination for organization studies using the work of Cornelius Castoriadis". *Organization Studies* 36: 321–342.

Koontz, H., O'Donnell, C. (1972) *Principles of management: An analysis of managerial functions*. New York: McGraw-Hill.

Korakandy, R. (2008) *Fisheries development in India. The political economy of unsustainable development*. Delhi: Kalpaz Publications.

Kraut, R. (2014) "Aristotle's ethics". In E.N. Zalta (Ed.) *The Stanford encyclopedia of philosophy*.

Krentz, A.A., Malloy, D.C. (2005) "Opening people to possibilities: A Heideggerian approach to leadership". *Philosophy of Management* 5 (1): 25–44.

Kreuter, M.W., de Rosa, C., Howze, E.H., Baldwin, G.T. (2004) "Understanding wicked problems: A key to advancing environmental health promotion". *Health, Education, and Behavior* 31: 441–454.

Ladd, J. (1985) "The quest for a code of professional ethics". In D.G. Johnson, J.W. Snapper (Eds.) *Ethical issues in the use of computers*. Belmont: Wadsworth.

Lans, T., Blok, V., Wesselink, R. (2014) "Learning apart and together: Towards an integrated competence framework for sustainable entrepreneurship in higher education". *Journal of Cleaner Production* 62: 37–47.

Law, E. (2009). *Oxford dictionary of business and management*. Oxford: Oxford University Press.

Le Ber, M.J., Branzei, O. (2010) "Value frame fusion in cross-sector interactions". *Journal of Business Ethics* 94: 163–195.

Lee, J., Berleur, J. (1994) "Progress towards a world-wide code of conduct". Proceedings of the conference on ethics in the computer age.

Lee, K.-H. (2009) "Why and how to adopt green management: Principles and examples". *Management Decision* 47 (7): 1101–1121.

Levin, K., Cashore, B., Bernstein, S., Auld, G. (2010) *Playing it forward: Path dependency, progressive incrementalism, and the "super wicked" problem of global climate change* (accessible via: http://citeseerx.ist.psu.edu/viewdoc/download?doi¼10.1.1.464.5287&rep¼rep1&type¼pdf).

Levinas, E. (1969) *Totality and infinity*. Pittsburgh: Duquesne.

Lewicki, R., Gray, B., Elliott, M. (2003) *Making sense of intractable environmental conflicts: Concepts and cases*. Washington, DC: Island Press.

Lewis, M. (2000) "Exploring paradox: Toward a more comprehensive guide?". *Academy of Management Review* 25 (4): 760–776.

Lezaun, E.J., Soneryd, L. (2007) "Consulting citizens: Technologies of elicitation and the mobility of publics". *Public Understanding of Science* 16 (3): 279–297.

Lim, M. (2007) "The ethics of alterity and the teaching of otherness". *Business Ethics: A European Review* 16 (3): 251–263.

Logsdon, J.M. (1991) "Interests and interdependence in the formation of social problem-solving collaborations". *Journal of Applied Behavioral Science* 27(1): 23–37.

Lopatta, K., Buchholz, F., Kaspereit, T. (2015) "Asymmetric information and corporate social responsibility". *Business and Society* 55 (3): 1–31.

Loumansky, A., Lewis, D. (2013) "A Levinasian approach to whistleblowing". *Philosophy of Management* 12 (3): 27–48.

Lowry, S.T. (1979) "Recent literature on Ancient Greek economic thought". *Journal of Economic Literature* 17 (1): 65–86.

MacAulay, M., Lawton, A. (2006) "From virtue to competence: Changing the principles of public service". *Public Administration Review* 66 (5): 702–710.

MacIntyre, A. (1985) *After virtue*. London: Duckworth.

Majone, G. (1994) "Paradoxes of privatization and deregulation". *Journal of European Public Policy* 1 (1): 53–69.

Maloni, M., Brown, M. (2006) "Corporate social responsibility in the supply chain: An application in the food industry". *Journal of Business Ethics* 68 (1): 35–62.

Málovics, G., Csigéné, N.N., Kraus, S. (2006) "The role of corporate social responsibility in strong sustainability". *The Journal of Socio-Economics* 37: 907–918.

Mamic, I. (2005) "Managing global supply chain: The sports footwear, appare and retail sectors". *Journal of Business Ethics* 59 (1): 81–100.

Mansfield, B., Mitchell, L. (1996) *Towards a competent workforce*. London: Gower.

Marcus, A., Geffen, D. (1998) "The dialectics of competency acquisition: Pollution prevention in electric generation". *Strategic Management Journal* 19: 1145–1168.

Mathews, M.C. (1988) *Strategic intervention in organisations*. London: Sage.

Mayo, G.E. (2003) *"The human problems of an industrial civilization"*. London: Routledge.

McDonald, G., Nijhof, A. (1999) "Beyond codes of ethics: An integrated framework for stimulating morally responsible behaviour in organisations". *Leadership & Organisation Development Journal* 20 (3): 133–146

McMahon, C. (1995) "The ontological and moral status of organizations". *Business Ethics Quarterly* 5: 541–554.

McMullen, J., Shepherd, D. (2006) "Entrepreneurial action and the role of uncertainty in the theory of the entrepreneur". *Academy of Management Review* 31 (1): 132–152.

Meara, N. M., Schmidt L. D., Day, J. D. (1996) "Principles and virtues: A foundation for ethical decisions, policies, and character". *The Counseling Psychologist* 24 (1): 4–77.

Meinhold, J.L., Malkus, A.J. (2005) "Adolescent environmental behaviours". *Environmental Behaviour* 37: 511–532.

Melewar, T.C., Karaosmanoglu, E. (2006) "Seven dimensions of corporate identity: A categorisation from the practitioner's perspective". *European Journal of Marketing* 40(7/8): 846–869.

Midttun, A. (2005) "Realigning business, government and civil society". *Corporate Governance* 5 (3): 159–174.

Millar, C., Udalov, Y., Millar, H. (2012) "The ethical dilemma of information asymmetry in innovation: Reputation, investors and noise in the innovation channel". *Creativity and Innovation Management* 21 (2): 224–237.

Milne, G.R., Iyer, E.S., Gooding-Williams, S. (1996) "Environmental organization alliance relationships within and across nonprofit, business, and government sectors". *Journal of Public Policy and Marketing* 15 (2): 203–215.

Miner, R. (2002) *Organizational behaviour. Foundations, theories and analysis.* Oxford: Oxford University Press.

Mintzberg, H. (2005) *Managers not MBAs: A hard look at the soft practice of managing and management development.* Broadway: Berrett-Koehler.

Mogensen, F., Schnack, K. (2010) "The action competence approach and the "new" discourses of education for sustainable development, competence and quality criteria". *Environmental Education Research* 16 (1): 59–74.

Mohamed, S., Mynors, D., Grantham, A., Walsh, K., Chan, P. (2006) "Understanding one aspect of the knowledge leakage concept: People". Paper presented at the Proceedings of the European and Mediterranean Conference on Information (Working Paper).

Mohr, J. and Spekman, R. (1994) "Characteristics of partnership success: Partnership attributes, communication behaviour, and conflict resolution techniques". *Strategic Management Journal* 15 (2): 135–152.

Molnar, E., Mulvihill, P. (2003) "Sustainability-focused organizational learning: Recent experiences and new challenges". *Journal of Environmental Planning & Management* 46 (2): 167–176.

Mondzain, M.J. (2005) *Image, icon, economy: The byzantine origins of the contemporary imaginary.* Stanford: Stanford University Press.

Moon, J. (2002). "The social responsibility of business and new governance". *Government and Opposition* 37: 385–408.

Moore, G. (2005) "Humanising business: A modern virtue ethics approach". *Business Ethics Quarterly* 15 (2): 237–255.

Moore, G., Beadle, R. (2006) "In search of organizational virtue in business: Agents, goods, practices, institutions and environments". *Organization Studies* 27 (3): 369–389.

Mouffe, C. (2009) "Democracy in a multipolar world". *Millennium: Journal of International Studies* 37 (3): 549–561.

Mulder, M. (2001) *Competence development in organizations.* Den Haag: Elsevier.

Murphy, P.E. (1991) "Character and virtue ethics in international marketing: An agenda for managers, researchers and educators". *Journal of Business Ethics* 18 (1): 117–124.

Nancy, J.L. (2007) *The creation of the world or globalization.* New York: SUNY.

Narvaez, D. (2008) "Triune ethics: The Neurobiological roots of our multiple moralities". *New Ideas in Psychology* 26 (1): 95–119.

Nayyar, P. (1990) "Information asymmetries: A source of competitive advantage for diversified service firms". *Strategic Management Journal* 11 (7): 513–519.

Nijhof, A., Bruijn, T., de Honders, H. (2008) "Partnerships for corporate social responsibility: A review of concepts and strategic options". *Management Decision* 46 (1): 152–167.

Noland, J., Phillips, R. (2010) "Stakeholder engagement, discourse ethics and strategic management". *International Journal of Management Reviews* 12 (1): 39–49.

Noonan, H. (2011) "Identity". In E.N. Zalta (Ed.) *The Stanford encyclopedia of philosophy*.

Norton, B.G. (2000) "Biodiversity and environmental values: In search of a universal earth ethic". *Biodiversity and Conservation* 9: 1029–1044.

Nowell, B. (2010) "Out of sync and unaware? Exploring the effects of problem frame alignment and discordance in community collaboratives". *Journal of Public Administration Research and Theory* 20 (1): 91–116.

O'Driscoll, A., Claudy, M., Peterson, M. (2013) "Understanding the attitude-behavior gap for renewable energy systems using behavioral reasoning theory". *Journal of Macromarketing* 33 (4): 273–287.

Oels, A. (2012). "From 'securitization' of climate change to 'climatization' of the security field: Comparing three theoretical perspectices". In J. Scheffran, M. Brzoska, H.G. Brauch, P.M. Link, J. Schilling (Eds.) *Climate change, human security and violent conflict*. Dordrecht: Springer.

Osagie, E., Blok, V., Wesselink, R., Mulder, M. (2019) "Contextualizing individual competencies for managing the corporate social responsibility adaptation process: The apparent influence of the business case logic".*Business & Society* 58 (2): 369–403.

Osagie, E., Wesselink, R., Blok, V., Lans, T., Mulder, M. (2016) "Individual competencies for corporate social responsibility: A literature and practice perspective". *Journal of Business Ethics* 135 (2): 233–252.

Owen, R., Stilgoe, J., Macnaghten, P., Gorman, M., Fisher, E., Guston, D. (2013) "A framework for responsible innovation". In R. Owen, J. Bessant, M. Heintz (Eds.) *Responsible innovation. Managing the responsible emergence of science and innovation in society*. Chichester: Wiley, 27–50.

Paine, L., Deshpande, R., Margolis, J.D., Bettcher, K.E. (2005) "Up to code. Does your company's conduct meet world-class standards?". *Harvard Business Review* 83 (12): 122–133.

Painter-Morland, M. (2010) "Questioning corporate codes of ethics". *Business Ethics: A European Review* 19 (3): 265–279.

Parrish, B. (2010) "Sustainability-driven entrepreneurship: Principles of organisation design". *Journal of Business Venturing* 25: 510–523.

Passmore, J. (1984) "Academic Ethics". *Journal of Applied Philosophy* 1 (1).

Pater, A., Van Gils, A. (2003) "Stimulating ethical decision-making in a business context: Effects of ethical and professional codes". *European Management Journal* 21 (6): 762–772.

Peterson, C. (2009) "Transformational supply chains and the 'wicked problem' of sustainability: Aligning knowledge, innovation, entrepreneurship, and leadership". *Journal of Chain and Network Science* 9 (2): 71–82.

Plato (2013) *Rebublic*. Loeb classical library. Harvard: Harvard University Press.

Ploum, L., Blok, V., Lans, T., Omta, O. (2017) "Toward a validated competence framework for sustainable entrepreneurship". *Organization & Environment* 31(2): 113–132. doi: 10.1177/1086026617697039.

Poole, M., Van de Ven, A. (1989) "Using paradox to build management and organization theories". *Academy of Management Review* 14 (4): 562–578.

Popa, E., Blok, V., Wesselink, R. (2020) "An agonistic approach to technological conflict". *Philosophy and Technology* (published online). doi: 10.1007/s1334 7-020-00430-7

Porter, M. (2006) "Strategy and society. The link between competitive advantage and corporate social responsibility". *Harvard Business Review* 84 (12): 78–92.

Post, J.E., Preston, L.E., Sachs, S. (2002) "Managing the extended enterprise: The new stakeholder view". *California Management Review* 45 (1): 6–28.

Raiborn, C.A. Payne, D. (1990) "Corporate codes of ethics: A collective conscience and continuum". *Journal of Business Ethics* 9 (11): 879–889.

Rauch, A., Frese, M. (2007) "Let's put the person back into entrepreneurship research: A meta-analysis on the relationship between business owners' personality traits, business creation, and success". *European Journal of Work and Organizational Psychology* 16 (4): 353–385.

Raulff, U., Agamben, G. (2004) "An interview with Giorgio Agamben". *German Law Journal* 5 (5): 609–614.

Reed, A.M., Reed, D., (2009) "Partnership for development: Four models of business involvement". *Journal of Business Ethics* 90: 3–37.

Rest, J.R. (1979) *Development in judging moral issues*. Minneapolis: University of Minnesota Press.

Rest, J.R., Narvaez, D., Thoma, S.J. Bebeau, M.J. (2000) "A Neo-Kohlbergian approach to morality research". *Journal of Moral Education* 29 (4): 381–395.

Rieckmann, M. (2012) "Future-oriented higher education: Which key competencies should be fostered through university teaching and learning?". *Futures* 44: 127–135.

Rip, A. (1986) "Controversies as informal technology assessment". *Knowledge: Creation, Diffusion, Utilization* 8 (2): 349–371.

Rittel, H.W.J., Webber, M.M. (1973) "Dilemmas in a general theory of planning". *Policy Sciences* 4: 155–169.

Robert, J. (2001). "Corporate governance and the ethics of narcissus". *Business Ethics Quarterly* 11 (1): 109–127.

Roelofsen, M., Blok, V., Wubben, E. (2015) "Maintaining the CSR-identity of sustainable entrepreneurial firms. The role of corporate governance in periods of business growth". In S.O. Idowu, C.S. Frederiksen, A.Y. Mermod, and M.E.J. Nielsen (Eds.) *Corporate social responsibility and governance. Theory and practice*. Dordrecht: Springer, 63–88.

Rondinelli, D., London, T. (2003) "How corporations and environmental groups cooperate: Assessing cross-sector alliances and collaborations". *Academy of Management Journal* 17 (1): 61–76.

Salzani, C. (2012) "The kingdom and the glory", book review. *Journal of Contemporary European Studies* 20 (2): 229–230.

Sanchez, R., Heene, A., Thomas, H. (1996). "Introduction: Towards the theory and practice of competence-based competition". In Sanchez, R., Heene, A., Thomas, H. (Eds.) *Dynamics of competence-based competition: Theory and practice in the new strategic management*. Oxford: Elsevier.

Sandler, R. (2007) *Character and environment*. New York: Columbia University Press.

Schaltegger, S., Wagner, M. (2011) "Sustainable entrepreneurship and sustainability innovation: Categories and interactions". *Business Strategy and the Environment* 20: 222–237.

Scherer, A.G., Palazzo, G. (2011) "The new political role of business in a globalized world: A review of a new perspective on CSR and its implications for the firm, governance, and democracy: Political role of business in a globalized world". *Journal of Management Studies* 48 (4): 899–931.

Scherer, F., Ross, D. (1990). *Industrial market structure and economic performance*. Boston: Houghton Mifflin.

Schnack, K. (1996) "Internationalisation, democracy and environmental education". In S. Breiting K. Nielsen (Eds.) *Environmental education research in the Nordic countries: Proceedings from the research centre for environmental and health education*. Copenhagen: The Royal Danish School for Educational Studies, 7–19.

Schneider, F., Kallis, G., Martinez-Alier, J. (2010) "Crisis or opportunity? Economic degrowth for social equity and ecological sustainability. Introduction to this special issue". *Journal of Cleaner Production* 18 (6): 511–518.

Schwartz, M. S. (2002) "A code of ethics for corporate code of ethics". *Journal of Business Ethics* 41 (1): 27–43.

Seitanidi, M.M., Crane, A., (2009) "Implementing CSR through partnerships: Understanding the selection, design and institutionalisation of nonprofit-business partnerships". *Journal of Business Ethics* 85: 413–429.

Selsky, J.W., Parker, B. (2005) "Cross-sector partnerships to address social issues: Challenges to theory and practice". *Journal of Management* 31 (6): 849–873.

Selsky, J.W., Parker, B. (2010) "Platforms for cross-sector social partnerships: Prospective sensemaking devices for social benefit". *Journal of Business Ethics* 94 (Suppl. 1): 21–37.

Shane, S. (2000) "Prior knowledge and the discovery of entrepreneurial opportunities". *Organization Science* 11 (4): 448–469.

Shane, S. (2003) *A general theory of entrepreneurship: The individual-opportunity nexus*. Northampton: Edward Elgar.

Shane, S., Venkataraman, S. (2000) "The promise of entrepreneurship as a field of research". *Academy of Management Review* 25 (1): 217–226.

Shearman, D., Smith, J.W. (2007). *The climate change challenge and the failure of democracy*. London: Praeger.

Smith, W. (2014) "Dynamic decision making: A model of senior leaders managing strategic paradoxes". *Academy of Management Journal* 57 (6): 1592–1623.

Solomon, R.C. (1992) *Ethics and excellence: Cooperation and integrity in business*. Oxford: Oxford University Press.

Statt, D.A. (2004). *The Routledge dictionary of business management*. London: Routledge.

Stevens, B. (1994) "An analysis of corporate ethical code studies: 'Where do we go from here?'". *Journal of Business Ethics* 13 (1): 63–69.

Stiegler, B. (2005) *Symbolic misery, volume 2: The catastrophe of the sensible*. Cambridge: Polity.

Stirling, A. (2007) "A general framework for analysing diversity in science, technology and society". *Journal of the Royal Society, Interface* 4 (15): 707–719.

Stirling, A. (2008), ""Opening up" and "closing down": Power, participation, and pluralism in the social appraisal of technology". *Science Technology and Human Values* 33 (2): 262–294.

Stirling, A. Mayer, S. (2001) "A novel approach to the appraisal of technological risk: A multicriteria mapping study of a genetically modified crop". *Environment and Planning C: Government and Policy* 19 (4): 529–555.

Strauss, L. (1989) *Xenophon's Socratic discourse. An interpretation of the Oeconomicus*. Sound Bend: St. Augustine Press.

Sulmasy, D.P. (1999) "What is an oath and why should a physician swear one?" *Theoretical Medicine and Bioethics* 20 (4): 329–346.

Swanson, D. (1999) "Towards an integrative theory of business and society: A research strategy for corporate social performance". *Academy of Management Review* 24: 506–521.

Swart, R.J., Raskin, P., Robinson, J. (2004) "The problem of the future: Sustainability science and scenario analysis". *Global Environmental Change* 14 (2): 137–146.

Taneja, S.S., Taneja, P.K., Gupta, R.K. (2011) "Researches in corporate social responsibility: A review of shifting focus, paradigms, and methodologies". *Journal of Business Ethics* 101 (3): 343–364.

Taylor, F.W. (1911) *The principles of scientific management*. New York: Harper & Brothers.

Teece, D.J., Pisano, G., Shuen, A. (1997) "Dynamic capabilities and strategic management". *Strategic Management Journal*, 18 (7): 509–533.

Tempels, T., Verweij, M., Blok, V. (2017a) "Big food's ambivalence: Seeking profit and responsibility for health". *American Journal of Public Health* 107 (3): 402–406.

Tempels, T., Blok, V., Verweij, M. (2017b) "Understanding political responsibility in corporate citizenship: Towards a shared responsibility for the common good". *Journal of Global Ethics* 13 (1): 90–108.

Tempels, T., Blok, V., Verweij, M. (2020) "Injustice in food-related public health problems: A matter of corporate responsibility". *Business Ethics Quarterly* 30 (3): 388–413.

Thompson, L.J. (2010) "The global moral compass for business leaders". *Journal of Business Ethics* 93 (Suppl. 1): 15–32.

Thompson, N., Herrman, A., Hekkert, M. (2015) "How sustainable entrepreneurs engage in institutional change. Insights from biomass torrefaction in the Netherlands". *Journal of Cleaner Production* 106: 608–618.

Trevino, L.K., Nelson, K.A. (2007) *Managing business ethics: Straight talk about how to do it right*. Hoboken: Wiley.

Trivedi, C., Stokols, D. (2011) "Social enterprises and corporate enterprises: Fundamental differences and defining features". *Journal of Entrepreneurship* 20 (1): 1–32.

Tsoukas, H., Cummings, S. (1997) "Marginalization and recovery: The emergence of Aristotelian themes in organization studies". *Organization Studies* 18: 655–683.

Uhlaner, L., Wright, M., Huse, M. (2007) "Private firms and corporate governance: An integrated economic and management perspective". *Small Business Economics* 29 (3): 225–241.

Urwick, L.F. (1952) *Notes on the theory of organization*. New York: American Management Association.

Utting, P., Zammit, A. (2009) "United nations-business partnerships: Good intentions and contradictory agendas". *Journal of Business Ethics* 90 (1): 39–56.

Valasquez, M.G. (1983) "Debunking corporate moral responsibility". *Business Ethics Quarterly* 13: 531–562.

Van den Bergh, J. (2001) "Ecological economics: Themes, approaches, and differences with environmental economics". *Regional Environmental Change* 2 (1): 13–23.

Van der Byl, C., Slawinski, N. (2015) "Embracing tensions in corporate sustainability: A review of research from win-wins and trade-offs to paradoxes and beyond". *Organization & Environment* 28 (1): 54–79.

Van Griethuysen, P. (2010) "Why are we growth-addicted? The hard way towards degrowth in the involutionary western development path". *Journal of Cleaner Production* 18: 590–595.

Van Huijstee, M.M., Francken, M., Leroy, P. (2007) "Partnerships for sustainable development: A review of current literature". *Environmental Sciences* 4 (2): 75–89.

Van Oosterhout, J., Heugens, P., Kaptein, M. (2006) "The internal morality of contracting: Advancing the contractualist endeavor in business ethics". *Academy of Management Review* 31: 521–539.

Von Schomberg, R. (2013) "A vision of responsible research and innovation". In R. Owen, J. Bessant, M. Heintz (Eds.) *Responsible innovation*. Chichester: Wiley, 51–74.

Vucetich, J.A., Nelson, M.P. (2010) "Sustainability: Virtuous or vulgar?". *BioScience*, 60 (7): 539–544.

Wall, R., Devine-Wright, P., Mill, G.A. (2007) "Comparing and combining theories to explain proenvironmental intentions". *Environmental Behaviour* 39: 731–753.

Wals, A.J. (2010) "Between knowing what is right and knowing that it is wrong to tell others what is right: On relativism, uncertainty and democracy in environmental and sustainability education". *Environmental Education Research* 16 (1): 143–151.

Wals, A., Jicklin, B. (2002) ""Sustainability" in higher education: From doublethink and newspeak to critical thinking and meaningful learning." *International Journal of Sustainability in Higher Education* 3 (3): 1467–6370.

Warren, R.C. (1993) "Codes of ethics: Bricks without straw". *Business Ethics A European Review* 2 (4): 185–191.

Werhane, P.H. (1985) *Persons, rights, and corporations*. Englewood Cliffs: Prentice Hall.

Werhane, P.H. (2002) "Moral imagination and systems thinking". *Journal of Business Ethics* 38 (1–2): 33–42.

Wesselink, R., Blok, V., Dentoni, D., Leur, S., van der Lans, T. (2015) "Individual competencies for managers engaged in corporate sustainable management practices". *Journal of Cleaner Production*. doi: 10.1016/ j.jclepro.2014.10.093.

Westley, F., Vredenburg, H. (1997) "Interorganizational collaboration and the preservation of global biodiversity". *Organization Science* 8 (4): 381–403.

Whyte, J. (2013) "The king reigns but he doesn't govern'. Thinking sovereignty and government with Agamben, Foucault and Rousseau". In T. Frost (Ed.) *Giorgio Agamben. Legal, political and philosophical perspectives*. London/New York: Routledge.

Wiek, A., Withycombe, L., Redman, C. L. (2011) "Key competencies in sustainability: A reference framework for academic program development". *Sustainable Science* 6: 203–218.

Wilburn, K.M., Wilburn, R. (2011). "Achieving social license to operate using stakeholder theory". *Journal of International Business Ethics* 4 (2): 1–14.

Willard, M., Wiedmeyer, C., Flint, R.W., Weedon, J.S., Woodward, R., Feldman, I., Edwards, M. (2010). "The sustainability professional: 2010 competency survey report". *Environmental Quality Management* 20 (1): 49–83.

Wood, D. J. (1991). "Corporate social performance revisited". *Academy of Management Review* 16: 691–718.

Wood, G. (2002) "A partnership model of corporate ethics". *Journal of Business Ethics* 40: 61–73.

World Commission on Environment and Development (1987) *Our common future*. Oxford: Oxford University Press.

Wubben, E.F.M., Runge, N.A., Blok, V. (2012) "From waste to profit: An interorganisational perspective on drivers for biomass valorization". *Journal on Chain and Network Science* 12 (3): 261–272.

Xenophon (1989) *Anabasis*. Loeb classical library. Harvard: Harvard University Press.

Xenophon (2013) *Memorabilia, oeconomicus, symposium, apology*. Loeb classical library. Harvard: Harvard University Press.

Yaziji, M., Doh, J. (2009) *NGOs and corporations: Conflict and collaboration*. Cambridge: Cambridge University Press.

Zwier, J., Blok, V. (2017) "Saving earth: Encountering Heidegger's philosophy of technology in the Anthropocene". *Techne: Research in Philosophy and Technology* 21 (2–3): 122–142.

Index

For Product Safety Concerns and Information please contact our EU
representative GPSR@taylorandfrancis.com
Taylor & Francis Verlag GmbH, Kaufingerstraße 24, 80331 München, Germany

www.ingramcontent.com/pod-product-compliance
Lightning Source LLC
LaVergne TN
LVHW020801230425
809368LV00003B/227